HISTORY OF THE KONKAN

HISTORY
OF
THE KONKAN

ALEXANDER KYD NAIRNE

GYAN

Published by

GYAN

Gyan Publishing House
5, Ansari Road
Daryaganj, New Delhi-110002
Phone: 011-47034999, 9811692060
E-mail: books@gyanbooks.com

Distribution Network
gyanbooks.com
India, USA, Canada, UK, Australia, France

ISBN : 978-81-212-3543-3 (PB)
First Published, Bombay, 1894

2nd Impression 2020

Printed at: Gyan Press, Delhi.

History of the Konkan
Author: Alexander Kyd Nairne

HISTORY OF THE KONKAN

ALEXANDER KYD NAIRNE

ASIAN EDUCATIONAL SERVICES
NEW DELHI ★ CHENNAI ★ 2008

HISTORY OF THE KONKAN

BY THE

REVEREND ALEXANDER KYD NAIRNE

LATE OF THE

BOMBAY CIVIL SERVICE.

"Hills with peaky tops engrailed,
and many a tract of palm and rice."
Tennyson.

BOMBAY:
PRINTED AT THE GOVERNMENT CENTRAL PRESS.

1894.

CONTENTS.

AUTHORITIES.

AITCHISON—Collection of Treaties, Engagements, and Sanads relating to India. Calcutta, 1864.

ANNAES MARITIMOS E COLONIAES (4th Series). Lisboa, 1844.

ARCHIVO PORTUGUEZ ORIENTAL. Nova Goa, 1866.

ASIATIC ANNUAL REGISTER, 1799 to 1811. London.

ASIATIC JOURNAL, 1816 to 1830.

ASIATIC RESEARCHES, 1799 to 1836. London.

ASTLEY—New General Collection ot Voyages and Travels, 1745.

BARBOSA—Description of the Coasts of East Africa and Malabár in the Sixteenth Century. Hakluyt Society.

BIRD—History of Gujarát. London, 1835.

BLACKER—Memoir of the Operations during the Marátha War, 1817-19. London, 1821.

BLUE BOOK—Pindáree and Marátha War.

Do. War in India, 1819.

BOHOURS—Life of St. Francis Xavier, translated by Dryden—WORKS, Vol. 16, Ed. 1808.

BOMBAY GOVERNMENT SELECTIONS—New Series :

No. VII.—Statistical Account of the Kolába Agency, by W. Hearn.

No. VIII.—Statistical Report on the Principality of Kolhápur, by Colonel Graham.

No. X.—Memoir on the Sávantvádi State, by Major Hutchinson and others.

No. XVI.—Tours in Gujarát and the Konkan, by Dr. Hové.

No. XXVI.—Miscellaneous information connected with the petty States of the Konkan.

No. XCVI.—Papers relating to the assessment of part of the Thána Collectorate.

No. CIV.—Military Papers by Hon. M. Elphinstone.

BOMBAY QUARTERLY REVIEW, 1855 to 1858.

BOMBAY REGULATIONS, 1799 to 1816.

BRIGGS—History of the Mahommedan Power in India, 4 vols., 1832.

BRUCE—Annals of the East India Company from 1661 to 1708, 3 vols., 1810.

CHAPLIN—Report on the Deccan, 1824. Bombay, 1877.

CLUVERIUS—Introductio in Universam Geographiam. Amsterdam, 1697.

CORREA (GASPAR)—Lendas da India. Lisboa, 1858.

CHURCHILL—Collection of Voyages, 6 vols., 1732.

CUNNINGHAM—Ancient Geography of India, 2 vols., 1871.

DACUNHA (J. GERSON)—Chaul and Bassein. Bombay, 1876.

DEBARROS—Decada da Asia, 9 vols. } Lisboa, 1778.

DECOUTTO— Do. 15 vols. } Lisboa, 1778.

DELA VALLE—Viaggi. 4 vols. Venetia, 1662.

DELLON—Relation de l'Inquisition de Goa. Paris, 1688.

DUPERRON (ANQUETIL)—Zendavesta (Vol. 1, Discours Préliminaire). Paris, 1771

EAST INDIA PAPERS relating to the Marátha War of 1803.

ELLIOT (SIR H. M.)—History of India as told by its own Historians, 7 vols. 1867.

ELPHINSTONE—History of India. Edn. London, 1854.

ERSKINE—History of India under Báber and Humáyun, 2 vols. London, 1854.

FERGUSON (J.)—Rock-cut Temples of India, 1864.

FIELD OFFICER—Memoirs of the Early Life and Services of a—. London, 1839.

FORBES (JAMES)—Oriental Memoirs. 4 vols. quarto, 1813.

FORBES, A. K.—Rás Málá. London, 1856.
FREIRE DE ANDRADE—Vida de Dom Joao deCastro. Edn. Paris, 1869.
FRYER—New Account of East India and Persia. London, 1691.
GILDEMEISTER—Scriptorum Arabum de Rebus Indicis. Bonn, 1838.
GRANT DUFF—History of the Maráthás. Edn. Bombay, 1873.
HAKLUYT—Collection of Voyages, 5 vols. Edn. London, 1809.
HAMILTON (W.)—Geographical, Statistical, and Historical Description of Hindustán, 2 vols. 1820.
HEBER (BISHOP)—Indian Journal, 2 vols. Edn. London, 1849.
HEEREN—Historical Researches, 3 vols. Oxford, 1833.
HERBERT (SIR T.)—Some Years' Travels into the divers parts of Africa and Asia, London, 1665.
HISTORICAL ACCOUNT OF THE SETTLEMENT AND POSSESSION OF BOMBAY BY THE ENGLISH EAST-INDIA COMPANY. Loudon, 1776.
HOUGH—History of Christianity in India, 2 vols. 1839.
IARRIC (PIERRE DU)—L'histoire des choses plus Memorables &c. Troisiéme partie. Bordeaux, 1614.
IBN BATUTA—Travels of. Translation by Lee. 1829.
INDIA IN THE FIFTEENTH CENTURY. Hakluyt Society, 1857.
INDIAN ANTIQUARY. Bombay, 1871 to 1874.
INSTITUTO VASCO DA GAMA. Nova Goa, 1866.
IVES—A Voyage from England to India in 1754 and an historical narrative. London, 1773.
JERVIS (T. B.)—Geographical and Statistical Memoir of the Konkan. Calcutta, 1840.
JOURNAL ROYAL ASIATIC SOCIETY OF GREAT BRITAIN.
Do. do. do. Bombay Branch.
Do. ASIATIC SOCIETY OF BENGAL.
KERR'S GENERAL HISTORY AND COLLECTION OF VOYAGES AND TRAVELS, 1812.
KNOX—New Collection of Voyages, 7 vols. London, 1767.
LINSCHOTEN (T. H.)—Histoire de la Navigation aux Indes Orientales. Amsterdam, 1638.
MACPHERSON (DAVID)—History of European Commerce with India. 1812.
MALCOLM (SIR J.)—Government of India. 1833.
MANDELSLO—Voyages and Travels of the Holstein Ambassadors. London, 1669.
MARCO POLO—Travels of. (Colonel Yule.) 2 vols. 1871.
MICKLE—The Lusiad, 2 vols. 1798.
MILBURN—Oriental Commerce, 2 vols. 1813.
MILL (JAMES)—History of British India, 6 vols. Edn. 1840.
MOOR—Narrative of the Operations of Captain Little's Detachment against Tipu Sultán. London, 1794.
MURRAY—Historical Account of Discoveries in Asia. Edinburgh, 1820.
O CHRONISTA DE TISSUARY. Nova Goa, 1866 to 1869.
OGILBY—English Atlas, 5 vols. About 1670.
ORME—History of the Military Transactions in Indostán, 2 vols. London, 1778.
Do.—Historical Fragments of the Mogul Empire. London, 1805.
OVINGTON—A Voyage to Surat in 1689. London, 1696.
PARSONS—Travels in Asia and Africa. London, 1808.
PINKERTON—General Collection of Voyages, 17 vols. 1808.
PRIAULX—Indian Travels of Apollonius of Tyana &c. 1873.
PYRARD (F.)—Viagen (Portuguese translation). Nova Goa, 1862.
REINAUD—Fragments Arabes et Persans inédits relatifs à l'Inde. Paris, 14.
RENNELL—Memoir of a Map of Hindustán. London, 1788.
REPORT ON PAST FAMINES IN THE BOMBAY PRESIDENCY. Bombay, 1868.
REPORTS FROM COMMITTEES OF THE HOUSE OF COMMONS, 1806.

Reports of Civil Causes adjudged by the Court of Sadar Adálat. Bombay, 1825.
Robertson (Rev. James)—Historical Disquisition on Ancient India. London, 1809.
Rule (Rev. Dr.)—History of the Inquisition.
Scott (Jonathan)—Ferishta's History of the Deccan, 2 vols. Shrewsbury, 1794.
Seely—Journey to the Temple of Ellora, 1812.
Selection of Papers from Records of the East India House, 4 vols 1826.
Shamráo Moroji Nayak—History of the Páttána Prabhus. Bombay, 1877.
Stanley (Hon. H.)—Three Voyages of Vasco da Gama. Hakluyt Society.
Stavorinus—Voyages to the East Indies, 3 vols. 1798.
Thomas—Treaties, Agreements, and Engagements. Bombay, 1851
Thornton—History of British India. 4 vols. 1841.
Tod—Travels in Western India. 1839.
Tohfat al Mujahidin—Translated by Rowlandson.
Transactions Bombay Geographical Society.
Do. Bombay Literary Society.
Do. Bombay Medical and Physical Society.
Valentia (Lord)—Voyages and Travels to India &c. 1809.
Vincent—Voyage of Nearchus and Periplus of the Erythræan Sea, 2 vols. 1805.
Wilson (H. H.)—Works, 12 vols. 1868.
Do. History of British India, 3 vols. 1845.
Wilson (Rev. Dr.)—The Bene-Israel of Bombay.
Do. Sermon to Pársis.
Do. Account of Warlees and Kátkaries.
Do. Caves of Western India.
Yule—Cathay and the Way Thither. Hakluyt Society.
Do. Mirabilia Descripta. Hakluyt Society.
Xavier (F. N.)—Resumo Historico da Vida S. Francisco Xavier. Goa, 1861.
Manuscript Records from Bombay Secretariat, &c.

Note—The references to Faria y Souza are either to the Summary of his book in Briggs' History or to that in Kerr's Voyages.

INTRODUCTION.

Introduction.

THE Konkan is now held to include all the land which lies between the Western Gháts and the Indian Ocean, from the latitude of Daman on the north to that of Terekhol, on the Goa frontier, on the south. This tract is about 320 miles in length, with a varying breadth of thirty to sixty miles, and is divided into the British districts of Thána Kolába and Ratnágiri, and the Native States of Jawhár Janjira and Sávantvadi.[1] The Pant Sachiv of Bhor in Poona has also a group of villages below the Gháts.

The word Konkan is of Indian origin and of considerable antiquity, but its meaning as the name of a country is not obvious and has never been satisfactorily explained, although various interpretations of it have been given. The district known under the name appears to have had very different limits at different periods. The seven Konkans of Hindu mythology are mentioned in a Hindu history of Kashmir, and are said by Professor H. H. Wilson[2] to have included nearly the whole of the west coast of India. Grant Duff[3] considered the Konkan to extend along the coast from the Tápti to Sadáshivgad, and inland as far as the open plains of the Dakhan, and he thus included in it part of both Gujarát and Kánara, and of the country above the Gháts. This latter he called Konkan Ghát-mátha as opposed to Tal-Konkan or the lowlands: and he inferred that the Musalmáns were the first who limited the name to the low country.[4] Ferishta[5] also speaks of the Konkan under the name of Tal-Ghát, and Khafi Khán calls it Tal-Konkan. This inclusion of the hilly district above and near the edge of the Gháts is very reasonable: for any one who passes from west to east will see that the country immediately above and immediately below the Gháts is of exactly the same character, although so different in elevation, while it is a few miles further east that the great bare plains which characterise the Dakhan begin. This narrow district above the Gháts is made up of the *Mávals*, the *Khorás*, and the *Murhás*, but it should be stated that neither the name Konkan-Ghát-Mátha,

---

[1] As the Sávantvádi state has always been closely connected with Kolhápur, the main part of its history must be looked for in the account of Kolhápur and not in this work.
[2] Asiatic Researches, XV. 47.
[3] History, 3.
[4] History, 33.
[5] Briggs, II. 338.

Introduction.

nor the meaning of the words describing its divisions is now generally known.[1] As opposed to this extended interpretation of the Konkan, Bird states that according to Sanskrit writers the Konkan stretched only from Devgad to Sadáshivgad (that is a distance altogether of only about ninety miles), from the Tápti to Devgad being Abhir, or the country of the shepherds: that the divisions of Abhir were Berbera or Marátha from the Tápti to Bassein, Virát from Bassein to Bánkot, and Kirát from Bánkot to Devgad.[2] It is curious that the limits thus assigned to the provinces of Virát, Kirát, and Konkan should exactly coincide with those generally given for the districts of the Parbhus, Bráhmans, and Shenvis respectively.

Whatever the old signification of the word may have been, the name Konkan is now used in the sense first mentioned, and the modern division of the district is into North and South Konkan, meaning the parts north and south of Bombay.[3] The boundary between the North and South Konkan is, however, sometimes considered to be the Sávitri river, which divides the Habshi's territory from Ratnágiri, as, for some years after the English conquest, the district of the North Konkan included the sub-divisions as far south as the Sávitri.

Of this district it may be said generally that the parts near the coast are fertile, highly cultivated, and populous, and the inland parts rocky and rugged, not much favoured by nature nor improved by man. Compared with other parts of India the climate is moist, the rainfall being very heavy, and hot winds but little felt. Although enervating it is much more equable than that of the Dakhan: and the district, especially the southern part, may be called decidedly healthy. North of Bombay the coast is low and sandy, containing in many places great expanses of salt swamp, the rivers few and shallow, and the harbours insignificant. South of Bombay the coast is bold with a line of hills often bordering the sea, never receding more than two or three miles from it; there are many navigable rivers and commodious harbours, and in most parts deep water near the shore. At various places along the coast are small rocky islands, generally within a quarter of a mile of the mainland, and which

[1] The meaning of *Mával, Khora,* and *Murha* has been thus explained to the writer: The *Murhás* are the comparatively level parts of the Ghát country found at the top; the *Khorás* the narrow gorges and ravines (*Khora* being similarly used throughout the Konkan) stretching towards the bottom; and the *Mávals* (the word meaning west) the lowest slopes of the hills extending quite into the Konkan.

[2] History of Gujarát, 8.

[3] Grant Duff, 168.

were in earlier times, and especially under the Maráthás, fortified and highly valued. Such are Arnála, Kolába, Dánda-Rájápur, and Suvarndurg. At Málvan, besides one or two islands of this sort, there are a great number of smaller rocks and reefs, and the whole sea between that port and the Vengurla rocks (formerly called by the Portuguese Ilheos Queimados, and thence shown in old English maps under the name of 'The burnt rocks')[1] is made dangerous by rocks of all sorts and sizes. Passing inland, the North Konkan is less rugged, and contains far more arable land though a thinner population than the South Konkan, which is, speaking generally, a rocky plateau slightly elevated, and from want of soil exceedingly sterile. But it is intersected by many great rivers and arms of the sea, and the valleys through which these and their tributary streams flow, partly make up by their fertility for the barrenness of the surrounding plateaux. The North Konkan is still in most parts well wooded, and in the coast districts the palmyra and the date palm spring up spontaneously in every direction. Parts of the Southern Konkan are also well covered with trees, though, from the nature of the soil, many parts are bare. On this part of the coast neither palmyra nor date tree is seen, but their place is better supplied by great groves of cocoanut trees planted along all the sandy parts of the coast and the banks of the creeks. The villages throughout the Konkan are almost invariably shaded with trees, and wherever there is room enough the houses stand in their own compounds, while in many of the inland districts they are found in scattered hamlets, several of which go to make up a village.

"The Konkan in early times seems to have been a thinly inhabited forest, from which character it has even now but partially emerged."[2] The last remark is at the present day true of part of the North Konkan only, the South possessing a population very thick compared with its arable area. It may be considered certain, however, that the whole was to a comparatively late period a district "where beasts with man divided empire claimed." The population Elphinstone considers to have been always Marátha,[3] but there is a great difference between the inhabitants of the northern and those of the southern half. In the latter the population is purely Marátha, and the castes are few and very exactly defined; but in the north there are large tribes more or less aboriginal, several somewhat

---

[1] From their colour and ruggedness. De la Valle, III. 143.

[2] Elphinstone, 220. [3] Elphinstone 220.

Introduction.

mixed castes, and, except for comparatively recent settlers, a total absence of pure Maráthás and Bráhmans. The whole tract is agricultural, the largest town having little over 14,000 inhabitants. Until the accession of the British Government the population had always a distinctly warlike character, and the South Konkan still supplies so great a number of recruits to the Bombay Army, that there are as many military pensioners in this district as in the whole of the rest of the Presidency. Besides this, all castes of the South Konkan are much more in the habit of seeking their living abroad than the natives of other parts, though they almost invariably return home to end their days. Both coast and interior are remarkable for the number of forts, so that it is little exaggeration to say that in some parts every rock and promontory, mountain and hill, were fortified. These forts are now all in ruins, but the beauty of the creeks and hills and valleys remains, and in many cases the forts themselves

"As stately seem but lovelier far
Than in the panoply of war."

Though the Konkan can scarcely be called historically famous, its long coast line and convenient harbours, together with its comparative nearness to the Arabian coast, made it known to the earliest travellers, while the natural strength of the country and the character of its inhabitants gave it in later days much greater importance than its wealth or extent would have justified. The Buddhists and after them the Bráhmans chose Sálsette for one of their greatest monastic establishments, and in other parts of the Konkan their cave temples are remarkable. The descendants of immigrant Pársis Jews Abyssinians and probably Arabs are still found in considerable numbers. The Musalmáns had two or three famous marts on this coast, and when the Portuguese began to make settlements in India the coast of the North Konkan was one of their early acquisitions; and in the South Konkan, factories of the English Dutch and French were established early in the seventeenth century. A little later the great founder of the Marátha empire chose a Konkan hill-fort as his capital. And when, after two or three generations, the pure Marátha dynasty lost its power, the Konkani Bráhmans better known as Konkanasths or Chitpavans inherited it and extended the Marátha conquests over the greatest part of India. Thus, though the Konkan has never been more than a province of some inland kingdom, it has many famous associations. And if, as geographically it does, the island of Bombay be considered to belong to it, the Konkan may be said to possess also one of the greatest centres of modern commerce. But the history of Bombay does not come within the scope of this memoir, and it must be admitted that the Konkan generally has for the last hundred years lost the greater part of such importance as it formerly had, and, except for its nearness to Bombay, would be even less regarded than it is. The Thána district has, indeed, benefited by both the railways which end at Bombay, and roads run through almost every part of it. But it is only within the last few years that roads fit for wheeled vehicles have been commenced in any of the districts south of Bombay, and many parts of the south, as well as the whole of the Jawhár and Janjira states, are still without cart roads. The Gháts separate the Konkan like a wall from the great plains of the Dakhan, and in the whole length of these mountains there are but eight cart roads leading from the Dakhan to the coast, and of these the two principal have been to some extent superseded by the railways that run close to them. In fact, none of the influences which have spread wealth over the rest of the Presidency in the last few years have affected the Konkan, except as regards a comparatively small part of the northern half. The interest of the country must depend therefore on the beauty of its scenery, its past history, and the character of its inhabitants, and in these respects it need not fear comparison with the more favoured and celebrated provinces of India.

Note 1.—Owing to the Konkan, though geographically so distinct, having been from the earliest times divided, and its various parts attached first to one kingdom and then to another, no history of it either by a Native or European author is known to exist. This accounts for the great number of references to the works of historians and travellers which will be found in this short sketch.

Note 2.—In the Second Section (Antiquities and Traditions) great additions have been made to Mr. Nairne's narrative for which he is not responsible. These refer in some cases to discoveries made since Mr. Nairne left India.

NOTE.

With regard to the present state of the districts as given in the Introduction and at the end it should be remembered that the time referred to is the year 1884.

ADDENDA AND ERRATA.

Page 2, line 19, Sir H. Yule (Hobson-Jobson, Art. Choul) confidently identifies Semulla of Ptolemy and Saimur of the old Arab Geographers with Choul.

Page 7, for "the last section" read Vol. XI. page 85.

Page 45, line 7 from bottom, for "1608" read "1508."

Page 62, note 3, is part of page 63, note 4.

Page 87, line 21, after "attacked Colába but failed," add "and the *Shoreham* Man-of-War was lost on the rocks."

Page 88, line 12 from bottom, after "principal station," add "In February 1754 Angria's fleet burnt or captured three Dutch ships, one of 50, one of 36, and one of 18 guns; and having set on the stocks two ships, one of which was to carry 40 guns, he boasted that he should soon be superior to whatever could be brought against him in the Indian seas." These particulars are from Cambridge's "Account of the War in India from 1750 to 1761," 2nd Ed., London, 1762, in which there are plates of the attacks on Suvarndrug and Gheriah.

Page 92, para. 1, at end, enter inverted commas;
para. 2, at beginning, remove inverted commas.

Page 94, para. 1, at end, enter inverted commas;
para. 2, at beginning, remove inverted commas.

Page 95, para. 1, at end, enter inverted commas;
para. 2, at beginning, remove inverted commas.

SECTION I.

EARLY TRAVELLERS.

Section I. Early Travellers.

THE earliest certain mention of the country now called the Konkan is in the geography of Ptolemy about A.D. 150, and in the Greek work called "The Periplus of the Erythræan Sea," the authorship of which is uncertain, and the date variously calculated from A.D. 66 to A.D. 240. Ptolemy makes of this part of the coast two provinces, Larika (Sk. Lâtaka or Lâtadesh[1]) which is identified with Gujarát and part of the North Konkan, and Ariaka which includes the rest of the Konkan.[2] The author of the Periplus does not mention Larika, but applies the name of Barugaza or Broach to this province as well as to the port of Broach, and states that Ariaka included "the land of the pirates."[3] This is the first mention of the pirates, who down to the present century were the terror of the coast between Bombay and Goa. With reference to them Rennell about 1780 wrote: "Few countries with so straight a general outline are so much broken into bays and harbours. The multitude of shallow ports, an uninterrupted view along the shore, and an elevated coast favourable to distant vision, have always fitted this tract of country for piracy. The land and sea breezes blow alternately and divide the day, so that vessels sailing along the coast are obliged to keep within sight of land."[4] The pirates of Suvarndurg are also mentioned by Strabo.[5] Vincent in collating the various descriptions of the coast assigns to Ariaka the limits from Goa to the Tápti, and of course includes in this the land of the pirates, and he considers that as the province can thus be identified with tolerable certainty, it is of little use to try to ascertain the exact position of the different ports named, most of which were places of only local trade.[6] The two identifications, however, which he makes without any doubt are Kalyán (Kalliéna) and the Vengular rocks, the first a port which was already decayed in the time of the Periplus, as Sandanes the king admitted no Egyptian vessels, and if any entered the harbour by accident or stress of weather he compelled them to go to Broach. The Vengurla rocks are mentioned as islands off the southern extremity of Ariaka and called Sesekrienai.[7] The ports given both by Ptolemy and in the Periplus between Broach and these islands are Oopára or Sopára near Bassein where interesting Buddhist remains of about A.D. 50 were discovered in 1882,[8] Semulla, Mandagora, Palaipotamai (Balapatna in Ptolemy), Melizigara, and Toparon

[1] Compare Bombay Gazetteer, XII. 57 note; XIII. Part II., 112, 431, 435 & note 4.
[2] Heeren, II. 239; Tod, 187. [3] Vincent, II. 418. [4] Memoir, xxx.-xxxviii.
[5] Vincent, I. 178. [6] Vincent, II. 428. [7] Vincent, II. 422, 432.
[8] Bom. Gaz. XIV. Sopára.

Section I.

Early Travellers.

of the Byzantians (Byzantium) in Ptolemy.[1] Besides these Ptolemy alone mentions the river Binda between Sopára and Semulla, Hippocura south of that, and the islands called Heptanesia.[2] These last are identified by Lassen with the islands of Bombay and Sálsette.[3] Semulla he puts at Bassein, Balipatna about Cheul or Dánda Rájápur, and Manadagora a little further south. Melizigaris, called by Pliny Zizerus, he puts at Suvarndurg, Vincent at Jaygad. Ptolemy calls this place an island, Pliny a river and a port, and the author of the Periplus a place on the continent. A tolerable agreement can be found between these three apparently contradictory descriptions if it is remembered that the Arabic word Janjira, which may be evidently traced in the two names given, is still used not only for the rocky island off Dánda-Rájápur, but also for the similar rocks at Suvarndurg and Málvan, either of which places, with the towns on the mainland which they protect, might then be identified with Melizigara or Zizerus.[4] Byzantium Lassen puts at Vijaydurg. And Nitrias, mentioned by Pliny as a chief station of the pirates, Rennell identifies with Nivti, between Málvan and Vengurla.[5]

The identification of all these places is an interesting study for those who are well acquainted with the district, and there are certain resemblances of names which will probably strike every reader; but the speculations made by different geographers are almost endless, and the means of ascertaining the real situation of the places mentioned are so small, owing to Ptolemy's mistake of making the coast from Broach to the Ganges run almost due east, and to no manuscript of the Periplus being known to exist, that it seems useless to go deep into the subject. Except Kalyán the places mentioned in the Periplus are all given as country ports frequented only by the natives.[6] From Barugaza (Broach) and Ariaka to the coast of Africa were exported corn, rice, butter, oil of sesame, coarse and fine cotton goods, and cane-honey (sugar). And ships with these cargoes sometimes went on from the African to the Arabian ports.[7] Whether this African trade was in the hands of Arabs or of the natives of India is doubtful, but all writers are agreed that the traffic from the west coast of India to the Red Sea was mainly in the hands of the Arabs.[8] The trade of the ancient Egyptians with India is to be looked on as previous to history and a matter only of speculation.[9] The Greeks from Egypt may occasionally have gone across the Indian Ocean, but in general they contented themselves with getting Indian goods from the

---

[1] Vincent, II. 427, 431. [2] Liber, VII. Cap. I. Bom. Gaz. XIII. Part II. 414.

[3] Map to Indische Altherthumskunde. [4] Vincent, II. 430.

[5] Memoir, 31; Vincent, II. 449; Bom. Gaz. XV. Part II. 336. The similarity of the name and position suggest that Mandagora is Mandangad, a lofty and prominent hill close to Mahápral, a village on the Bánkot creek, to which large native craft still pass.

[6] Vincent, II. 428. Compare Bom. Gaz. X. 192; XI. 136, 137, note 6; XIII. Part II. 414-418; XV. Part II. 78 and note 1. [7] Vincent, II. 282, 423.

[8] Heeren, II. 301; Elphinstone 166; Vincent, I. 43; II. 35, 119; Robertson, 38.

[9] Vincent, I. 281.

Section I.

Early Travellers.

Arabs in the ports of the Red Sea.[1] Authorities differ as to whether the Romans ever traded with this coast at all.[2] As regards the ports of the Konkan in the earliest times it may be taken as proved that the larger ones were frequented by the Arabs and the smaller ones by the natives who carried on the coasting trade.[3] The author of the Periplus also mentions that Muziris, which is generally identified with Mangalore, was a great place of resort for vessels from the Konkan.[4]

The conclusion is that, notwithstanding the pirates, this coast was not devoid of trade or shunned by foreigners in the earliest times of which we have any record, though it had no place of such importance as Cambay, Broach, or the ports of Malabár; and that the exports were not very different from what they now are, cotton cloth, muslin, indigo, chintz, spices, and sugar.[5] It must also be mentioned that the metropolis to which Ariaka was subject was Tagara, a place formerly identified with Divgiri or Daulatabad, about which there is now a difference of opinion.[6]

After the author of the Periplus no authority can be mentioned until Cosmas, a Greek merchant of the sixth century, who described India, though it is very doubtful if he had visited it himself.[7] He speaks of Calliana as a place of great trade, and states that the return cargoes from there to Ceylon consisted of native brass, sesamum, wood, and articles of clothing.[8] He also speaks of a king of Calliana, and of there being a bishop's see and a Christian community at Kalyán subject to the Persian metropolitan. In these respects Kalyán was not different from the other considerable ports of India, most of which were frequented by Persian traders.[9] The conjecture has been made, though the evidence is certainly weak, that the Buddhist priest Fa Hian at the end of the fourth century and Hiuen Tsiang in the seventh century both visited the Buddhist caves of Kanheri, and that the latter on his return embarked at Kalyán or Bánkot.[10]

After Cosmas there is a long break before any other European writer mentions this part of India, but the gap is supplied by several Arabian geographers, by whom the name is variously given as Kemkem, Kourkam, Kaukan, Konkan, and Konkan-Tana, which last compound is given by Ibn Batuta (1340), and is conjectured by Colonel Yule to have been the proper name of the province. The compound is reproduced by an Italian writer of the fourteeth century

---

[1] Vincent, II. 119, 35; Priaulx, 84. [2] Priaulx, 234. [3] Elphinstone, 166. [4] Vincent, II. 448. [5] Elphinstone, 169.

[6] Wilford in Asiatic Res. I. 373; Vincent, II. 403, 414. Compare Bom. Gaz. XIII. Part II. 423 note 4; XVI. 181 note 2; XVIII. Part II. 211 note 2; Fleet's Dynasties of the Kánarese Districts, 99-103. [7] Priaulx, 226.

[8] Heeren, II. 442. Heeren's sesame and wood should probably be *sisu* or blackwood.

[9] It must be acknowledged that the description here given by Cosmas seems to point rather to Quilon than Callian, and some writers have also considered the Kalyán of the Periplus to be Quilon. See Paulini a S. Bartolomeo in India Orientalis Christiana. Vincent's account of the whole coast, however, renders this supposition untenable. [10] R. A. S. Journal, VI. 329; Cunningham, I. 554.

Section I.

Early Travellers.

as Cocintana. It appears in what is called the Catalan map of 1375 as Cocintaga.[1]

Reinaud[2] gives an extract from an Arab writer named Beladori to the effect that in A.D. 636 the Khalif Omar sent an army to Tanna and he thinks that this was probably our Thána. But he acknowledges that the diacritical marks of the initial letter are wanting and he gives no other particulars. In the travels of the merchant Suleiman written in A.D. 851 the country of Komkam is given as part of the kingdom of the Balhára.[3] But Alberuni, of whom Colonel Yule says that "in Indian matters he knew what he was talking about a great deal better than other old Arabic writers," says nothing of Balhára. He mentions a kingdom of Konkan with its capital at Tálah and gives the itinerary along the coast as Broach, Sindan 50 parasangs, Soubarah 6 parasangs, Tana 5 parasangs. Then the country of Láran and in that Djymowr, Malyah, Kandjy; then the Dravira which Reinaud says is the Coromandel Coast. Alberuni also mentions the plains of the Konkan as containing the animal called Scharan, a quadruped with four extra legs standing up above its back.[4]

Rashid-ud-Din about A.D. 1300 mentions Konkan, of which the capital is Tana on the sea-shore. But further on he mentions Gujarát as a large country within which are Cambay, Somnát Kankan, 'Tana and several other cities and towns;' and again 'Beyond Gujarát are Kankan and Tana, beyond them the country of Malabar.'[5] The question as to the dependence of the Konkan on Gujarát will be considered in the next section. It is sufficient here to say that the above extracts prove that the Konkan was a separate province with a capital called Thána, which is mentioned as a town on the coast by the traveller Al Masudi who died in A.D. 956.[6] By Al Idrisi in the twelfth century the following itinerary of the coast is given: "From Baruk (Broach) to Sindhábur[7] along the coast four days. From hence to Bana (Thána) upon the coast four days. This is a pretty town upon a great gulf where vessels anchor and from whence they set sail."[8] Gildemeister has no doubt that the ancient and modern places are the same, and thinks that Thána is the only port known to the Arabs between Broach and Goa of which the situation can be exactly ascertained.[9] When it is considered that, at no very distant time, the sea must have filled the whole space between the hills on the east of the Thána creek and those on the west of it, and must have flowed also over a very wide expanse of country between Thána and Bassein, it seems that these descriptions may have been tolerably correct for the Thána of eight hundred years ago. The last of these early Arabian

---

[1] R. A. S. Journal (New Series), IV. 340; Yule's Cathay, I. ccxxx.

[2] Fragments, 1826.

[3] Elliot, I. 4.

[4] Yule's Cathay, I. clxxxiv; Reinaud, 109, 121.

[5] Elliot, I. 60, 67.

[6] Elliot, I. 24.

[7] There is some confusion among travellers as to Sindabur. Colonel Yule thinks it was Goa, but that Al Idrisi and others confounded it with Sanjan. Indian Antiquary, III. 116.

[8] Elliot, I. 89.

[9] De Rebus Indicis, 46.

travellers is Ibn Batuta in the fourteeth century, who did not visit the Konkan, but mentions Thána as one of the ports from which great ships used to go to Aden.[1] But this last traveller was later in date than the famous Venetian Marco Polo (1290). His description of this part is unfortunately rather vague, nor does he mention the name Konkan. But he divides all this coast into the kingdom of Tanna and the kingdom of Lar. Of the latter his account is very indefinite, but Tanna he calls "a great kingdom with a language of its own and a king of its own, tributary to nobody; many ships and merchants frequent the place." He mentions leather, buckram, and cotton as the exports, and then he comes to the pirates, and their custom of giving up all the horses they take to the king, and keeping the rest of the plunder to themselves. With so much specified it is not difficult to assume Lar to be the Larika of Ptolemy, and to have included the northern part of the Konkan and part, at all events, of Gujarát. Colonel Yule adds that all the sea, west of this coast, was in early times called the sea of Lar.[2] The account of the martyrdom of the four friars at Thána, which is believed to have taken place on the Thursday before Palm Sunday 1322, is so curious that it cannot be omitted. It is given by the Friar Odoricus who himself visited Thána, and, though full of wonders anachronisms and absurdities, seems from some of the local details to be founded on fact. It is not clear whether the friars ever received the official beatification of Rome, but they appear as Beati in the Acta Sanctorum and are commemorated in one of the churches at Goa.

The account given by Odoricus is as follows: "I passed over (from Ormuz) in 28 days to Thána, where for the faith of Christ four of our minor friars had suffered a glorious martyrdom. The city is excellent in position, and hath great store of bread and wine, and aboundeth in trees. This was a great place in days of old, for it was the city of king Porus who waged so great a battle with Alexander. The people thereof are idolators, for they worship fire and serpents and trees also. The land is under the dominion of the Saracens, who have taken it by the force of arms, and they are now subject to the Emperor of Delhi. Here be found sundry kinds of beasts, and especially black lions in very great numbers, besides monkeys and babcons and bats as big as pigeons are here. There be also rats as big as are our dogs called *scherpi*. In this country there are trees which give wine which they call *loahe*, and which is very intoxicating. And here they do not bury the dead but carry them in great pomp to the fields, and cast them to the beasts and birds to be devoured. And they have here very fine oxen which have horns a good half pace in length, and have a hump on the back like a camel. And it was in this place called Tanna that the four minor friars suffered a glorious martyrdom for the sake of Christ."

They hired a ship at Ormuz to take them to Polumbum, but it took them to Thána instead. "Here there be fifteen houses of

---

[1] Travels, II. 177. [2] Yule's Marco Polo, II. 230, 302.

Section I.

Early Travellers.

Christians, that is to say, of Nestorians, who are schismatics and heretics." The friars were apparently hidden in one of these Nestorian houses, and the Kadi accidently heard of it, and sent for them, and Friar Thomas of Tolentino, Friar James of Padua, and Friar Demetrius a Georgian lay brother "good at the tongues" went, but Friar Peter of Sienna was left at home to take care of their things. There they began to dispute, and Friar Thomas confounded the Saracens as to Christ. Then the Kadi and the Saracens urged them to say what they thought of Mahomet. So, after trying to evade the question, Friar Thomas at last said, "Mahomet is the son of perdition, and hath his place in hell with the devil his father." Then the Saracens tied the friars up in the sun, that they might die a dreadful death by the intense heat. But after six hours they were cheerful and unscathed. So then they selected to burn them, and kindled a great fire "on the maidan, that is the Piazza of the city," and threw in Friar James first, and it blazed so high and wide that they could not see him, but they heard him invoking the Virgin. And when the fire was spent there he was unhurt. Then they made a much larger fire, and stripped him naked, and covered him and the wood with oil and threw him in again, while Thomas and Demetrius prayed fervently. But he again came out unhurt. Then the Malik (or podesta) tried to rescue them, and conveyed them "across a certain arm of the sea, that was a little distance from the city where there was a certain suburb," and there they were received into the house of an idolator. But the Kadi overpersuaded the Malik, and sent four men to kill the friars, and caused all the Christians to be imprisoned; and after talking in a friendly way to the friars, the four men cut off the heads of Thomas, James, and Demetrius. And the air was illuminated, and there was wonderful thunder and lightning, and the ship the friars had come in went to the bottom. And next day they found Friar Peter and tried to convert him, and on his refusing tortured him and then hung him up to a tree, and as he came down unhurt they clove him asunder and in the morning no trace of him could be found. Then a vision appeared to the Malik which disturbed him so much that he released the Christians, and "caused four mosques to be built in honour of the Friars, and put Saracen priests in each of them to abide continually." But the Emperor of Delhi sent for the Malik and put him to death, and the Kadi fled.

"Now in that country it is the custom never to bury the dead, but bodies are cast into the fields, and thus are speedily destroyed and consumed by the excessive heat; so the bodies of these friars lay for fourteen days in the sun and yet were found quite fresh and undecayed as if on the very day of their glorious martyrdom." So the Christians buried them. Afterwards Odoric came, and took their bones which worked various miracles.[1]

[1] The above description is from Yule's Cathay, I. 57. There is another account not much differing from this, but taken from a Latin manuscript in the preface to Yule's Mirabilia Descripta, page ix., and another differing as to dates and other particulars in Hakluyt's Voyages, II. 160.

It cannot escape notice that among all these later travellers no mention is made either of Kalyán, which had been so frequently mentioned in earlier times, or of Dábhol and Cheul, which are spoken of as great places very shortly afterwards. Ample time had certainly elapsed for Kalyán to have decayed, nor is it likely that two cities of any great pretensions should at the same time have flourished in such proximity as Kalyán and the modern Thána. The absence of any mention of Dábhol and Cheul is more difficult to explain; but until any account of their rise can be found it may perhaps be assumed that they emerged from obscurity only when the Musalmáns took possession of the Dakhan and required sea ports. It is also an allowable conjecture that Cheul did not rise to importance until the gradual drying up of the shallow waters around it Thána rendered less advantageous as a seaport.

The Arabs are said not only to have monopolised the early carrying trade between Arabia and Malabár, but also to have made many settlements on the Malabár and Konkan coasts.[1] Although some of these colonies in Kánara and Malabár are well known,[2] nothing certain can be adduced as to any in the Konkan. Still, in treating of the different races and castes of the district, reasons will be given for believing the very distinct class of Mahomedans known in Bombay as "Konkani Musalmáns" to be descended from the old Arab settlers. It is also stated, but the authority is not given, that the Abyssinians had planted colonies along the whole western coast of India from Cape Comorin upwards at a very early period of the Christian era, of which Rájpuri is one of the last remaining.[3]

The Muhammadan conquest is so distinct an era in all Indian history that it has seemed better to bring together all the descriptions of the country up to that period. In the same way the next section will contain all that can be made out as to its government and territorial divisions up to the Musalmán conquest; but this seems the best place in which to mention the immigration of two parties of foreigners from across the sea. The first of these were the ancestors of the interesting people called the Bene-Israel who are found scattered over the northern parts of the Kolába Collectorate and are believed to have arrived in India from Yemen during the sixth century of the Christian era.[4] Unfortunately no record ancient or recent of their history remains. Still the Jews of Cochin say that they found the Bene-Israel at Rájpuri when they first came to India, and their distinct position among the various native races taken with their partial adoption of Hindu usages points to a very ancient occupation. A further account of their present condition will be found in the last section.

The other immigrants who in India first found a home in the Konkan were the Pársis. They are believed to have arrived about

---

[1] Heeren, II. 438. [2] Vincent, II. 452, 283; Faria in Briggs, IV. 508.
[3] Jervis' Report on Konkan Weights and Measures (1829), 145.
[4] Dr. Wilson's Bene-Israel, 10-16. Details are given in Bom. Gaz. XI. 85-86; XVIII. 506-536.

Section I.

Early Travellers.

the end of the eighth century. It is certain that after living for some years at Diu they first settled on the continent of India at Sanján, now an utterly insignificant village, but which is believed then to have extended nearly to the sea coast.[1] Here they were permitted to settle by the Ràna, who is called Jáde, and whom Dr. Wilson believes to have been Jayadeva, a chief subordinate to the Rajput kings of Champáner or Pátan. In the next three hundred years they were dispersed through Hindustán; but the places mentioned as receiving them are all north of Sanján, which agrees with the present facts of their settlements, for it is about Dáhánu, twenty miles south of Sanján, that Pársis begin to be found in considerable numbers, and not merely as settlers for purposes of trade. Tárápur, ten miles south of Dáhánu, has also a large settlement of Parsis; but Kalyán is the only place south of that where their settlement is believed to be of earlier date than the British occupation of Bombay. Nargol, at the mouth of the Sanján creek, is still one of their largest villages, but Sanján itself does not now contain a single Pársi resident.

[1] Wilson's Sermon to Parsis, 6; Bom. R. A. S. Journal, I. 170. Compare Bom. Gaz. XIV. 506-536.

SECTION II.

ANTIQUITIES AND TRADITIONS.

Section II.

Antiquities.

In this section will be collected the little that is known of the history of the district previous to the Musalmáns coming to it at the beginning of the fourteenth century. And as the greater part of that little is to be found in cave temples and in inscriptions on copperplates and stones, the section will be in great part occupied by a description of these antiquarian remains. To this will be added some traditions bearing on the history of the district.

The large number of cave temples in the Konkan, especially in Sálsette, give the district a very high interest from an antiquarian point of view. But until a connected history of all the cave temples of Western India is written it is impossible to come to any satisfactory conclusion about those of the Konkan. Here nothing more can be done than to mention all that have been hitherto found, with all that is known as to their age and purpose, and the general purport of the inscriptions which still exist in them.

In the small island of Sálsette in the neighbourhood of Bombay, which is about eighteen miles long with an average breadth of ten miles, there are five groups of caves; at Kanheri, Kondivte, Jogeshvari, Mandapeshvar, and Mágáthan.[1] In the island of Ghárápuri are the well-known caves of Elephanta. In the neighbouring island of Karanja are also some small caves. In the Thána district north of Sálsette there are small caves at Jambrug, Kondáne, and Chandansár. In the Kolába district are the caves of Pál near Mahád and the large series of Kuda. In the Ratnágiri district there are caves at Chiplun, Khed, Dábhol, Sangameshvar, Gavháne-Velgaum, and Váde-Pádel. By far the greater part of these are small and apparently of no significance, having neither sculpture nor inscriptions, and may properly be called hermit's cells, generally two or three together. The caves of Elephanta have been so often and so thoroughly described[2] that they need no further mention here, for they are in no respect so remarkable as those of Kanheri which until Elura and Ajanta became so easily accessible were among the chief objects of interest on this side of India. Of them Bishop Heber wrote: "They are in every way remarkable from their number, their beautiful situation, their elaborate carving, and their marked connection with Buddh and his religion." Even to those who have visited Elura and Ajanta there are points of interest at Kanheri which the others want. "The excavations in Sálsette, especially those at Kanheri, are probably the most perfect specimens in India of a

[1] Dr. Wilson, 2, 3; Journal, II. 130.   [2] Bom. Gaz. XIV. 59-97.

Section II. Antiquities.

genuine Buddhist temple, college, and monastery. The great temple is not equal in beauty to that of Kárle in Poona but it exceeds that called Vishvakarma at Elura, and every other on this side of India."[1] "It is not only the numerous caves that give an idea of what the population of this barren rock must have been, but the tanks the terraces and the flights of steps which lead from one place to another."[2] The caves of Kanheri indeed are not a mere series of temples and halls without any trace of the existence of the worshippers who should have filled them, but the excavations include arrangements such as were required for a resident community. There are here in close proximity several *vihárs* or monasteries for associations of devotees, a great number of solitary cells or *grihás* for hermits, with *shálás* or halls for lectures and meetings, and *chaityas* or temples with relic-shrines not out of proportion in number or size to the dwelling-places. Outside the caves are reservoirs for water, a separate one for each cell, and couches or benches for the monks to recline on, carved out of the rock like everything else, while flights of steps and paths worn in the rock lead like streets from one series of caves to another; for the excavations are not only at different elevations in the face of the same hill, but also in several different hills and ravines. Here

> "All things in their place remain
> As all were ordered ages since,"

and the effect is that of a town carved out of the solid rock, which, although "life and thought here no longer dwell," would, if the monks and worshippers returned, be in a day or two as complete as when first inhabited.

The excavations are 102 in number, besides a good many now fallen in or choked with rubbish. They are all distinctly Buddhist, and contain fifty-four inscriptions, which vary in date from the first to the ninth century.[3] Only two of the inscriptions, however, contain dates, *Shak* 775 (A.D. 853) and *Shak* 779 (A.D. 877). They belong to the Silhára kings of the Konkan who were tributaries of the Ráshtrakutas of Málkhet.[4] These inscriptions have been all more or less completely deciphered. Except the Pahlavi inscriptions in cave 66, two, in caves 10 and 78, in Sanskrit, and one in cave 70 in peculiar Prákrit, the language of all is the Prákrit ordinarily used in cave writings. The letters, except in an ornamental looking inscription in cave 84, are the ordinary cave characters. As regards their age, ten appear from the form of the letters to belong to the time of the Andhrabhritya or Shátakarni king Vasishthiputra (A.D. 133-162), twenty to the Gotamiputra II. period (A.D. 177-196), ten to the fifth and sixth centuries, one to the eighth, three to the ninth or tenth, and one to the eleventh. Three inscriptions in caves 10 and 78, bear dates and names of kings and three in caves 3, 36, and 81 give the names of kings but no dates. The dates

---

[1] W. Erskine in Bom. Lit. Trans. III. 394. [2] Lord Valentia, II. 198.

[3] Details of the Kanheri caves are given in Bom. Gaz. XIV. 121-190.

[4] See below page 11.

of the rest have been calculated from the form of the letters. Though almost all are mutilated, enough is in most cases left to show the name of the giver, the place where he lived, and the character of the gift. Of the fifty-four inscriptions, twenty-eight give the names of donors, which especially in their terminations differ from the names now in use. In twenty-one the profession of the giver is mentioned; the majority were merchants or goldsmiths, some were recluses, and one was a minister or leading officer of the state. Except seven women, four of whom were nuns, all the givers were men. The places mentioned in the neighbourhood of the caves are the cities of Kalyán Sopára and Chemula, and the villages of Mangalsthán or Mágáthan, Sákapadra probably Sáki near Tulsi, and Saphád. Of more distant places there are Násik, Pratisthán or Paithan near Ahmadnagar, Dhanakot or Dharnikot near the mouth of the Krishna, Gaud or Bengal, and Dáttámitri in Sindh. The gifts were caves, cisterns, pathways, images, and endowments in cash or land. Of the six inscriptions which give the names of kings, one in cave 36 gives the name of Madharipntra and one in cave 3 gives Yajnashri Sátakarni or Gotamiputra II. two Andhrabhritya rulers of about the first or second century after Christ. Of the two, Madhariputra is believed to be the older and Yajnashri Shátakarni to be one of his successors. Madhariputra's coins have been found near Kolhápur and Professor Bhándárkar believes him to be the son and successor of Pudumáyi Vasishthiputra who is believed to have flourished about A.D. 130 and to be the S'ri Pulimai whom Ptolemy (A.D. 150) places at Paithan near Ahmadnagar. Yajnashri Shátakarni or Gotamiputra II. appears in the Násik inscriptions and his coins have been found at Kolhápur, at Dharnikot near the mouth of the Krishna the old capital of the Andhrabhrityas, and on the 9th April 1882 in a stupa or relic mound in Sopára near Bassein. Two of the other inscriptions in which mention is made of the names of kings are caves 10 and 78. These are among the latest inscriptions at Kanheri both belonging to the ninth century, and the names given are of Siláhára kings of the Konkan. They are interesting as giving the names of two kings in each of these dynasties as well as two dates twenty-four years apart in the contemporary rule of one sovereign in each family. Kapardi II. the Siláhára king, the son of Pulashakti, whose capital was probably Chemula, was reigning for the twenty-four years between 853 and 878, and apparently Amoghvarsh ruled at Málkhet during the same period. This Amoghvarsh is mentioned as the son and successor of Jagattung; Amoghvarsh I. was the son of Govind III. one of whose titles was Jagattung; and he must have ruled from 810 to 830. Amoghvarsh II. was the son of Indra himself who may have borne the title of Amoghvarsh and he succeeded Jagattung about 850.

The nearest caves to Kanheri, those of Mandapeshvar and Mágáthan, are Bráhmanical. This may be attributed either to the Bráhmans, after the overthrow of Buddhism in Western India, having taken a pride in attempting to rival the works

Section II.

Antiquities.

of their predecessors,[1] or to the fact that in the early years of our era Bráhmans and Buddhists lived at peace with one another, and were equally favoured and protected by the reigning sovereigns.[2] In accordance with this view Colonel Sykes records of the Chálukya kings that, though mostly votaries of Shiv, they extended the most perfect toleration to other creeds.[3] The caves at Mandapeshvar are rendered more curious by their having been occupied by the Portuguese, who called the place Mont Pezier, and erected a church and college on the hill in which the caves are, and set up an altar in the caves, so that they became, as it were, a crypt to the church above.

The caves of Kuda are purely Buddhist, and form a large series of twenty-six. Almost all of them are plain and, except in size, much alike. Five of them, one unfinished, are *chaityas* or temple caves containing the secred relic-shrine or *dághoba;* the other twenty-one are dwelling caves or *lenás* as they are called in the inscriptions. These *lenás* generally consist of a veranda with a door and window opening into a cell or cells in which are rock-cut benches for the monks to sleep on. The doors are almost all grooved for wooden frames. The walls of almost all the caves were plastered with earth and rice chaff and on several of them are remains of painting. There are in all twenty-four inscriptions, six of them in one cave, the sixth, which is the only cave with sculpture. Five of these six inscriptions belong to the fifth or sixth century after Christ; all the rest are in letters of about the first century before Christ and record the names of the giver and the nature of the gift, whether a cave, a cistern, or both. Several of the figures are women and one of them is a Bráhman's wife. It is worthy of note that the name Shiv forms part of the name of several of the givers. The caves in the neighbourhood of Mahád are mere cells. One group of twenty-nine of about the first or second century after Christ are at Pále about two miles north-west of Mahád, and two groups of the same age at Kol, about a mile to the south. The Pále group has one inscription of about A.D. 130 and the second Kole group has three short inscriptions of about the same time. There is a third group of a few cells and cisterns in a hill to the north-east of Mahád, and one cell in a hill to the south near the road leading to Nágothna. In the hills above the old port of Cheul are ten caves of about A.D. 150, all plain and much ruined. It is probable that, besides those mentioned above, many other small caves exist in hills and other places not generally accessible, and one such may be mentioned in the hill-fort of Asheri.

The conclusion undoubtedly is that Sálsette and a part of the Konkan south of Bombay were strongholds of Buddhism. It is not so certain that this would involve any considerable degree of civilization. On the contrary it is known that the Buddhist leaders inclined to establish their great monasteries in places remote

---

[1] Dr. Wilson in Bom. R. A. S. Journal, III. 6.
[2] Dr. Stevenson in Bom. R. A. S. Journal, V. 41. [3] R. A. S. Journal, IV. 18.

Section II.

Antiquities.

from cities, and chiefly remarkable, as Kánheri undoubtedly is, for beauty of situation. Here indeed we may believe that to many "the calm life of the hermit seemed a haven of peace where a life of self-denial and earnest meditation might lead to some solution of the strange enigmas of life."[1]

It should be mentioned that when the Portuguese took possession of Sálsette they found the Kánheri caves inhabited by *Jogis*, about whom as well as about the caves themselves the early historians made many wonderful statements. Thus the cells exceeded 3000 in number, each with a cistern supplied by one conduit; the chief *Jogi* was 150 years old; and from the caves at Kanheri an underground passage some said to Cambay, some to Agra, in which a number of Portuguese explorers travelled for seven days without seeing any sign of an outlet, and so were obliged at last to turn back.[2] The elephant at Elephanta was the work of a king in whose time a shower of golden rain fell for three hours.[3] Even to an English traveller of the sixteenth century it seemed scarcely incredible that the water there ran uphill in order to supply the wants of the monks.

Of considerably later date than that given to the Kanheri and other cave inscriptions are the inscribed stones and copperplates which have been found in the Konkan in considerable numbers, and which from the ninth century downwards afford some evidence as to the civilization and divisions of the country.

A copperplate found by Dr. Bird in 1839, in a relic mound at Kanheri in front of the great chapel cave No. 3 is dated in the 245th year of the Trikutakas, a dynasty of kings who, about the fourth or fifth century, appear to have held Central and South Gujarát and the North Konkan.[4] From the form of the letters, which seem to belong to the fifth century, Dr. Burgess considers the era to be the Gupta commencing in A.D. 219 and thus makes the date of the plate A.D. 464.[5] Two hoards of silver coins bearing the legend, "The illustrious Krishnarája the great lord meditating on the feet of his mother and father" were found in 1881-82, one in the island of Bombay the other at Mulgaon in Sálsette. This seems to show that the early Ráshtrakuta king Krishna (A.D. 375-400), whose coins have already been found in Báglán in Násik and Karhád in Sátára, also held possession of the North Konkan.[6]

About the middle of the sixth century kings of the Maurya and Nala dynasties appear to have been ruling in the Konkan. Kirtivarma (A.D. 550-567), the first Chálukya king who turned his arms against the Konkan, is described as the night of death to the Nalas and

[1] Rhys David's Buddhism. [2] DeCoutto, VII. 238. [3] DeCoutto, VII. 261.

[4] A copperplate of the Trikutaka king Darhasena was in 1884 found in Párdi in the Surat district.

[5] Trikuta or The Three Hills is mentioned by Kálidás (A.D. 500) as a city on a lofty site built by Raghu when he conquered the Konkan. The name is the same as Trigiri the Sanskrit form of Tagar, and Pandit Bhagvánlál identifies the city with Junnar in west Poona, a place of great importance on a high site, and between the three hills of Shivneri, Ganeshlena, and Mánmodi.

[6] Compare Cunningham's Archæological Survey Report, IX. 30; Fleet's Kánarese Dynasties, 31 note 2.

Section II.
Antiquities.

Mauryas.[1] And an inscription of Kirtivarma's grandson Pulikeshi II. (A.D. 610-640) under whom the Konkan was conquered, describes his general Chanda-danda, as a great wave which drove before it the watery stores of the pools, that is the Mauryas. The Chálukya general with hundreds of ships attacked the Maurya capital Puri, the goddess of the fortunes of the western ocean.[2] A stone inscription from Váda in the north of the Thána district shows that a Mauryan king of the name of Suketuvarma was then ruling in the Konkan.[3]

During the reign of the great Naushervan (531-578), when the Persians were the rulers of the commerce of the eastern seas, the relations between Western India and Persia were extremely close.[4] On the Arab overthrow of Yezdejard III. (638) the last of the Sassanians, several bands of Persians sought refuge on the Thána coast and were kindly received by Jádav Ràna, apparently a Yádav chief of Sanján.[5] In the years immediately after their conquest of Persia the Arabs made several raids on the coasts of Western India; one of these in 637 from Bahrein and Oman in the Persian gulf plundered the Konkan coast near Thána.[6]

---

[1] Ind. Ant. VIII. 244.

[2] Dr. Burgess' Archæological Survey Report, III. 26. Puri has not been identified. Bom. Gaz. XIV. 401-402.

[3] Dr. Bhagvánlál Indràji. Compare Bom. Gaz. XIII. Part II. 420 note 8; XIV. 372-373.

[4] Yule (Cathay, I. 56) notices that about this time the lower Euphrates was called Hind or India, but this seems to have been an ancient practice. Rawlinson in J. R. G. S. XXVII. 186. As to the extent of the Persian trade at this time, see Reinaud's Mémoire Sur l'Inde, 124. In the fifth and sixth centuries, besides the Persian trade, there was an active Arab-trade up the Persian gulf and the Euphrates to Hira on the right or west bank of the river, not far from the ruins of Babylon. There was also much traffic with Obollah near the mouth of the joint river not far from Basra. Reinaud's Abu-l-fida, ccclxxxii. Obollah is also at this time (A.D. 400-600) noticed as the terminus of the Indian and Chinese vessels which were too large to pass up the river to Hira. (Ditto and Yule's Cathay, lxxvii. 55.) So close was its connection with India that the Talmud writers always speak of it as Hindike or Indian Obillah (Rawlinson in J. R. G. S. XXVII. 186). According to Masudi (915) Obollah was the only port under the Sassanian kings (Prairies d'Or, III. 164). McCrindle (Periplus, 103; compare Vincent, II. 377) identifies it with the Apologos of the Periplus (A.D. 247) which he holds took the place of Ptolemy's (A.D. 150) Teredon or Diridotus. Reinaud (Ind. Ant. VIII. 330) holds that Obollah is a corruption of the Greek Apologos, a custom house. But Vincent's view (II. 355) that Apologos is a Greek form of the original Obollah or Obollegh seems more likely. In Vincent's opinion (Ditto, II. 356) Obollah was founded by the Parthians. At the time of the Arab conquest of Persia (637) Abillah is mentioned as the port of entry at the mouth of the Euphrates (J. R. A. S. XII. 208). In spite of the rivalry of the new Arab port of Basrah, Obollah continued a considerable centre of trade. It is mentioned by Tabari in the ninth century (Reinaud's Abu-l-fida, ccclxxxii.): Masudi (913) notices it as a leading town (Prairies d'Or, I. 230-231); Idrisi (1135) as a very rich and flourishing city (Jaubert's Ed. I. 369); and it appears in the fourteenth century in Abu-l-fida (Reinaud's Abu-l-fida, 72). It was important enough to give the Persian gulf the name of the Gulf of Obollah (D'Herbelot's Bibliotheque Orientale, III. 61). According to D'Herbelot when he wrote (about 1670) Obollah was still a strong well peopled town (Ditto). The importance of the town and the likeness of the names suggest that Obollah is the Abulamah from which came the Persian or Parthian Harpharan of Abulamah who records the gift of a cave in Kárli inscription 20. This identification supports the close connection by sea between the Parthians and the west coast of India in the centuries before and after the Christian era.

[5] See above page 8.

[6] Elliot and Dowson's History, I. 415, 416. As the companion fleet which was sent to Dibal or Diul in Sindh made a trade settlement at that town, this attack on Thána

Section II.
Antiquities.

No further notice[1] of the North Konkan has been traced till the rise of the Siláháras, twenty of whom, so far as present information goes, ruled in the North Konkan from about A.D. 810 to A.D. 1260, a period of 450 years.

So far as at present known, the family tree of the Thána Siláháras was:

(1) Kapardi.
(2) Pulashakti.
(3) Kapardi (II.) named Laghu or the Younger, (*Shak* 775-799, A.D. 853-877).
(4) Vappuvanna.

(5) Jhanjha (A.D. 916).
Lasthiyavva (married Bhillama the fourth Chándor Yádav king).

(6) Goggi.
(7) Vajjadadev.
(8) Aparájit (*Shak* 919, A.D. 997).

(9) Vajjadadev (II.).
(10) Arikeshari (*Shak* 939, A.D. 1017).

(11) Chhittaráj (*Shak* 948, A.D. 1026).
(12) Nágárjun.
(13) Mummuni (*Shak* 982, A.D. 1060).

(14) Anantdev (*Shak* 1003 and 1016, A.D. 1081 and 1094).
?
(15) Aparáditya (*Shak* 1060, A.D. 1198).
?
(16) Haripáldev (*Shak* 1071, 1072, and 1075, A.D. 1149, 1150, and 1153).
?
(17) Mallikárjun (*Shak* 1078 and 1082, A.D. 1156 and 1160).
?
(18) Aparáditya (II.) (*Shak* 1106 and 1109, A.D. 1184 and 1187).
?
(19) Keshidev (*Shak* 1125 and 1161, A.D. 1203 and 1238).
?
(20) Someshvar (*Shak* 1171 and 1182, A.D. 1249 and 1260).

Who the Siláháras were has not been ascertained. The name is variously spelt Siláhára, Shailáhára, Shrilára, Shilára, and Silára; even the same inscription has more than one form, and one inscription has the three forms Silára, Shilára, and Shrilára.[2] Lassen suggests that the Siláháras are of Afghán origin, as Silár Káfirs are still found in Afghanistán.[3] But the southern ending Ayya of the names of almost all their ministers and the un-Sanskrit names of some of the chiefs favour the view that they were of southern or Dravidian origin.[4]

---

was probably more than a plundering raid. The Kaliph Umar (634-643), who had not been consulted, was displeased with the expedition and forbad any further attempt.

[1] Hiuen Tsiang's (642) Konkanapura, about 330 miles from the Drávid country, was thought by General Cunningham (Anc. Geog. 552) to be Kalyán, or some other place in the Konkan. Dr. Burnell (Ind. Ant. VII. 39) has identified it with Konkanhalli in Mysore.

[2] Ind. Ant. IX. 33, 34, 35; Jour. B. B. R. A. S. XIII. 2, 3, 5.

[3] Lassen's Ind. Alt. IV. 113.

[4] It seems probable that Siláhára and Shailáhára are Sanskritised forms of the common Maráthi surname Selar. The story of the origin of the name is that Jimutváhan the mythical founder was the son of a spirit or Vidyádhara, who under a curse became a man. At this time Vishnu's eagle, Garuda, conquered the serpent king Vásuki and forced Vásuki to give him one of his serpent subjects for his daily food. After a time it came to the lot of the serpent Shankhachuda to be sacrificed. He was taken to a stone, *shila*, and left for the eagle to devour. Jimutváhan resolved to save the victim, and placed himself on the rock instead of the serpent. When Garuda came, Jimutváhan said he was the victim and Garuda devoured him except his head. Meantime Jimutváhan's wife came, and finding her husband slain, reproach-

Section II.

Antiquities.

The Siláháras seem to have remained under the Ráshtrakutas till about the close of the tenth century A.D. 997, when Aparájit assumed independent power.[1] The Thána Siláháras seem to have held the greater part of the present districts of Thána and Kolába. Their capital seems to have been Puri,[2] and their places of note were Hamjaman probably Sanján in Dáhánu, Thána (Shristhának), Sopára (Shurpárak), Chaul (Chemuli), Lonád (Lavanatata), and Uran.[3] As the Yádavs call themselves lords of the excellent city of Dvárávatipura or Dwárka and the Kadambas call themselves lords of the excellent city of Banavásipura or Banavási, so the Siláháras call themselves lords of the excellent city of Tagarapura or Tagar. This title would furnish a clue to the origin of the Siláháras if, unfortunately, the site of Tagar was not uncertain.[4]

---

ed Garuda, who restored him to life and at her request ceased to devour the serpents. For this act of self-sacrifice Jimutváhan gained the name of the Rock-devoured *Shiláhára*. J. R. A. S. (Old Series), IV. 113. Tawney's Kathá Sarit Ságara, I. 174-186. A stanza from this story forms the beginning of all Siláhára copperplate inscriptions.

[1] See below page 18. The early Siláháras, though they call themselves Rájás and Konkan Chakravartis, seem to have been only Mahámandleshvaras or Mahásámantádhipatis, that is great nobles. In two Kanheri cave inscriptions (Arch. Sur. X. 61, 62) the third Siláhára king Kapardi II. (A.D. 853 to 877) is mentioned as a subordinate of the Ráshtrakutas. Of the later Siláháras Anantapál, A.D. 1094, and Aparáditya, A.D. 1138, claim to be independent. Ind. Ant. IX. 45.

[2] The Siláhára Puri, if, as seems likely, it is the same as the Maurya Puri (Ind. Ant. VIII. 244), was a coast town. Of the possible coast towns Thána and Chaul may be rejected, as they appear under the names of Shristhának and Chemuli in inscriptions in which Puri also occurs (As. Res. I. 361, 364; Ind. Ant. IX. 38). Kalyán and Sopára may be given up as unsuitable for an attack by sea, and to Sopára there is the further objection that it appears in the same copperplate in which Puri occurs. (Ind. Ant. IX. 38.) There remain Mangalpuri or Mágáthan in Sálsette, Ghárápuri or Elephanta, and Rájápuri or Janjira. As neither Mangalpuri nor Rájápuri has remains of an old capital, perhaps the most likely identification of Puri is the Moreh landing or Bandar on the north-east corner of Ghárápuri or Elephanta, where many ancient remains have been found. Compare Bom. Gaz. XIV. Places and Appendix A.

[3] Other places of less note mentioned in the inscriptions are Bhádán, Padgha, and Bábgaon villages, and the Kumbhári river in Bhiwndi, Kanher in Bassein, and Chanje (Chadiche) village near Uran.

[4] Tagar has been identified by Wilford (As. Res. I. 369) with Devgiri or Daulatabad and by Dr. Burgess with Roza about four miles from Daulatabad (Bidar and Aurangabad, 55); Lassen and Yule place it doubtfully at Kulburga (Ditto); Pandit Bhagvánlál, as already stated, at Junnar; Grant Duff (Maráthás, 11) near Bhir on the Godávari; and Mr. J. F. Fleet, I. C. S. (Kánarese Dynasties, 99-103) at Kolhápur. Prof. Bhandárkar observes: 'The identification of Tagar with Devgiri is based on the supposition that the former name is a corruption of the latter. But that it is not so is proved by its occurrence as Tagar in the Siláhára grants (A.D. 997-1094), and in a Chalukya grant of A.D. 612, the language of all of which is Sanskrit. The modern Junnar cannot have been Tagar, since the Greeks place Tagar ten days' journey to the east of Paithan. On the supposition that Junnar was Tagar, one would expect the Chálukya plate issued to a Bráhman of Tagar to have been found at or near Junnar. But it was found at Haidarabad in the Dakhan. The author of the Periplus calls Tagar "the greatest city" in Dakhinabades or Dakshinápath. The Siláhára princes or chiefs, who formed three distinct branches of a dynasty that ruled over two parts of the Konkan and the country about Kolhápur, trace their origin to Jimutváhan the Vidyadhar or demigod and style themselves "The lords of the excellent city of Tagar." From this it would appear that the Siláháras were an ancient family, and that their original seat was Tagar whence they spread to the confines of the country. Tagar therefore was probably the centre of one of the earliest Aryan settlements in the Dandakáranya or 'forest of Dandaka,' as the Dakhan or Maháráshtra was called. These early settlements followed the course of the Godávari. Hence it is that in the formula repeated at the beginning of any religious

Besides the Siláhára references, the only known Sanskrit notice of Tagar is in a Chálukya copperplate found near Haidarabad in the Dakhan and dated A.D. 612.[1] As has been already noticed, the references to Tagar in Ptolemy and in the Periplus point to a city considerably to the east of Paithan, and the phrase in the Periplus,[2] 'That many articles brought into Tagar from the parts along the coast were sent by wagons to Broach,' seems to show that Tagar was in communication with the Bay of Bengal, and was supported by the eastern trade, which in later times enriched Málkhet, Kalyán, Bidar, Golkonda, and Haidarabad.

From numerous references and grants the Thána Siláháras seem to have been worshippers of Shiv.[3]

Of Kapardi, the first of the Thána Siláháras, nothing is known except that he claims descent from Jimutváhan. Pulashakti his son and successor, in an undated inscription in Kanheri Cave 78, is mentioned as the governor of Mangalpuri in the Konkan, and as the humble servant of (the Ráshtrakuta king) Amoghvarsh. The third king, Pulashakti's son, Kapardi II. was called the Younger *Laghu*. Two inscriptions in Kanheri Caves 10 and 78, dated A.D. 853 and 877, seem to show that he was subordinate to the Ráshtrakutas. The son of Kapardi II. was the fourth king Vappuvanna, and his son was Jhanjha the fifth king. Jhanjha is mentioned by the Arab historian Masudi as ruling over Saimur (Cheul) in A.D. 916.[4] He must have been a staunch Shaivite, as, according to a Siláhára copperplate of A.D. 1094, he built twelve temples of Shambhu.[5] According to an unpublished copperplate in the possession of Pandit Bhagvánlál, Jhanjha had a daughter named Lasthiyavva, who was married to Bhillama the fourth of the Chándor Yádavs.[6]

The next king was Jhanjha's brother Goggi, and after him came Goggi's son Vajjadadev. Of the eighth king, Vajjadadev's son

---

ceremony in Maháráshtra, the place where the ceremony is performed is alluded to by giving its bearing from the Godávari. People in Khándesh use the words '*Godávárya uttara tire*' that is 'on the northern bank of the Godávari,' while those to the south of the river, as far as the borders of the country, use the expression '*Godávarya dakshine tire*' that is 'on the southern bank of the Godávari.' If then Tagar was one of the earliest of the Aryan settlements, it must be situated on or near the banks of the Godávari, as the ancient town of Paithan is; and its bearing from Paithan given by the Greek geographers agrees with this supposition, as the course of the Godávari from that point is nearly easterly. Tagar must therefore be looked for to the east of Paithan. If the name has undergone corruption, it must, by the Prákrit law of dropping the initial mutes, be first changed to Taaraura, and thence to Tárur or Terur. Can it be the modern Dárur or Dhárur in the Nizám's dominions, twenty-five miles east of Grant Duff's Bhir and seventy miles south-east of Paithan?

[1] Ind. Ant. VI. 75. [2] McCrindle, 126.

[3] The most marked passages are in a copperplate of A.D. 1094, where the fifth king Jhanjha is mentioned as having built twelve temples to Shambhu, and the tenth king Arikeshari as having, by direction of his father, visited Someshvar or Somnáth, offering up before him the whole earth (Ind. Ant. IX. 37). The Kolhápur Siláháras appear to have been tolerant kings, as one copperplate records grants to Mahádev, Buddha, and Arhat (Jour. B. B. R. A. S. XIII. 17). Compare Fleet's Kánarese Dynasties, 103. [4] Prairies d'Or, II. 85. [5] Ind. Ant. IX. 35.

[6] The text is, "*Bháryá yasya cha Jhanjharájatanayá shri Lasthiyavvávhayá.*" A short account of the Chándor Yádavs is given in the Násik Statistical Account, Bom. Gaz. XVI. 185.

Section II.

Antiquities.

Aparájit or Birundakarám, a copperplate dated 997 (*Shak* 919) has lately been found at Bher, about ten miles north of Bhiwndi.[1] It appears from this plate that during Aparájit's reign, his Ráshtrakuta overlord Karkarája or Kakkala was overthrown and slain by the Chálukyan Tailapa, and that Aparájit became independent some time between 972 and 997.[2]

In a copperplate of A.D. 1094, recording a grant by the fourteenth king Anantdev, Aparájit is mentioned as having welcomed Gomma, confirmed to Aiyapdev the sovereignty which had been shaken, and afforded security to Bhillamámmamanambudha ?[3] The next king was Aparájit's son Vajjadadev. The next king Arikeshari, Vajjadadev's brother, in a copperplate grant dated A.D. 1017, is styled the lord of fourteen hundred Konkan villages. Mention is also made of the cities of Shristhának, Puri, and Hamyaman probably Sanján.[4] The eleventh king was Vajjadadev's son Chhittarájdev. In a copperplate dated *Shak* 948 (A.D. 1025) he is styled the ruler of the fourteen hundred Konkan villages, the chief of which were Puri and Hamyaman.[5] The twelfth king was Nágárjun, the younger brother of Chhittarájdev. After him came Nágárjun's younger brother Mummuni or Mámváni, who is mentioned in an inscription dated A.D. 1060 (*Shak* 982).[6] The fourteenth king was Mummuni or Mámváni's son Anantpál or Anantdev, whose name occurs in two grants dated A.D. 1081 and 1096.[7] In the 1096 grant Anantpál is mentioned as ruling over the whole Konkan fourteen hundred

---

[1] The copperplate records the grant at Shristhának or Thána, of Bhadáne village about eight miles east of Bhiwndi for the worship of Lonáditya residing in (whose temple is in) Lavanatata (Lonád), on the fourth of the dark half of *Ashádh* (June-July) *Shak* 919 (A.D. 997), as a *Dakshináyan* gift, that is a gift made on the occasion of the sun beginning to pass to the south. Aparájita's ministers were Sangalaiya and Siuhapaiya. The inscription was written by Sangalaiya's son Annapai. The grant was settled in Thána, *Tachcha Shristhánake dhruvam*. [2] Pandit Bhagvánlál Indraji.

[3] Ind. Ant. IX. 36. Of Gomma and Aiyapdev nothing is known; of the third name only Bhillam the son-in-law of Jhanjha can be made out.

[4] Asiatic Researches, I. 357-367. This grant was found in 1787 while digging foundations in Thána fort. Arikeshari's ministers were Vásapaiya and Várdhapaiya. The grant consists of several villages given to a family priest, the illustrious Tikkapaiya son of the illustrious astrologer Chchhinpaiya, an inhabitant of Shristhának (Thána) on the occasion of a full eclipse of the moon in *Kártik* (October-November) *Shak* 939 (A.D. 1017) Pingala *Samvatsara*. The grant was written by the illustrious Nágalaiya, the great bard, and engraved on plates of copper by Vedapaiya's son Mándhárpaiya.

[5] Ind. Ant. V. 276-281. His ministers were the chief functionary *Sarvádhikári* the illustrious Náganaiya, the minister for peace and war the illustrious Sihapaiya, and the minister for peace and war for Karnáta (Kanara) the illustrious Kapardi. The grant, which is dated Sunday the fifteenth of the bright half of *Kártik* (October-November) *Shak* 948 (A.D. 1026) Kshaya *Samvatsara* is of a field in the village of Nour (the modern Naura two miles north of Bhándup) in the *táluka* of Shatshashthi (Sálsette) included in Shristhának (Thána). The donee is a Bráhman Amadevaiya the son of Vipranodamaiya, who belonged to the Chhandogashákha of the Sámved.

[6] Jour. B. B. R. A. S. XII. 329-332. In this inscription, which is in the Ambarnáth temple near Kalyán, he is called Mámvánirájadev and his ministers are named Vinta(paiya), Náganaiya, Vakadaiya, Jogalaiya, Padhisena, and Bháilaiya. The inscription records the construction of a temple of Chhittarájdev, that is a temple, the merit of building which counts to Chhittarájdev.

[7] The A.D. 1081 grant was found in Vehár in Sálsette and the 1096 grant in Khárepátan in Devgad in the Ratnágiri district. The Vehár stone was found in 1881 and

Section II.
Antiquities.

villages, the chief of which was Puri and next to it Hanjamana probably Sanján, and as having cast into the ocean of the edge of his sword those wicked heaps of sin, who at a time of misfortune, caused by the rise to power of hostile relatives, devastated the whole Konkan, harassing gods and Bráhmans.[1]

The names of six Siláhára kings later than Anantdev have been made out from land-grant stones. As these stones do not give a pedigree, the order and relationship of the kings cannot be determined.

The first of these kings is Aparáditya, who is mentioned in a stone dated A.D. 1138 (*Shak* 1060).[2] The next king is Haripáldev, who is mentioned in three stones dated A.D. 1149, 1150, and 1153 (*Shak* 1071, 1072, and 1075).[3]

The next king is Mallikárjun, of whom two grants are recorded, one from Chiplún in Ratnágiri dated 1156 (*Shak* 1078), the other from Bassein dated 1160 (*Shak* 1082). This Mallikárjun seems to be the Konkan king, who was defeated near Balsár by Ámbada the general

---

records a grant by Anantdev in *Shak* 1003 (A.D. 1081), the chief minister being Rudrapai. The inscription mentions Ajapálaiya, son of Mátaiya of the Vyádika family, and the grant of some *drammas* to *khárdsán mandli*[?] (Pandit Bhagvánlál). The Khárepátan copperplates were found several years ago and give the names of all the thirteen Siláhára kings before Anantdev. Ind. Ant. IX. 33-46.

[1] This account refers to some civil strife of which nothing is known (Ind. Ant. IX. 41). Anantdev's ministers were the illustrious Nauvitaka Vásaida, Rishibhatta, the illustrious Pádhisen Mahádevaiya prabhu, and Somanaiya prabhu. The grant is dated the first day of the bright half of *Mágh* (January-February) in the year *Shak* 1016 (A.D. 1094), Bháv *Samvatsara*. It consists of an exemption from tolls for all carts belonging to the great minister the illustrious Bhábhana *shreshthi*, the son of the great minister Durgashreshthi of Valipavana, probably Pálpattna or the city of Pál near Mahád in Kolába, and his brother the illustrious Dhanamshreshthi. Their carts may come into any of the ports, Shristhának, Nágpur perhaps Nágothna, Shurparak, Chemuli, and others included within the Konkan Fourteen Hundred. They are also freed from the toll on the ingress or egress of those who carry on the business of *norika* (?)

[2] This stone, which was found in 1881 at Chánje near Uran in the Karanja petty division, records the grant of a field in Nágum, probably the modern Nágaon about four miles west of Uran, for the merit of his mother Liládevi; and another grant of a garden in Chadija (Chánje) village. This is the Aparáditya 'king of the Konkan,' who is mentioned in Mankha's Shrikanthacharita (a book found by Dr. Buhler in Káshmir and ascribed by him to A.D. 1135-1145) as sending Tejakanth from Shurpárak (Sopára) to the literary congress held at Káshmir, of which details are given in that book. Jour. B. B. R. A. S. XII. Extra Number, 51. cxv.

[3] The 1149 stone is built into the plinth of the back veranda of the house of one Jairám Bháskar Sonár at Sopára. It records a gift. The name of the king is doubtful. It may be also read Kurpáldev. The 1150 stone was found near Agáshi in 1881. It is dated 1st *Márgshirsh* (December-January), in the Pramoda *Samvatsara*, *Shak* 1072 (A.D. 1150). Haripál's ministers were Vesupadval, Lakhsman prabhu, Padmashivrául, and Vásugi náyak. The grant is of the permanent income of Shrinevadi in charge of a Pattakil (Pátil) named Rája, to the family priest Brahmadevbhatt son of Divákarbhatt and grandson of Govardhanbhatt by prince A'havamalla enjoying the village of Vattárak (Vatár) in Shurpárak (Sopára). The witnesses to the grant are Risi Mhátara, head of Vattárak village, Náguji Mhátara, Anantnáyak, and Chángdev Mhátara. [Pandit Bhagvánlál.] Another inscription of Haripáldev has been found on a stone in Karanjon in Bassein. The inscription is of thirteen lines which are very hard to read. In the third and fourth lines can be read very doubtfully 'the illustrious Haripáldev, the chief of the Mahámandaleshvaras, adorned with all the royal titles.' The 1153 stone was found near Borivli station in 1882. The inscription is in nine lines, and bears date *Shak* 1075, Shrimukh *Samvatsara* and the name of king Haripál.

Section II. Antiquities.

of the Gujarát king Kumárpál Solanki (A.D. 1143-1174).[1] Next comes Aparáditya II. of whom there are four land-grant stones, three of them dated, one in 1184 (*Shak* 1106) and two in 1187 (*Shak* 1109), and one undated.[2]

The next king is Keshidev, son of Aparárka (Aparáditya II. ?), two of whose land-grant stones have been found, one dated 1203 (*Shak* 1125) the other 1238 (*Shak* 1161).[3]

---

[1] The Kumárpál Charitra (A.D. 1170) which gives details of this defeat of Mallikárjun, see below page 24, describes Mallikárjun's father as Mahánand, and his capital as Shatánandpur 'surrounded by the ocean' (*Shatánapure jaladhiveshtite Mahánando rája*). Mahánand is an addition to the Siláhára table, but the form appears doubtful and does not correspond with the name of any of the preceding or succeeding kings. 'Surrounded by the ocean' might apply to a town either in Sálsette or on Sopára island. But the epithet applies much better to a town on Elephanta island, and the similarity in name suggests that Shatánandpur may be Santapur, an old name for Elephanta. See Bom. Gaz. XIV. Thána Places of Interest, 81-82. Mallikárjun's Chiplún stone was found in 1880 by Mr. Falle, of the Marine Survey, under a wall in Chiplún (Jour. B. B. R. A. S. XIV. 35). It is now in the museum of the Bombay Branch of the Royal Asiatic Society. The writing gives the name of Mallikárjun and bears date *Shak* 1078 (A.D. 1156). His ministers were Nágalaiya and Lakshmanaiya's son Anantugi (Pandit Bhagvánlál). The Bassein stone styles the king 'Shri-Siláhára Mallikárjun' and the date given is *Shak* 1082 (A.D. 1160), Vishva *Samvatsara*, his ministers being Prabhákar náyak and Anantpai prabhu. The grant is of a field (?) or garden (?) called Shilárvátak in Padhálasak in Katakhadi by two royal priests, for the restoration of a temple. Pandit Bhagvánlál.

[2] The 1184 (*Shak* 1106) stone was found in February 1882 about a mile south-west of Lonád in Bhiwndi. Of the two *Shak* 1109 (A.D. 1187) stones, one found near Government House, Parel, records a grant by Aparáditya, the ruler of the Konkan, of 24 *dramma* coins after exempting other taxes, the fixed revenue of one cart in the village of Máhuli (probably the modern Máhul near Kurla) connected with Shatshashthi, which is in the possession of Anantapai prabhu, for performing the worship by five rites of (the god) Vaidyanáth, lord of Darbhávati. The last line of the inscription shows that it was written by a Káyasth named Válig Pandit (Jour. B. B. R. A. S. XII. 335). The second *Shak* 1109 (A.D. 1187) stone is in the museum of the Bombay Branch of the Royal Asiatic Society. It is dated *Shak* 1109 (A.D. 1187) Vishvávasu *Samvatsara*, on Sunday the sixth of the bright half of *Chaitra* (April-May). The grantor is the great minister Lakshmannáyaka son of Bháskarnáyaka, and something is said in the grant about the god Somnáth of Suráshtra (Ind. Ant. IX. 49). The fourth stone, which bears no date, was found near Kalambhom in Bassein in 1882. It gives the name of Aparáditya, and from the late form of the letters probably belongs to this king. A fifth stone has recently been found near Bassein. The date is doubtful; it looks like *Shak* 1107 (A.D. 1185), Pandit Bhagvánlál.

[3] The *Shak* 1125 (A.D. 1203) stone was found in 1881 near Mándvi in Bassein. It records the grant of something for offerings, *naivedya*, to the god Lakshminárayan in the reign of the illustrious Keshidev. [Pandit Bhagvánlál.] The *Shak* 1161 (A.D. 1238) stone was found near Lonád village in Bhiwndi in February 1882. It bears date the thirteenth of the dark half of *Mágh* (February-March) and records the grant by Keshidev, the son of Aparárka of the village of Brahmapuri, to one Kavi Soman, devoted to the worship of Shompeshvar Mahádev. The inscription describes Brahmapuri as 'pleasing by reason of its Shaiv temples.' A field or hamlet called Májaspalli in Bápgrám, the modern Bábgaon near Lonád, is granted by the same inscription to four worshippers in front of the image of Shompeshvar. Aparárka, Keshidev's father, is probably the Aparáditya (*arka* and *áditya* both meaning sun) the author of the commentary called *Aparárka* on Yájnavalkya's law book the Mitákshara. At the end of the commentary is written: Thus ends the Penance Chapter in the commentary on the Hindu law of Yájnavalkya made by the illustrious Aparáditya of the family of Jimutvahán, the Shiláhára king of the dynasty of the illustrious Vidyádhara. Jour B. B. R. A. S. XII. 335 and Extra Number, 52. Aparárka is cited by an author of the beginning of the thirteenth century. Jour. B. B. R. A. S. IX. 161.

The next is Someshvar, two of whose land-grant stones have been found, one dated 1249 (*Shak* 1171) the other 1260 (*Shak* 1182).[1]

Though, with few exceptions, the names of the Thána Siláháras are Sanskrit the names of almost all their ministers and of many of the grantees point to a Kánarese or a Telugu source. They appear to be southerners, and *ayyas* or high-caste Dravidian Hindus seem to have had considerable influence at their court.[2] Káyasths, probably the ancestors of the present Káyasth Prabhus, are also mentioned.

Though their grants are written in Sanskrit, sometimes pure sometimes faulty, from the last three lines of one of their stone inscriptions, the language of the country appears to have been a corrupt Prákrit, the mother of the modern Maráthi.[3] The same remark applies to the names of towns. For, though inscriptions give such Sanskritised forms as Shri-Sthának, Shurpárak, and Hanjaman or Hamyaman, the writings of contemporary Arab travellers show that the present names Thána, Sopára, and Sanján were then in use.[4]

On the condition of the Silábára kingdom the inscriptions throw little light. The administration appears to have been carried on by the king assisted by a great councillor or great minister, a great minister for peace and war, two treasury lords, and sometimes a (chief) secretary. The subordinate machinery seems to have consisted of heads of districts *ráshtras*, heads of sub-divisions *vishayas*, heads of towns, and heads of villages.[5] They had a king's high road *rájpath*, passing to the west of the village of Gomvani a little north of Bhándup, following nearly the same line as the present road from Bombay to Thána; and there was another king's high road near Uran. At their ports, among which Sopára, Thána, Chaul, and perhaps Nágothna are mentioned, a customs duty was levied. The *dramma* was the current coin.[6] The Siláháras seem to have been

---

[1] The *Shak* 1171 (A.D. 1249) stone was found in Ránvad near Uran. In this stone the Siláhára king Someshvar grants land in Padivase village in Uran to purify him from sins. The *Shak* 1182 (A.D. 1260) stone was found in Chánje also near Uran. It records the grant by the Konkan monarch Someshvar of 162 *Páruttha* (Parthian ?) *dramma* coins, being the fixed income of a garden in Konthalesthán in Chadiche (Chánje) village in Uran, to Uttareshvar Mahádev of Shri-Sthának (Thána). The boundary on the west is the royal or high road *rájpath*. Someshvar's ministers were Jhámpadprabhu, Mainákn, Bebalaprabhu, Peramde Pandit, and Pádhigovenaku. Pandit Bhagvánlál.

[2] Ind. Ant. IX. 46. This southern element is one reason for looking for Tagar in the Telugu-speaking districts. *Ayya*, the Kánarese for master, is the term in ordinary use in the Bombay Karnátak for Jangam or Lingáyat priests. The Sárasvat Bráhmans of North Kánara are at present passing through the stage, which the upper classes of the North Konkan seem to have passed through about 500 years ago, of discarding the southern *ayya* for the northern *ráo*. [3] Jour. B. B. R. A. S. XII. 334.

[4] Elliot and Dowson, I. 24, 27, 30, 34, 38, 60, 61, 66, 67, 77, 85; Masudi's Prairies d'Or, I. 254, 330, 381 and III. 47.

[5] Asiatic Researches, I. 361; Ind. Ant. V. 280 and IX. 38. The name *pattákil* (modern *pátil*) used in stone inscriptions seems to show that the villages were in charge of headmen.

[6] *Drammas*, which are still found in the Konkan, are believed by Pandit Bhagvánlál to be the coins of a corrupt Sassanian type which are better known as Gadhia *paisa* or ass-money. Jour. B. B. R. A. S. XII. 325-328. The *Páruttha Drammas* mentioned in note 1 above seem to be Parthian drammas. Perhaps they

Section II. Antiquities.

fond of building. The Muhammadans in the beginning of the thirteenth century and the Portuguese in the sixteenth century destroyed temples and stone-faced reservoirs by the score. The statements of travellers and the remains at Ambarnáth, Pelar, Átgaon, Párol, Wálukeshvar in Bombay, and Lonád prove that the masonry was of well-dressed close-fitting blocks of stone, and that the sculptures were carved with much skill and richness. Many of them seem to have been disfigured by indecency.[1] Some of the Siláháras seem to have encouraged learning. One of them Aparáditya II. (1187) was an author, and another Aparáditya I. (1138) is mentioned as sending a Konkan representative to a great meeting of learned men in Káshmir.

While its local rulers were the Siláháras, the overlords of the Konkan, to whom the Siláháras paid obeisance during the latter part of the eighth and the ninth centuries, were the Ráshtrakutas of Málkhet, sixty miles south-east of Sholápur.[2] Their power for a time included a great part of the present Gujarát where their head-quarters were at Broach.[3] The Arab merchant Sulaimán (A.D. 850) found the Konkan (Komkam) under the Balhára, the chief of Indian princes. The Balhára and his people were most friendly to Arabs. He was at war with the Gujar (Juzr) king, who, except in the matter of cavalry, was greatly his inferior.[4] Sixty years later Masudi (916) makes the whole province of Lár, from Chaul (Saimur) to Cambay, subject to the Balhára, whose capital was Mankir (Málkhet) the 'great centre' in the Kánarese-speaking country about 640 miles from the coast.[5] He was overlord of the Konkan (Kemken) and of the whole province of Lár in which were Chaul (Saimur), Thána, and Supára, where the Láriya language was spoken. The Balhára was the most friendly to Musalmáns of all Indian kings. He was exposed to the attacks of the Gujar (Juzr) king who was rich in camels and horses. The name Balhára was the name of the founder of the dynasty, and all the princes took it on succeeding to the

---

are the same as the coins mentioned by Abu-l-fida as Khurásani dirhems, and by Masudi (Prairies d'Or, I. 382) and Sulaimán (Elliot and Dowson, I. 3) as Tátariya or Tahiriyeh dirhems. General Cunningham (Anc. Geog. 313) identifies these Tátariya dirhems with the Skythic or Indo-Sassanian coins of Kábul and North-West India of the centuries before and after Christ, and Mr. Thomas (Elliot and Dowson, I. 4) with the Musalmán dynasty of Tahirides who ruled in Khurásan in the ninth century.

[1] Details of these remains are given in the fourteenth volume of the Bombay Gazetteer. The only place not mentioned in that volume of the Gazetteer is Wálukeshvar in Bombay. The remains at Wálukeshvar consist of about sixty richly carved stones, pillar capitals, statues, and other temple fragments, one of them about 6'×3', apparently of the tenth century, which lie near the present Wálukeshvar temple on Malabár Point. The memorial stones or *páliyás*, which are interesting and generally spirited, seem almost all to belong to Silábára times. The handsomest specimens are near Borivli in Sálsette. Details of the sculptures on memorial stones are given in Bombay Gazetteer, XIV. under Eksar and Sháhápur.

[2] Like the Siláháras the Ráshtrakutas seem to have been a Dravidian tribe. Ráshtra is believed (Dr. Burnell in Fleet's Kánarese Dynasties, 31-32) to be a Sanskrit form of Ratta or Reddi the tribe to which the mass of the people in many parts of the Dakhan and Bombay Karnátak belong.

[3] Ind. Ant. VI. 145. [4] Sulaimán in Elliot, I. 4. [5] Prairies d'Or, I. 254, 381.

throne.[1] When Masudi (916) was in the Konkan, the province of Lár was governed by Jhanja the fifth of the Siláhara rulers.[2]

For fifty years more (950) the Ráshtrakutas continued overlords of the Konkan, and of Lár as far north as Cambay.[3] Soon after the beginning of the reign of Mulráj (943-997), the Chaulukya or Solanki ruler of North Gujarát, his dominions were invaded from the south by Bárap or Dvárap, the general of Tailap II. (973-997) the Dakhan Chálukya who afterwards (980) destroyed the power of the Ráshtrakutas. Bárap established himself in South Gujarát or Lát, and, according to Gujarát accounts, towards the close of Mulráj's reign, was attacked and defeated, though after his victory Mulráj withdrew north of the Narbada. In this war Bárap is said to have been helped by the chiefs of the islands, perhaps a reference to the Thána Siláháras.[4] It appears from a copperplate lately (1881) found in Surat, that, after Mulráj's invasion, Bárap and four successors continued to rule Lát till 1050.[5]

---

[1] Prairies d'Or, I. 254, 383 & II. 85; Elliot and Dowson, I. 24, 25. Tod (Western India, 147, 160) held that Balhara meant the leaders of the Balla tribe, whose name appears in the ancient capital Valabhi (A.D. 480), probably the present village of Valleh about twenty miles west of Bhávnagar in Káthiáwár. Elliot (History, I. 354) has adopted Tod's suggestion, modifying it slightly so as to make Balhára stand for the Ballabhi or Ballabh, Rái. Reinaud (Mémoire Sur l'Inde, 145) explained Bálhara by Malvarai lord of Málwa, and Mr. Thomas has lately adopted the view that Balhára is Bara Rái or great king, and holds that his capital was Monghir in Behár (Numismata Orientalia, III.) The objection to these views is, as the following passages show, that the two Arab travellers who knew the country of the Balháras, Sulaimán (850) and Masudi (915), agree in placing it in the Konkan and Dakhan. Sulaimán (Elliot and Dowson, I. 4) says the Balhára's territory begins at the Komkam or Konkan. Masudi says (Pariries d'Or, I. 177, 381), the capital of the Balhára is Mankir, the sea-board Saimur or Chaul, Sopára, and Thána, and again (I. 383) the Balhára's kingdom is called the Konkar (Kemker). Again the Balhara of Mankir ruled in Sindán, Sanján in north Thána, and the neighbourhood of Cambay in Gujarát (Ditto, I. 254 & III. 47. This Gujarát power of the Ráshtrakutas at the opening of the tenth century is proved by local inscriptions. Ind. Ant. VI. 145). Finally Lár, or the North Konkan coast, was under the Balhára, and Masudi in 916 (H. 304) visited Saimur or Chaul, one of the chief of the Balhára towns (Ditto, II. 85), which was then under a local prince named Jandja. This is the Siláhára Jhanja. (See above page 17.) Idrisi (1135) is the only authority who places the seat of Balhara power in Gujarát (Jaubert, I. 176; Elliot, I. 87, 88). The Anahilaváda sovereigns had before this (Rás Málá, 62) adopted the title of King of Kings *Rája of Rájás*, and Idrisi seems to have taken for granted that this title was Balhára, which Ibn Khurdádba (912), who never was in India, had, by mistake, translated king of kings (Elliot, I. 13). The true origin of the title Balhára, that it was the name of the founder of the dynasty, is given by Masudi (Prairies d'Or, I. 162), and neither Sulaimán (850), Al Istakhir (951), nor Ibn Haukal (970), all of whom visited India, translates Balhara king of kings (see Elliot I. 4, 27, 34). The details of the Balhára kings given by Sulaiman, Masudi, Al Istakhir, and Ibn Haukal, show that their territory began from the Konkan and stretched across India, and that their capital was Mankir, inland in the Kánarese (Kiriah) speaking country. These details point to the Ráshtrakutas of Málkhet, who were overlords of the Konkan from about 750 to 970, and among the earliest of whom, as Professor Bhandárkar has shewn, Valabh the Beloved was a favourite personal name. At the same time the Ráshtrakutas seem to have no claim to the title Balhára.

[2] Prairies d'Or. II. 85. Jhanjha (see above page 17) is the fifth Siláhára king.

[3] See Al Istakhir (950) and Ibn Haukal (943-976) in Elliot, I. 27, 34.

[4] Ind. Ant. V. 317, VI. 184; Rás Málá, 38, 46.

[5] The kings are Bárappa, who is described as having obtained Látdesh; (2) Agniráj (Gongiráj?), who freed and reconquered the land encroached on by his enemies; (3) Kirtiraj, who became the king of Látdesh; (4) Vatsaráj, the opening part of

Section II.
Antiquities.

Between the overthrow of the power of Málkhet (A.D. 970) and the establishment of the overlordship of Gujarát (A.D. 1151, the Siláhára rulers of the North Konkan claim independence, and, during part at least of this time, Thána was the capital of the Konkan.[1] Between the death of Mulráj (997) and the succession of Bhimdev I. (1022-1072), the power of Gujarát did not increase. But Bhimdev took the title of Rája of Rájás, and spent most of his reign in spreading his power northwards and in a great contest with Visaldev of Ajmir.[2] Neither Bhimráj nor his successor Karan (1072-1094) advanced his borders to the south. Nor does Sidhráj (1094-1143), the glory of the Gujarát Chálukyas, though he spread his arms over so much of the Dakhan as to fill with fear the chief of Kolhápur, seem to have exercised control over the Konkan.[3] Idrisi (1135), whose details of Anahilaváda (Nahrwára) seem to belong to Sidhráj's reign, calls him King of Kings.[4] He shows how wealthy and prosperous Gujarát then was,[5] but gives no information regarding the extent of Sidhráj's power. Idrisi's mention of Thána (Bana) seems to show that it was unconnected with Gujarát and this is borne out by the account of Kumár Pál's (1143-1174) invasion of the Konkan. Hearing that Mallikárjun (a Siláhára) king of the Konkan, the son of king Mahánand who was ruling in the seagirt city of Shatánand had adopted the title of Grandfather of Kings *Rájapitámaha*, Kumár Pál sent his general Ámbad against him.[6] Ámbada advanced as far as the Káveri (Kalvini) near Navsári, crossed the river, and in a battle fought with Mallikárjun on the south bank of the river, was defeated and forced to retire. A second expedition was more successful. The Káveri was bridged, Mallikárjun defeated and slain, his capital taken and plundered, and the authority of the Anahilaváda sovereign proclaimed. A'mbad returned laden with gold, jewels, vessels of precious metals, pearls, elephants, and coined money. He was received graciously and ennobled with Mallikárjun's title of Grandfather of Kings.[7] The Konkan is included among the eighteen

whose reign and the closing part of whose father's reign were occupied in foreign wars; (6) Trilochanpál (1050) the grantor, whose reign also was disturbed by wars. There are three copperplates, the middle plate inscribed on both sides and the outer plates on the inner sides. They are well preserved and held by a copper ring bearing upon it the royal seal, stamped with a figure of the god Shiv. The date is the fifteenth of the dark half of *Paush* (January-February) *Shak* 972 (A.D. 1050). The plate states that the king bathed at Agastitirth, the modern Bhagvádándi twenty miles north-west of Surat, and granted the village of Erathána, modern Erthán, six miles north-east of Olpád in Surat. Mr. Harilál H. Dhruva. A list of references to Lát Desh is given in Bom. Gaz. XII. 57 note 1.

[1] Rashid-ud-din in Elliot, I. 60. This independence of the Siláháras is doubtful. In an inscription dated 1034 Jayasimha the fourth western Chálukya (1018-1040) claims to have seized the seven Konkans. Bom. Arch. Sur. Rep. III. 34; Fleet's Kánarese Dynasties, 44. [2] Rás Málá, 62, 70-75. [3] Rás Málá, 138.

[4] Idrisi calls the ruler of Nahrwala Balhára. He says the title means King of Kings. He seems to have heard from Musalmán merchants that Sidhráj had the title of King of Kings, and concluded that this title was Balhára which Ibn Khurdádba (912) had translated king of kings, apparently without reason. Jaubert's Idrisi, I. 177; Elliot, I. 75, 93. [5] See Rás Málá, 188, 189, 192; Tod's Western India, 156.

[6] Rás Málá, 145. For the mention of the Siláháras as one of the thirty-six tribes subject to Kumár Pál, see Tod's Western India, 181, 188.

[7] The title 'Grandfather of Kings *Rájapitámaha*,' occurs along with their other titles in three Siláhára copperplates (As. Res. I. 359; Jour. R. A. S. [O. S.], V. 186;

districts, and the Siláháras are mentioned among the thirty-six tribes who were subject to Kumár Pál. But Gujarát power was shortlived, if the Siláhára ruler of Kolhápur is right in his boast that in 1151 he replaced the dethroned kings of Thána.

Section II. Antiquities

During at least the latter part of the thirteenth century the North Konkan seems to have been ruled by viceroys of the Devgiri Yádavs, whose head-quarters were at Karnála and Bassein. Two grants dated 1273 and 1291, found near Thána, record the gift of two villages Anjor in Kalyán and Vávla in Sálsette (called Shatshasthi in the inscription), by two Konkan viceroys of Rámchandradev (1271-1309) the fifth Yádav ruler of Devgiri. Two stone inscriptions dated 1280 (S. 1202) and 1288 (S. 1210), recording gifts by Rámchandradev's officers have also recently (1882) been found near Bhiwndi and Bassein.[1]

In the thirteenth century, while the Devgiri Yádavs held the inland parts of the district, it seems probable that the Anahilaváda kings kept a hold on certain places along the coast.[2] At the close of the thirteenth century Gujarát, according to Rashid-ud-din (1310), included Cambay Somnáth and Konkan-Thána. But his statements are confused,[3] and, according to Marco Polo, in his time (1290) there was a prince of Thána who was tributary to no one. The people were idolators with a language of their own. The harbour was harassed by corsairs, with whom the chief of Thána had a covenant.[4] There were other petty chiefs on the coast, *náiks*, *rájás*, or *ráis*, who were probably more or less dependent on the Anahiláváda kings.

The South Konkan branch of the Siláháras appears, from the single copperplate inscription which has been found of them in the Ratnágiri district, to have consisted of ten kings who ruled from

Ind. Ant. IX. 35, 38). Mr. Wathen suggests, 'Like a Brahmadeva among kings' that is 'First among kings,' and Mr. Telang, while translating the phrase as 'The grandfather of the king' suggests the same meaning as Mr. Wathen. The Kumárpál Charitra, which gives a detailed account of this invasion, has the following passage in explanation of the term *Rájapitámaha*: 'One day while the Chálukya universal ruler (Kumár Pál) was sitting at ease, he heard a bard pronounce *Rájapitámaha* as the title of Mallikárjun king of the Konkan' (in the verse), 'Thus shines king Mallikárjun who bears the title *Rájapitámaha*, having conquered all great kings by the irresistible might of his arms and made them obedient to himself like grandsons.'

[1] J. R. A. S. [O. S.], II. 388; V. 178-187. The text of one of the inscriptions runs, 'Under the orders of Shri Rám this Shrikrishnadev governs the whole province of the Konkan.' This would show that the Yádavs had overthrown the Siláháras and were governing the Konkan by their own viceroys about 1270. How long before this the Yádavs had ceased to hold the Konkan as overlords and begun to govern through viceroys is not difficult to determine, as the Siláhára Someshvara calls himself king of the Konkan in 1260. For the Bhiwndi (Kalwár) and Bassein stones recently found see Bom. Gaz. XIV. Appendix A.

[2] Rás Málá, 188, 189. They seem to have had considerable power at sea. Bhimdev II. (1179-1225) had ships that went to Sindh, and Arjundev (1260) had a Musalmán admiral. Tod's Western India, 207; Ras Mála, 161.

[3] Elliot, I. 67. In another passage of the same section he makes Konkan-Thána separate from Gujarát.

[4] Yule's Marco Polo, II. 330. More than two hundred years later Barbosa complains of the same piratical tribe at the port of Thána. 'And there are in this port (Tanamayambu) small vessels of rovers like watch-boats, which go out to sea, and, if they meet with any small ship less strong than themselves, they capture and plunder it, and sometimes kill their crews.' Barbosa's East Africa and Malabár, 69.

Section II.
Antiquities.

about A.D. 808 to 1008, at first under the Ráshtrakutas and then under the Chálukyas until eventually the Devgiri Yadavs became supreme over the whole Konkan.[1]

Of the state of the country these inscriptions give us no information. At the same time it is safe to infer that land must have been of considerable value when grants of it were recorded by engravings on copper, and also that a community among which the art of engraving on metal existed, and was apparently not uncommon (for the inscriptions are not only numerous but lengthy), must have attained a considerable degree of civilization. It may also be remarked that all these grants refer to those parts of the Konkan which are still the most valuable, as well as the most naturally fertile, Sálsette and the villages on the coast and on the great creeks.

Finally a caution is necessary. It is as well to be guarded in believing the grandeur which these inscriptions record by remembering that "the princes in all parts of India who are commemorated by these grants are all represented as victorious warriors and surrounded by enemies over whom they have triumphed. Though not pretending to be more than sovereigns of some particular district, they are described as conquerors and sovereigns of the whole world[2]."

Before coming to the period of undeniable history it is worth while to give some early Konkan traditions. The following is the traditional account of the creation of the Konkan:

During the constant wars between the Bráhmans and the Kshatriyas, the Bráhmans had been so reduced that at length they could live only in caves and forests. To restore them to power the sixth *avatár* of Vishnu appeared under the form of the son of a Bráhman named Jamadagni. This *avatár*, who was afterwards known as Parashurám, from *parashu* an axe which was his usual weapon, standing on a projecting peak of the Sahyádris, which were then washed by the sea and were a great place of retreat for the persecuted Bráhmans, shot an arrow westward, and commanded the sea to retreat. The sea retreated and gave up a strip about thirty miles in breadth, which has since been known as the Konkan, and of which the persecuted Bráhmans immediately took possession. Parashurám then led them to battle and to victory, and the Kshatriyas in their turn were reduced to extremity.

The hill from which the *avatár* is said to have shot his arrow is named after him Parshurám, and overlooks the fertile and very beautiful valley in which Chiplún stands, with "a full-fed river winding slow" to the distant sea. The temple, though not outwardly remarkable, is one of the most famous in the Konkan and is constantly visited by pilgrims on their way from Dwárka to Cape Comorin. Those who believe in Parshurám as a historical character say that he was never in this part of India at all, and Dr. Stevenson states that, though this is the first place where the legends of Parshurám affect the names of places, yet they are

[1] Journal B. B. R. A. S. XIII. 1-16.

[2] Mill, II. 179.

Section II.
Antiquities.

frequently found further south.[1] The severe historical interpretation is that, "This legend of the creation of the Konkan and the subjection of a great part of its territory to the Bráhmans by Parshurám is nothing more nor less than a faint tradition of the first triumphs of Hinduism over other forms of superstition prevalent in the province."[2] And to this it must be added that the Sahyádri Khand, in which the story of the creation of the Chitpávans at Chiplún is first mentioned, is by the best authorities believed to be not more than 300 years old. Yet those who like to hold by the legend may take it as in favour of their view that the district about Chiplún has certainly always been the great head-quarters of the Chitpávan caste. The cave temples as being beyond mere human power are believed by the common people to have been made by the Pándavs, but the first sovereign of the Konkan is said to have been Bhimdev. From some Marátha records, supposed to be a little later than the capture of Bassein in 1739, it is made out that at the end of the thirteenth century the Konkan was conquered by this Bhim Rája, who is said to have been a son of Rámdev Rája of Devgir, defeated by the Musalmáns in their first invasion of the Dakhan.[3] Other accounts give him a different origin, and his caste is also in dispute between the Parbhus Rajputs and Shudrás. He dispossessed the Náik princes, and seized upon Chichni, Tárápur, Asheri, Kelva Máhím, Thal, Sálsette, and (Bombay) Máhim, which he made his capital. He divided the whole into fifteen *maháls* or groups containing 444 villages. His chiefs received subordinate governments in Kelva, Bassein, and other places. His son Pratáp Sháh built another capital at Marol in Sálsette which he called Pratáppuri. He was, however, defeated and deprived of his kingdom by his brother-in-law, a chief of Cheul, named Nágar Sháh, whom the Muhammadans in their turn defeated. Now, as to the origin of Bhim Rája, Tod gives three Rájás of the Anahilaváda dynasty of this name between A.D. 1013 and 1250, and he connects this dynasty very closely with the Konkan and Kalyán.[4] Sir W. Elliot gives a Rája Bhimdev and his brother Haripáldev among the Yádav kings of Devgiri early in the fourteenth century.[5] It is easy to find support in the inscriptions already given to the theory of one or other of these Bhimdevs having been the first conqueror of the Konkan, but it seems scarcely worth while to try to connect these legends with real history when there is nothing to enable us to advance beyond the region of conjecture. But the name of Pratáp Sháh's capital is still preserved as Pardápur or Parjápur; a deserted village near the centre of Sálsette. There are no ancient remains there, but the caves of Kondivte are in a hill very near, and within a mile or two is a fine pond called Pasrák taláv and belonging to the villages of Marol, Kondivti, and Mulgaon, on the edge of which are the ruins of a fine Portuguese church and monastic buildings.

---

[1] Bom. R. A. S. Journal, V. 44. [2] Dr. Wilson's Account of Warlees, 2.
[3] Trans. Bom. Geo. Soc. VI. 132.
[4] Forbes in the Rás Málá gives the history of two Bhimdevs at length but says nothing about the third. Western India, 150. [5] R. A. S. Journal, IV. 31.

Section II.
Antiquities.

A tradition exists that the temple at Nirmal near Bassein was erected to commemorate the death there of the great Shankar-ácharya, the chief teacher of the Shaivite worship in the eighth or ninth century. But he is known to have died in Kashmir, and as there were twenty-seven of his spiritual descendants who assumed his name, and who are calculated to have lasted for about 650 years, it is probable that some one of these was the person in whose honour the original temple was built.[1] The present building dates only from the time of the Peshwás, having been built by one Náro Shankar, probably the same mentioned by Grant Duff.[2]

The hill and shrine of Tungár near Bassein are also mentioned in some of the Puráns,[3] but on these little reliance can be placed. Its mention, however, may be taken as evidence that Tungár was formerly a place of some pretensions, and there are remains of apparently ancient temples and buildings in various parts of the forest round the base of the hill which may perhaps, when properly investigated, throw more light on the ancient history of this neighbourhood.

So also the hill of Máchál in the Southern Konkan where the river Muchkundi rises is said to have been the scene of the exploit of the Rishi Muchkunda when he destroyed with a glance of his eye the rash person who awakened him from his sleep. This hill is close to Vishálgad, one of the most ancient and famous Sahyádri forts, but there is nothing in this legend having any bearing on the history of the district.

This section may be closed with a legend of a different sort. On the bare sheet rock of the Southern Konkan where scarcely a blade of grass will grow are to be found, in the rains, masses of a very beautiful little purple flower (Utricularia albocærulea) called by the common people 'Sitáchi Ásre' Sita's Tears. The story is that after Rám had recovered Sita from her captivity in Ceylon he reproached her with inconstancy. On his leaving her, or threatening to leave her, she appealed to his mercy with tears, which, falling on the bare rock, flowered forth then and for all time in this lovely form.

---

[1] H. H. Wilson's Works, I. 197. Compare Bom. Gaz. XIV. 292-293.
[2] History, 313, 327. [3] Dr. DaCunha's Chaul and Bassein, 124.

SECTION III.

THE MUSALMA'NS.

Section III.

The Musalmans.

IT has been already mentioned that the date of the Musalmán conquest is that from which the reliable history of the Konkan may be said to begin, and that the possession of Bombay and Sálsette by the Gujarát kings, although previous to that, cannot be traced to any particular conquest. Elphinstone's view that these islands had long been detached possessions of the Gujarát kingdom is confirmed by the legend given in the last section, and Forbes considers that they fell to the Muhammadan conquerors of Gujarát at the end of the thirteenth century as an undisputed part of the Anahilaváda possessions.

It was about the same time, namely A.D. 1294, that the first Musalmán army of the Dakhan arrived before Devgiri or Daulatabad, and they then found outside the walls a number of bags of salt which had just been brought from the Konkan,[1] and had probably come by the Nána Ghát. Salt is still the chief article carried from the Konkan to the Dakhan, the Nána Ghát being, it is said, the most ancient road from Devgiri to the coast, and having at the top the oldest inscription yet found on this side of India. The first direct mention of the extension of the Muhammadan power to this coast is in 1312, when Malik Káfur, who commanded the fourth great expedition into the Dakhan, laid waste the countries of Maháráshtra and Kánara from Dábhol and Cheul to Raichor and Modkal.[2] In 1318, after the reduction of Devgiri and the death of Harpáldev, son-in-law of the Ráje, the Emperor Mubárik I. ordered his garrisons to be extended[3] as far as the sea, and occupied Máhim and Sálsette.[4] It was soon after this that the Friar Odoricus wrote of this part: "Over all this land the Saracens rule, but the people of the country are idolators, worshipping fire, serpents, and trees."[5] Until the Musalmán occupation the Devgir kingdom is said to have included the Konkan north of the Sávitri and Bijnagar the part south of it,[6] the northern division being divided into the *pránts* or districts of Vasai (Bassein), Kalyán, Karnála, Chaul, and Rájápur, and the southern division into those of Dábhol, Rájápur, and Kudál.[7] When in 1347 the first Báhmani king established his independence

---

[1] Briggs, I. 306.
[2] Briggs, I. 379.
[3] Ferishta does not mention this extension to the coast, though he gives the expedition and death of Harpáldev. Briggs, I. 373.
[4] Bom. Geo. Soc. Trans. V. 129.
[5] Yule's Cathay, I. 58.
[6] Briggs, II. 338.
[7] Jervis, 81.

Section III. The Musalmans.

in the Dakhan it was natural that he should divide his kingdom into governments. Of these he made four; the first, which included Gulbarga the capital, extended to the sea at Dábhol, and the second from Daulatabad to Chaul.[1] Previous to this, about 1341, the Jawhár dynasty had been recognized by the Emperor of Delhi. He conferred the title of Rája on the son of Jayab Mukne, the founder of the family,[2] whose descendant is now one of the last of the Koli chiefs. His country contained twenty-two forts, and yielded nine lákhs of revenue.[3] There is no doubt that at this time, as earlier, there were a number of petty Rájás, sometimes called poligárs, Kolis in the north and Maráthás in the south, and it does not appear that at this time the whole either of the coast or of the inland parts was conquered by the Musalmáns. These local chiefs obeyed the Hindu Rájás of Bijnagar or the Muhammadan Sultáns of Golkonda as circumstances might require.[4]

These are all the materials of history that can be found in the fourteenth century. In 1429 Malik-ul-Tujár led a larger force into the Konkan, which Ferishta says brought the whole country under subjection. Briggs, however, thinks this was rather a marauding expedition than a conquest, and several elephant and camel-loads of gold and silver were sent as booty to the Báhmani king.[5] Malik-ul-Tujár then seized on Máhim (Bombay) and Sálsette. This aroused the hostility of the Gujarát king Ahmad Sháh, who to recover the islands sent an army, part of which embarked in seventeen vessels, while the rest went by land. The united force invested Thána by sea and land. The Dakhan general made some sallies, but eventually abandoned the siege of Thána and returned to Máhim. Being reinforced he marched back to Thána, but was there defeated and his army dispersed in an action which lasted all day, and the Gujarát fleet returned home carrying with it some beautiful gold and silver embroidered muslins taken on the island of Máhim.[6]

Erskine says[7] that Ahmad Sháh during his reign reduced under his power the lowlands to the south (of Gujarát) below the gháts, the Northern Konkan, and the island of Bombay, and in the Mirát-i-Ahmadi a list of the possessions of the Gujarát kings during the time the power and sovereignty of the monarchy continued to increase is given. These are made to include in the Konkan the districts of Bassein, Bombay, Daman, and Dánda-Rájápur, and the ports of Chaul, Dabhol, Beláwal (?), Bassein, Dánda, Panwelly, Akassi (Agási), Sorab (?), Kallian, Bhimry (Bhiwndi), Dánda-Rájápur, and Goba (Goa).[8]

This may be taken to refer generally to the fifteenth century, for the Gujarát monarchy was established in 1391 and Mahmúd Sháh Begada, who may be considered the last of its great sovereigns, died

---

[1] Briggs, II. 295; Grant Duff, 25, 29.
[2] Bombay Selections (New Series), VI. 14.
[3] Macintosh in Bom. Geo. Soc. Trans. V. 238.
[4] Jervis, 63.
[5] Briggs, II. 413.
[6] Briggs, IV. 29; Rás Málá, I. 350.
[7] History, II. 29.
[8] Bird, 110, 29.

Section III.

The Musalmans.

in 1511. It will be noticed that the places named are nearly all north of Bombay, and although this account is probably not altogether reliable in some of its details, it may safely be assumed that the Northern Konkan generally was at that time subject to Gujarát. Ludovico Varthema who travelled in India in 1503 has his ports on the West Coast so misplaced and confused that they are often hard to identify, but he went from Cambay to Cheul and says: "the land of Gujarát is interposed between these two cities," [1] which is in accordance with the other authorities given above.

Returning to the Southern Konkan we find that in 1436 another army was sent by the Báhmani king Alá-ud-din II. into the Konkan, which was successful, and on this occasion the Rájás of Rairi (Ráygad) and Sonkehr (the position of which has not been ascertained) were made tributary. The daughter of the latter Rája was sent to the king, and became famous under the title of Pari-chera or Fairy-face. The narrative of Ferishta however makes it clear that the Konkan Rájás were not all reduced on this occasion. In 1453, therefore, a plan for the subjection of all the coast fortresses was decided on, and a large army under Malik-al-Tujár, having its head-quarters at Junnar, sent detachments into the Konkan, and after a time moved down in force. A number of Rájás were reduced, and at last one of the Shirké family by the promise of becoming Musalmán induced Malik-al-Tujár to march against Shankar Rái, Rája of Khelna (Vishálgad), with whom he represented himself to have an old feud. Shirké for two days led the army along a broad road, probably across the plain between Sangameshvar and Lánja. On the third day they entered the woods and ravines, and by the evening were so entangled in them that when Shankar Rái, who had from the first been in league with Shirké, fell on the Musalmáns, they made but little resistance, and upwards of 7000 were massacred, among who were 500 Syeds of Arabia and some Abyssinian officers.[2] The survivors escaped above the gháts. The place where this massacre took place has not been ascertained, but it was probably somewhere below and not very far from Vishálgad.[3] The family of Shirké had, probably from very early time and up to 1768, their court at Bahirugal, a little north of Vishálgad, as Rájás of the surrounding country yielding at a later period a revenue of Rs. 75,000 a year.[4] Grant Duff states that the Konkan Ghát-Máthá from the neighbourhood of Poona to the Várna belonged to this family.[5]

This great disaster was not avenged for sixteen years, a fact which shows how little hold the Musalmáns had on the Konkan. About this time Nikitin, a Russian traveller,[6] speaks of Dábhol as the last seaport in Hindustán belonging to the Musalmáns. In the meantime the Rája of Vishálgad, who had a fleet of 300 vessels, harassed the commerce of the Musalmáns. In 1469 however the

---

[1] Kerr's Voyages, VII. 83. [2] Briggs, II. 424, 436. [3] Ind. Ant. II. 319.
[5] Sadar Adálat Reports (1825), II. 458. [4] History, 13.
[6] India in the Fifteenth Century, 15.

Section III.
The Musalmans.

Prime Minister Mahmúd Khwája Gawán took a force into the Konkan large enough to overcome all opposition, and being joined by troops from Dábhol and Chaul set to work systematically to reduce the country. He soon found that his cavalry was useless in the Konkan, and sent them back, but advancing slowly and steadily through the jungles he gradually reduced a great part of the country. Vishálgad, however, after a siege of five months still held out, when the rains forced the Musalmán army to retreat above the Ghấts. At the commencement of the fine season Vishálgad was again besieged, and shortly afterwards taken by treachery, and this Ferishta distinctly states was the first time the Musalmáns got possession of this famous fortress.[1] But the conquest of the Vishálgad district was still a work of time, and was not completed till after the second rains. The army then proceeded towards Goa, and the conquest of the Konkan was considered so important that on his return to the capital Mahmúd Khwája Gawán was received with the greatest distinction.[2] Though this conquest of the Konkan, or at all events of the southern part, must have been tolerably complete, it is not said to have been formed into a separate government, but from subsequent proceedings it would appear that the governor of Dábhol had very extensive authority.

In 1478 the four governments of the Dakhan were increased to eight, and in this division all that part of the Konkan which belonged to the Dakhan was put under the governor of Junnar,[3] which although sufficiently distant, was yet nearer to the Konkan than any previous provincial capital. Soon after this, however, Bahádur Khán Giláni, son of a governor of Goa, got possession of Dábhol and a great many places on the coast. In 1485 Malik Áhmad was appointed to the government of the two provinces of Daulatabad and Junnar and shortly afterwards he reduced a number of Ghát and Konkan forts, some of which had never before been subdued by the Musalmáns. Among these were Koári, Bharap or Sudhágad, Páli or Sarasgad, and Máhuli, and he laid siege to Dánda-Rájápur, but without success.[4] While thus engaged, his father Nizám-ul-Mulk was put to death, and Mulk Áhmad thereupon threw off his dependence on Bidar and established the Nizám Sháhi dynasty of Ahmadnagar. In like manner Yusúf Adil Khán in 1489 founded the Adil Sháhi dynasty of Bijápur. In 1490 the new king of Ahmadnagar took Dánda-Rájápur, and thus secured peaceable possession of that part of the Northern Konkan which did not belong to Gujarát.[5] But Bahádur Giláni was still unsubdued, and in 1493 he burnt Máhim (Bombay) and seized many ships belonging to the king of Gujarát. The latter thereupon sent both a land and sea force to Máhim, but most of his ships were wrecked there in a great storm: the admiral and those of the sailors who escaped

---

[1] Briggs, II. 483. As to this see Ind. Ant. II. 318 and III. 29. For further particulars as to the Shirké family see Section VII.
[2] Briggs, II. 483.
[3] Briggs, II. 502; Grant Duff, 29.
[4] Briggs, III. 191.
[5] Briggs, III. 199.

were either made prisoners or massacred by the enemy. The officer who commanded the army marched through the Northern Konkan, and hearing of the naval disaster on arriving near Máhim halted, and referred to Gujarát for orders. Eventually a large force, composed of troops of Bidar Ahmadnagar and Bijápur, went against Bahádur Khán who in a battle near Kholhápur was defeated and killed.[1] Mahmúd Sháh, king of Bidar, then went with a few of his nobles to Dábhol, called by the Musalmáns Mustáfabad, where they spent a short time sailing about the coast. Bahádur Khán's fleet was made over to the Gujarát admiral.[2]

About this time also the Gujarát kingdom was divided into five governments, one of which, including no doubt the whole of the North Konkan, had Thána as its capital. This arrangement, however, did not last long, as in 1561 a fresh division was made, in which no provincial capital is found nearer to the Konkan than Surat.[3] The reason though not mentioned is obvious: Sálsette and all the best parts of the North Konkan had in the meantime fallen into the hands of the Portuguese as will be shown further on.

The power of the Bidar kings having now entirely declined, their part of the Konkan was divided between the kings of Ahmadnagar and Bijápur. The Sávitri appears from the first to have been the boundary, and accordingly Chaul and Dábhol fell to different masters.[4] These ports were no doubt of greater importance than all the rest of the country, and as early as the fourteenth century they had been mentioned with Bidar, Gulburga, and other large towns as having had orphan schools established in them by Muhammad Sháh Báhmani I. It should be mentioned that Yusúf Adil Khán, the first king of Bijápur, believed to be the son of an Emperor of Constantinople, had first landed in India at Dábhol, and from there had been taken as a slave to Bidar. Mahmúd Khwája Gawán had also come by this route from Persia to Bidar, and a little earlier in the century the Báhmani king Ahmad Sháh Wali had sent two different deputations by way of Chaul to a celebrated saint in Persia, some of whose family came to India soon afterwards by the same route.[5] It may be supposed therefore that by this time more was known of the Konkan than before, and greater interest felt in it than was usual in these Dakhan courts. At all events it was in the time of Yusúf Adil Khán that the first steps were taken to improve the district, for in 1502 the Subhedár of the province of Dábhol, which extended from the Sávitri to Devgad, including therefore the whole of the Ratnágiri district with the exception of the Málvan sub-division and a very little more, gave grants to the first of the *khots* for the occupation and reclamation of waste lands. It is stated that at this time the country was in an exceedingly unsettled and impoverished condition, and that encouragement was

---

[1] Briggs, II. 523, 529, III. 345, IV. 71; Rás Málá, I. 797; Elphinstone, 680. There is some discrepancy between the different authorities as to the date.

[2] Briggs, IV. 62, 136.

[3] Jervis, 64; DeBarros, VIII. 172.

[4] Jervis, 64; DeBarros, VIII. 172.

[5] Briggs, II. 350, 419, 511.

Section III. The Musalmans.

now given to the former landholders to occupy their land at a light rent. Thus many of these grants confirmed in their *vatans* the old Hindu proprietors *desáis, deshpándes,* and *kulkarnis.*[1] It may be here mentioned that the origin of the Hindu institution of *desáis* or *deshpándes* and *deshmukhs* is unknown, but it is certain that the Moghals found them useful in their new conquests. Their authority was therefore confirmed and in some cases extended by the Bijápur government. It may be added that although higher offices under the name of *sardeshmukhs* and *sardesáis* are known to have existed, Elphinstone could hear of only two families enjoying the *sardeshmukhi,* and of no *sardesáis,* except in the Konkan.[2]

The date of the establishment of the Abyssinians in Janjira cannot be clearly made out. There is one legend which shows them to have got possession about 1489. Another account puts them a great deal later. Two of them were, however, admirals of the Nizám Sháhi fleet in the time of Malik Ambar, and another had charge of Ráiri.[3] The large number of Abyssinians and other foreigners employed in the armies of the Musalmán kings, not only as private soldiers but also in high command, is noticeable. In Daman there was a garrison of 3000 "Abyssinian Turks and other white men,"[4] and they are mentioned on several other occasions. In fact, it is evident from the various alliances of Egyptians and Turks with the Rájás of Cochin Cambay &c. and by the whole history of the first voyages of the Portuguese that the Musalmán powers of Europe and Africa were then much more closely connected with the Musalmáns of this coast than at any later time.[5] And this is not to be wondered at, seeing how entirely the followers of that creed had monopolised the trade of Asia.

A more definite account of the divisions of the country and of the importance of the various towns at the beginning of the sixteenth century is obtained from the early Portuguese historians, though there are still but few events recorded. The kingdom of Gujarát extended as far south as Nágothna; that of Ahmadnagar, the king of which the Portuguese always called Nizamaluco[6] from Nágothna to Shrívardhan or Bánkot; and Bijápur included all south of Bánkot.[7] Chaul and Dábhol[8] are called cities and ranked with Surat and Goa: the other places mentioned are Dáhánu, Tárápur, Kelva-Máhim, Agáshi, Bassein, Bándra, Máhim, Nágothna, Shrívardhan, Jaytápur, and Khárepátan.[9] Both Chaul and Dábhol were indeed great commercial marts, with a large trade with Persia and the Red

---

1 Jervis, 75, 83. 2 E. I. House Selections, IV. 667, 799; Elphinstone, 161.
3 Grant Duff, 63. 4 DeCoutto, VIII. 15, 208. 5 DeBarros, VIII. 407.
6 No doubt from Nizám-ul-Mulk, father of the founder of the kingdom.
7 DeBarros, VII. 537.
8 Ludovico Varthema in 1503 speaks of Chaul and Dábhol as both having kings who were idolators but with many Musalmán subjects. The inhabitants of both were much addicted to war and Dabhol had an army of 30,000 men. (Kerr, VII. 83.) It seems impossible to give any weight to these statements.
9 DeBarros, II. 294.

Section III.

The Musalmans.

Sea, by which route the whole of the Indian goods designed for Europe then passed. Of seventeen large ships on their way from the coast of India to the Red Sea, which were detained by Sir H. Middleton in 1612, two were from Dábhol and one from Chaul.[1] Dábhol is also spoken of by Nikitin as the great meeting place of all nations living on the coast of India,[2] which of course implies a large coasting trade. In the sixteenth century the Portuguese historians describe it as one of the most magnificent and populous maritime places of those parts, full of noble houses, fine buildings, superb temples, and old mosques, one of which with a vaulted roof standing on the hills above the town was destroyed in 1557.[3] Barbosa also mentions its very beautiful mosques, and says that the town was not very large, but the houses though thatched were handsome, and that from December to March there was a great commerce between the ships of Malabár and Cambay, which met here and exchanged their commodities, while great caravans of bullocks loaded with goods came down from the interior.[4] They went back with wheat and rice grown in the Konkan.[5] Up the river were many pretty towns plentifully supplied and owning much cultivated land and flocks. A route is given from Bijápur to Dábhol by the Kumbhárli pass, and on account of the traffic along this road Chiplún is said to have been a great village and very populous, stored with all manner of provisions.[6] The importation of horses from Mecca Aden and Ormuz is also mentioned. When Dábhol was first attacked by the Portuguese there were 6000 troops in garrison, but the defences were slight. It is said in 1547 to have had two forts and some redoubts which defended the entrance of the harbour, but these being destroyed the Portuguese in the following year attacked the upper town which was some distance from the sea.[7]

Chaul is spoken of in the same terms as Dábhol both as to size and trade, its weavers of silk and traffic in horses being particularly and frequently mentioned.[8] Indeed, from the time of Marco Polo the acquisition of horses from the ports of the Red Sea and the Persian Gulf is always spoken of as of the highest importance to the kings of the Dakhan, and in every treaty with the Portuguese stipulations were made as to the importation of horses for the cavalry of the native armies.[9] Later on, notwithstanding the prosperity of the Portuguese town (Lower Chaul), the traffic of the old city is said to have been very great, and the list of imports from Mecca includes many European commodities; while among the

---

[1] Orme's Fragments, 325. [2] India in the Fifteenth Century, 15.

[3] DeBarros, V. 266; DeCoutto, VI. 419 and VII. 289.

[4] Barbosa, 69. [5] Mandelslo, 75. [6] Ogilby, 5.

[7] Vida de J. deCastro, 264-269. Dábhol is mentioned in the Lusiad, Book X., but the lines are not very striking. In Ogilby's English Atlas published about 1670, there is an engraving of Dábhol, made apparently from a description of the place, for the natural features of this engraving are certainly very little like the reality. It shows wall all round the sea and river sides, and two or three large round buildings just inside the wall, which may be meant either for part of the fortifications or for mosques. [8] DeBarros, III. 56 and VI. 71; DeCoutto, XIII. 165.

[9] De Barros, VII. 501 and VIII. 69; DeCoutto, VI. 77.

Section III.

The Musalmans.

exports are found articles such as indigo and opium which must have come from a great distance inland.[1] And as to the silk Pyrard at the beginning of the seventeenth century says that sufficient was made there to supply Goa and all India, and that it was better than the China silk and much prized at Goa. It was all made in the Musalmán city, where were also made very fine boxes and other small carved articles.[2] Linschotten also mentions the silk, and says that the raw material was brought from China; he also speaks of the lacquer work of Chaul.[3] Feroz Sháh Báhmani is said to have despatched vessels every year from Goa and Chaul to procure manufactures and productions from all parts of the world, and to bring to his court persons celebrated for their talents.[4] De la Valle, who gives a detailed description of Chaul in 1623, mentions the groves and gardens of palm and other fruit trees which shaded the broad roads and adorned the Musalmán as well as the Portuguese city of Chaul. A long shady street connected the two towns, and in the shops all sorts of necessaries could be bought, and also fine silks and articles of luxury.[5]

With regard to the other ports, Bassein was apparently the most important place after Chaul and Dábhol; it had a garrison of 3000 infantry and 500 cavalry in 1529, but afterwards in 1533, when the Musalmáns were to some extent prepared for the Portuguese, there were no less than than 12,000 troops there. But more is said of the fertility and importance of the surrounding country than of the greatness of the town, the district which is called "one delicious garden" being the most productive in provisions and timber of all those belonging to Cambay. Many ships used to load there with timber and carry it to Mecca where the Turks used it for their fleets, and it was to exclude these as well as to strengthen themselves that the Portuguese took the place.[6] Pyrard says that all the timber required at Goa for building houses and ships came from Bassein, and also a very good building stone like granite, of which all the churches and palaces at Goa were built.[2] Agáshi is spoken of as a large and rich place, but poor in buildings, with a trade in timber. It was defended when first attacked by 5000 infantry and 4000 cavalry; and, as showing the equality on which these places stood with Portugal in the art of ship-building, it must be mentioned that in 1540 an expedition went from Bassein against Agáshi with the sole object of getting possession of a great ship, which was just built there, and was then ready for launching. The ship was taken and afterwards made several voyages to Portugal.[7] One of the Surat ships stopped by Sir H. Middleton on its voyage to the Red Sea in 1612 was 153 feet long 42 beam 31 deep, and said to be of 1500 tons burden.[8] One of the Dábhol ships stopped at the same time was of 1200 tons. Similarly Faria y Souza explicitly states

[1] Cæsar Frederick and Ralph Fitch in Hakluyt, II. 384, 398.
[2] Viagen, II. 227, 226. [3] Histoire, 21. [4] Briggs, II. 368.
[5] Viaggi, III. 409. [6] DeBarros, VII. 220, 194, 195, 499.
[7] DeCoutto, IV. 99. [8] Orme's Fragments, 326.

Section III.

The Musalmans.

that the Portuguese found their enemies in India much better supplied with guns and powder than they were themselves.[1]

Of Thána an Italian traveller of the fourteenth century, quoted by Colonel Yule, had written that there were the remains of an immense city to be seen, and that there were still 5000 velvet weavers there.[2] It is described in much the same way when the Portuguese arrived, as a decaying town and not so much resorted to by merchants as formerly, but it was full of people who lived by the silk trade, and there were more than a thousand silk looms there. From the description it would seem that Sálsette was to some extent independent of Gujarát, as the 'Xeque' sent an embassy offering a tribute.[3] This may, however, have been only the provincial governor. There were two forts commanding the narrow part of the creek between Bassein and Thána built by the Musalmáns, but afterwards taken by the Portuguese.[4] About the same time Cæsar Frederick called Thána a place "very populous with Portugals Moors and Gentiles."[5] There can be little doubt that the gradual silting of the creek reduced its value as a port, while at the same time the increased size of the ships built made it necessary to find harbours with deeper water than Thána could ever have had, and so both causes contributed to its decay.

About the middle of the century Kalyán is described as having a fine fort with a garrison of 1500 men; the Portuguese burnt the suburbs, and took from them a large booty. The river of Khárepátan is frequently mentioned as attracting a great number of Musalmán ships, and as a resort of pirates.[6] The Sangameshvar river is also mentioned as having on its banks a town of much commerce and merchandise, and afterwards as being a great stronghold of pirates. Pepper and iron were among its exports. A river twelve leagues south of Sangameshvar is mentioned under the name of Dobetala as having on its banks several small places with very pretty gardens and orchards of betel.[7] This may probably refer to the river on which Sátavali stands, where there are old paved roads and other Musalmán remains, and which would have been the nearest port to Vishálgad. Malundi, a little north of Málvan, is also stated to have been a place of trade at this time, with a high road leading to the Gháts.[8] Besides these, Barbosa states that there were many other small ports in which vessels from Malabár took inferior rice and vegetables, showing that at this time the Southern Konkan was an exporting district.

Of the inland parts of the Konkan under the Musalmáns very little can be known, but we may certainly apply to this district a remark of Elphinstone's[9] regarding the Musalmán power: "Many mountain and forest tribes throughout India were unsubdued,

[1] Briggs, III. 510. [2] Marco Polo, II. 330. [3] DeBarros, VII. 224.
[4] DeCoutto, VII. 237. [5] Hakluyt, II. 334.
[6] DeCoutto, VIII. 569; IX. 109, 427. [7] Barbosa 72, 74; DeCoutto, XII. 30.
[8] Bombay Selections, X. 156. [9] History, 421.

Section III.

The Musalmans.

though they could scarcely be called independent: they were left out of the pale of society, which they sometimes disturbed by their depredations."

The course of the Portuguese conquests will be given in detail in Section IV. but it seems better to give in this section the remainder of what is known about the Musalmán rule down to the time of Shiváji. The whole of the coast belonging to the kingdom of Gujarát fell to the Portuguese before the middle of the sixteenth century, and thus Kalyán was the only part of the district of any value to which the Moghals succeeded on the fall of the Gujarát sovereignty. The Nizám Sháhi kings of Ahmadnagar were always favourable to the Portuguese, the only exceptions being a misunderstanding in 1557 regarding the rock of Korlai opposite Chaul, their joining the alliance against the Portuguese in 1570, and the hostilities which ended in the capture of Korlai in 1594. Thus the cities of Upper and Lower Chaul, respectively Musalmán and Christian, flourished as long as the Ahmadnagar kingdom lasted, and for some time afterwards. But the Bijápur kings were always more or less at war with the Portuguese, and their coast was subjected to perpetual ravages, yet it remained entirely in the hands of the Musalmáns until the Maráthás took it. In the decline of the Nizám Sháhi kingdom Malik Ambar, the Abyssinian minister of Ahmadnagar, managed the revenues in the most enlightened spirit, and extended to the Konkan all the advantages of a good government. He abolished revenue farming and committed the management of the districts to Bráhman agents under Muhammadan superintendence.[1] He also carried out a survey on very excellent principles, and this in the Konkan extended from the Vaitarna to the Sávitri, except in the Habshi's territories.[2] His jurisdiction is said by Ferishta to have extended to within eight *kos* of Chaul,[3] and from this it may perhaps be assumed that that city and creek were under a separate governor. But in 1636, only ten years after Malik Ambar's death, the whole of the Konkan dominions of the Ahmadnagar kingdom were ceded to Bijápur. The cession is said by Kháfi Khán to have been made by the Emperor of Delhi in exchange for districts belonging to Bijápur in the neighbourhood of Aurangabad, and the part of the Konkan given up is described as "jungles and hills full of trees."[4] Sháhji Bhonsla had before this begun to overrun the Northern Konkan, and had taken a number of forts. An account of one of the expeditions made against him by a Musalmán force reads very like the history of the pursuit of Tátia Topi by our troops in 1858. The Imperial general Khán Zamán was ordered to co-operate with the Bijápur general Randaula against Sháhji. After investing Junnar the armies went towards Poona and Sháhji fled into the Konkan by the pass of Kumbha. Finding no support there he returned by the same pass. The Imperial force then went down the Kumbha pass into the Konkan, while the Bijápur general was closing Sháhji in on the other side.

---

[1] Grant Duff, 43. [2] Jervis, 68. [3] Briggs, III. 315. [4] Elliot, VII. 256.

Sháhji then went off to Máhuli, and from thence to Muranjan[1] where Khán Zamán followed him. Sháhji sent a part of his baggage and abandoned the rest, and the Imperial army overtook a number of his followers and put them to the sword. Sháhji again got off to Máhuli hoping to get away by Trimbak and Tringalwari, but found it best to stay at Máhuli and stand a siege with the best of his followers, disbanding the rest. His son was with him in the fort. Khán Zamán came up very soon and opened his trenches and a few days afterwards Randaula joined him. Sháhji soon began to treat, and after much fencing when the final attack was near, came out, met Randaula halfway down the hill and surrendered.[2] It is not stated how long the chase or the siege lasted, but this sort of warfare might have gone on for years. When the Emperor of Delhi had made peace with Bijápur there was no longer any excuse for Sháhji's resistance, and he entered into the service of Bijápur.[3] Before this the forts of Kolába, Suvarndurg, Anjanvel, Jaygad, Ratnágiri, and Vijaydurg had been built, but they were all apparently of little importance till enlarged and strengthened by Shiváji.[4]

The Bijápur state was now for a few years the paramount power in the Konkan, and in 1648 before the assaults of the Maráthás had weakened it its government was thus provided for. The forts of Dábhol, Anjanvel, Ratnágiri, and Rájápur, with the districts dependent on them, were held direct from the crown.[5] In Sir Henry Middleton's time the governor of Dábhol was a Persian and a great merchant owning many slaves. In 1612 Sir Henry Middleton stayed there with his ships for twelve days, got as much provisions as he wanted, and an eighteen-inch cable ninety-six fathoms long of Indian make for £8, but he obtained little trade owing to the duplicity of the governor.[6] The remainder of the Southern Konkan was farmed out to the hereditary Deshmukhs, of whom the Sávants of Kudál were the chief. As mentioned the Dábhol subhedári was very extensive, and it is stated that its capital was for some time at Prabánváli.[5] This place, now almost entirely deserted and with no ruins to tell of its former importance, lies at the foot of the great Ghát fortress of Vishálgad, and it is allowable to conjecture that the government of the subhedári was fixed in that secure but retired position in consequence of the ruin brought on Dábhol by the frequent attacks of the Portuguese, who in these later days never mention any Musalmán officer of high rank as commanding at Dábhol.[7] About 1540 the governor of the Konkan under Bijápur, Asad Khán, is said to have had his head-quarters at Sangameshvar[8] and to have made

---

[1] This is the old name of Prabal near Mátherán, but a fort called Muroanjan is much further south in the Gháts, which Sir H. Elliot supposes to be meant.
[2] Elliot, VII. 59. [3] Grant Duff, 52. [4] Jervis, 92, 93.
[5] Grant Duff, 40, 62. [6] Astley, I. 374, 418. [7] DeCoutto, VII. 289, IX. 326.
[8] There is some confusion about the place mentioned as Sanguicar. Faria speaks of it as on the Viziadurg river, and from DeBarros' description it would seem to be further south and nearer the sea than Sangameshvar. But Hamilton whose travels were published in 1727, says: "There is an excellent harbour for shipping eight leagues south of Dábul called Sanguseer." This evidently refers to Jaygad at the

Section III. The Musalmans.

overtures to the Portuguese with a view to getting their assistance if he made himself independent. The Portuguese, however, refused to help him.[1] In 1583 and again in 1585 the Portuguese in conjunction with Bijápur troops attacked the Naik of Sangameshvar, who had seven or eight villages and 600 sepoys, and lived by piracy and pillage. His lands were given to another naik.[2]

The remainder of the Konkan was divided into two subhedáris: the first, Kalyán, extended from the Vaitarna to Nágothna under a Musalmán officer; the rest down to the Sávitri was committed to the management of the Habshi of Janjira, whose own estate was in the middle of this district. His charge included the great forts of Tala, Ghosála, and Ráiri (afterwards Ráygad).[3] Thus the government was administered until Shiváji's invasion of the Konkan. The Northern Konkan was to so great an extent in the hands of the Portuguese that not much besides the inland and wild parts of it were left to the Moghals, and of this a great part, as already mentioned, was held by the tributary state of Jawhár. Although the Moghals in 1572 succeeded to the territories of Gujarát in the Northern Konkan, yet they did not much interfere with the Portuguese, and a treaty was soon made between the two powers.[4] In 1582 they invaded the Daman and Tárápur thánadáris, and attacked Dáhánu, where the captain and fifty men defended themselves in a tower.[5] At Máhim the captain and villagers fortified the church of the Dominican Fathers to resist them. Peace however was soon made. This moderation may have been attributable to the influence of a Portuguese lady of rank in the seraglio of Akbar, who is said to have obtained favourable concessions for her countrymen.[6]

In 1612 the Moghals besieged Daman Bassein and Chaul, and desolated the surrounding country, and peace was purchased only by concessions and presents,[7] although the Portuguese of the Máhim and Tárápur districts are said to have defended themselves valiantly.[8] Bassein is spoken of by a Muhammadan historian of that time as a Moghal port, though in the hands of the Portuguese.[9] The Emperor Sháh Jahán was however as favourable to the Portuguese as Akbar had been[10] and no further hostilities by the Moghals against them appear to have taken place till near the end of the century under Aurungzeb, when great cruelties were committed.

---

mouth of the Sangameshvar river, and even by Orme Sangameshvar is put for Jaygad. This and Hamilton's remark that "being inhabited by Raparees, it is not frequented," sufficiently identifies Jaygad with the piratical station of Musalmán and Portuguese times. Pinkerton, VIII. There is also some doubt about this Asad Khan, as in the frequent mention of the well-known soldier of that name in Musalmán history he is never said to have been governor of the Konkan, and his constant loyalty is particularly noticed. Scott, I. 275.

[1] DeCoutto, IV. 352, [2] DeCoutto, XII. 30; Faria in Briggs, III. 254.

[3] Grant Duff, 63; Jervis, 90. [4] DeCoutto, X. 84; Mickle, clxxx.

[5] DeCoutto, XI. 195.

[6] Jervis, 84. It is evident, however, that this could not have been the cause of the original cessions of territory to the Portuguese as Jervis states, since Akbar was born in 1542, before which time almost the whole of the possessions they ever had on the coast were in the hands of the Portuguese. [7] Mickle, ccii.

[8] O Chronista, III. 218. [9] Tohfat al Mujahidin, 174. [10] Jervis, 84.

Section III. The Musalmans.

Even then peace was soon made, and on more favourable terms than the Portuguese were then justified by their strength in demanding.[1] The Musalmáns had however by this time so little influence left in the Konkan that their future proceedings must be looked for in the account of the Maráthás.

The remains of Musalmán buildings in the Konkan are but few and unimportant. Dábhol was so frequently burnt by the Portuguese, and Chaul so thoroughly destroyed by Shiváji, that there is little more than enough to show that they were once great places. At both there are a number of tombs scattered about, but none of great pretensions. At Dábhol there is a fine mosque with dome and minarets standing close to the water's edge, and now almost buried in cocoanut trees. It is of considerable size, and its situation is striking, but it would not be thought very much of in Gujarát or any other district rich in Musalmán remains.[2] The site of the Musalmán city of Chaul is even more covered by cocoanut gardens than Dábhol. The most striking ruin is a *hamám khána* or bath, containing one large central chamber and two smaller ones, all octagonal, and each lighted by a circular opening in the cupola which covers it. There is also a mosque of some pretensions. At Kalyán, formerly called Islámabad, there is a large Musalman population and several mosques in use. There is however nothing either old or remarkable except one mosque, which would be very fine if it had a dome in proportion to its other parts. This stands on the edge of a noble pond, round which there are many tombs and other undistinguishable remains, as well as one considerable building said to be the tomb of a governor named Mohartaba Khán, on which is the date H. 1108. This is probably the person called by the Portuguese Mortaba Khán, Nawáb of Bhiwndi, who ravaged their territories at various times about 1690.[3] The absence of other buildings is due to the ravages to which this district was subjected in the early days of Shiváji. Fryer, who travelled in India from 1673 to 1676, speaks of the remains of the Musalmán city of Kalyán, then only recently destroyed, as noble and striking, and goes so far as to call them "the most glorious ruins the Mahommadans in the Deccan ever had occasion to deplore."[4] At Khárepátan there are the foundations of a large Musalmán town in a fine situation and a great number of tombs, but no building remains standing.[5] At Rájpuri near Janjira, now a wretched looking village, there are the tombs of four of the Nawábs situated in a pretty glen and close to the creek. There are, of course, tombs and mosques of an ordinary description in many places, but none architecturally remarkable. The tomb of a saint at Bhiwndi, said to have been previously a diwán of Bijápur, and that of a princess at Lánja, said to have been the daughter of one of the Bijápur kings, may be mentioned.

---

[1] Grant Duff, 168.

[2] It is said to have been built by a princess of Bijápur in 1659-60, but the real date was probably much earlier. See Ind. Ant. II. 280.

[3] O Chronista, II. 52.

[4] It is needless to say that he had not seen Bijápur or any of the Dakhan capitals.

[5] See Ind. Ant. III. 321.

Section III. The Musalmans.

When the forts are examined it will be found that from the much greater importance their successors attached to these than the Musalmáns did, the older work is generally hidden by the more modern. At Vizaydurg however the most massive of the buildings within and on the fort walls are evidently Musalmán. At Avchitgad the crenated battlements of the outer wall seem to prove the same origin. The island fort of Árnála near the mouth of the Vaitarna appears to be entirely Musalmán, with domes, Saracenic arches, octagonal recesses, and other features never seen in Marátha forts, though there are also marks inside of its Hindu occupation. But there is scarcely any mention to be found of any of the Konkan forts in the records of the Musalmán time.

One more Musalmán relic must be mentioned, the picturesque bridge at Nágothna. This is said to have been built about 1582 by one Káji Aláuddin of Chaul,[1] and as this date is between the siege of Chaul during the alliance of the Musalmán kings against the Portuguese and the activity of the Nizám Sháhi troops at the same place twenty years later,[2] it may without improbability be assumed that the bridge was built to facilitate the march of the troops from Ahmadnagar to Chaul, as from Nágothna there was a ghát by Koári considerably nearer to Poona than the Borghát.[3] The chief peculiarity of the bridge is its narrowness, the space between the parapets being only nine feet nine inches.

Villages with Musalmán names are often met with, of the origin of which nothing can be heard. Two small districts close to Dábhol retain the names they received from the Musalmáns, though everywhere else the ancient Hindu names of *pránts* and *tarafs* have been preserved. These are Haveli Jafarabad containing thirty-seven villages, and Haveli Ahmadabad containing twenty-one, and the probability is that when Dábhol was first taken by the Musalmáns these villages were assigned for the support of the governor and his establishment.

---

[1] East India House Selections (1826), III. 786.
[2] See pages 38, 39.
[3] Hamilton, II. 162.

SECTION IV.

THE PORTUGUESE IN THE SIXTEENTH CENTURY.

Section IV. The Portuguese, 1500-1600.

The proceedings of the Muslmáns, so far as they can be traced, have been brought down to the middle of the seventeenth century. It is now necessary to turn back to the first appearance on the coast of the Portuguese who here as over the whole of the east played so grand a part through the whole of the sixteenth century. It is impossible to understand the position which they held on this coast without considering the objects which they pursued as to the whole of Asia and the enmities which they thereby excited. For many centuries the Egyptians had held the monopoly of the Indian trade, and the Venetians were closely connected with them as the chief carriers of Indian goods from Alexandria to Europe.[1] But the Portuguese immediately after the discovery of the Cape of Good Hope and their first visit to Calicut in 1498, resolved to become the commercial masters of the East, and for that purpose they not only claimed the monopoly among European nations of trading by the Cape of Good Hope, but also undertook the wonderful enterprise of conquering the whole coast of Asia, from the Red Sea round the Persian Gulf, along all the shores of India, and away to the Straits China and Japan.[2] This of course brought them into immediate collision with the Egyptians in the Red Sea, and with the whole body of Musalmán traders spread along the shores of the Eastern seas, who soon saw the necessity of opposing the Europeans by every artifice and every force,[3] for the Musalmáns of those days had no more idea than the Christians of commerce being the right of all nations equally. Thus the Egyptians, who were the first enemies of the Portuguese, were entirely supported by the local traders; and the Venetians, seeing how seriously the defeat of the Egyptians would affect their prosperity, joined in the vain attempt to confine the Indian trade within its old bounds.[4] The Portuguese had gradually made their way up the coast from Calicut, and had had many more or less casual encounters with the Musalmán fleets.

Their first voyage north of Goa appears to have been in 1503 under Vincent Sodre, who sailed along the coast as far as Cambay.[5] This was just before their first voyage from India to the Red Sea, and no places in the Konkan are mentioned in the account of this voyage, nor anything of importance on this part of the coast until in 1507 Lorenzo d'Almeida destroyed seven vessels of the

---

[1] Robertson, 41. [2] Robertson, 151. [3] Mickle, lxxxviii.; Robertson, 153. [4] Mickle, cxviii. [5] Correa, I. 346.

Section IV.

The Portuguese, 1500-1600.

Moors in the port of Chaul because they entered without returning his salute. He then went to Dábhol, and found the Calicut fleet there, and having called a council of war and resolved not to attack it he went on to a river four leagues from Dábhol, and took all the vessels in the harbour, and burnt them, except two richly laden ships from Ormuz, which he took with him to Cochin. His father however expressed great anger against him for not having attacked the Calicut fleet, and it is said that the remembrance of this in the following year cost him his life in the famous sea fight at Chaul, for he refused to fly or surrender though there was no possibility of otherwise saving his life.[1] At that time he had conveyed some merchantmen to Chaul, where the governor under the king of Ahmadnagar received them kindly, and permitted them to trade. But while lying in the harbour[2] they were suddenly attacked by the combined fleets of Egypt and Gujarát.[3] The Portuguese were outnumbered, and lost the flagship with their commander, and one hundred and forty others killed and one hundred and twenty-four wounded. They put the Musalmán loss at six hundred and Ferishta at four hundred, and this was naturally claimed by the Musalmáns as a victory,[4] but the Portuguese were soon afterwards amply avenged by the fleet of the elder Almeida, who destroyed the Egyptian fleet and the Gujarát sea power at Diu. The account of the sea fight at Chaul is thus given by the Gujarát historians: "The infidel Europeans, who had of late years usurped the dominion of the ocean, endeavoured at this time to occupy for themselves some part of the coast of Gujarát, on which they wished to settle." Amir Husan, the admiral of the Turkish Emperor Bajazet II., arrived off the coast of Gujarát with a fleet of twelve sail carrying fifteen hundred men, and Mahmúd Sháh (Begada) anxious to aid in the expulsion of the foreigners sailed in person with his fleet to Daman and Máhim (Bombay). The Amir al Umra Malik Aiaz Sultáni sailed also from the port of Diu, and having united his squadron with that of the Turkish admiral attacked the Portuguese fleet then lying off the harbour of Chaul. The Portuguese fled with the loss of "three thousand or four thousand infidels."[5]

A war carried on against so many enemies, in so many seas, and along so vast an extent of coast, necessarily lasted for very many years; and when the Turks had conquered Egypt they considered the expulsion of the Portuguese from the Persian gulf and from India as not less important than the Mameluke rulers had done.[6] Therefore in 1538 Sulimán the Magnificent sent to this coast a fleet of seventy large vessels, on board of which were many Venetian galley-slaves and 7000 Janisaries.[7] This force besieged the Portuguese in Diu, but was beaten off after the garrison had defended

---

[1] Faria y Souza in Kerr's Voyages, VI. 98, 112.

[2] Mr. Talboys Wheeler without giving any authority puts the first fight as well as the second at Diu. History, III. 416.

[3] Robertson, 154; Mickle, cxx.; DeBarros, II. 294 and III. 186.

[4] Tohfat al Mujahidin, 92; Briggs, IV. 75. [5] Rás Málá, I. 378; Bird, 214.

[6] Robertson, 192. [7] Mickle, cliv.; DeBarros, VIII. 50.

Section IV.

The Portuguese, 1500-1600.

itself most heroically. A similar expedition and siege took place in 1546,[1] and that was apparently the last great attempt on the part of the former possessors of the Indian trade to cxpel the Portuguese. But as late as 1586 the Turks with ships built at Suez took two merchantmen of Chaul, and a fleet was accordingly sent against them, but was defeated by them at the entrance of the Red Sea.

It is not likely that the Portuguese in the beginning of the sixteenth century with all their great schemes would have troubled themselves about the Konkan, if there had not been in it ports and marts of too great importance to be left in the hands of their enemies. But Chaul and Dábhol could not be so left, while tho Portuguese could not spare men enough to establish themselves in these ports in the same way as they had determined to do at Goa. The state of the Musalmán kingdoms, which divided the Konkan among them, was however at this time eminently favourable to the designs of the Portuguese. The Northern Konkan as far south as Nágothua had always belonged to Gujarát[2] but the Southern Konkan had only just been divided (as narrated in the last section) between the dynasties of Bijápur and Ahmadnagar. The rivalry which existed between these two[3] was probably the cause of the Portuguese first obtaining a footing in the Konkan. The Ahmadnagar king, who had possession of the coast from Nágothna to Bánkot, admitted them into Chaul, and at a very early date accepted the protection of their fleets for the vessels which frequented his ports, and for that protection paid them a tribute, and allowed them to establish a factory at Chaul.[4] This was between 1512 and 1521.[5] And by the latter year the Portuguese had obtained permission to build a small fort there, and had command of the whole river.[6] The captaincy of the fortress was already an important appointment in 1524, when Vasco da Gama took charge of the Viceroyalty there, as the first port touched at.[7]

The good understanding between the Portuguese and the Ahmadnagar kingdom (or to speak more correctly the governors of Chaul) was scarcely broken during the sixteenth century. On the other hand the Bijápur king was too powerful on the coast to accept the protection or acknowledge the supremacy of the Portuguese fleet, and the consequence was that as early as 1608 his great port of Dábhol was destroyed bv the fleet of Francisco d'Almeida, consisting of nineteen vessels and 1600 men, half of whom were natives.[8] On several subsequent occasions the destruction was repeated;[9] for Dábhol was so great a place of resort for ships from Malabár and Arabia that it very soon recovered its importance.[10] The king of Gujarát also for some time felt no

---

1 DeCoutto, V. 120. 2 DeBarros, VII. 537. 3 Elphinstone, 416.
4 DeBarros, V. 316; DeCoutto, IV. 209.
5 The historians differ as to the exact year. Faria in Briggs, IV. 512; DeBarros, V. 316. 6 DeBarros, VI. 69, 81. 7 Three Voyages of Vasco da Gama, 384.
8 Faria in Briggs, IV. 507; DeBarros, III. 266.
9 DeCoutto, V. 418; VII. 198, 289; IX. 326. 10 Barbosa, 72.

Section IV.

The Portuguese, 1500-1600.

necessity for the Portuguese alliance, and as there was no great port in his part of the Konkan the Portuguese after punishing him at Diu did not trouble themselves much about him. But in 1521 his Admiral defeated the Portuguese off Chaul, and sank one of their vessels, and remained for twenty days off the port greatly harassing them.[1] In 1527 another Gujarát fleet was sent to Chaul, but a great number of its ships were destroyed by the allied forces of the Portuguese and Ahmadnagar.[2] In 1528 there was a decisive battle off Bándra, in which the Portuguese took seventy-three ships out of the eighty which composed the Cambay fleet.[3]

These attacks led to frequent marauding expeditions of the Portuguese along the coast of the North Konkan, in one of which in 1529 they burnt Nágothna Bassein and Agáshi. At this time also Thána Bándra and Karanja paid tribute to the Portuguese, these towns having sent a peaceable embassy instead of resisting as the others did.[4] The Portuguese possession of Sálsette appears to date from about this time,[5] though Faria puts it at the same time as Bassein,[2] but it seems unlikely that they had any more than a very precarious hold on any of these parts for many years after this, and it is expressly stated as regards the country round Bassein that the natives were masters of these villages in time of war.[6] The war between Gujarát and the Portuguese was continued in 1530, and the Portuguese suffered another repulse at Chaul.[7] In 1533 an expedition consisting of eighty vessels with 1800 Portuguese and 2000 Kánarese attacked Bassein, and stayed there ten days, destroying the fortifications: after which the fleet proceeded northwards and burnt all the places as far as Tárápur.[8] In the next year Bassein was ceded by the king of Gujarát; and he then, as Ahmadnagar had done before, put his ships entirely under the protection of the Portuguese, and agreed that none should sail from his ports without taking out Portuguese passes and paying port dues at Bassein. This[9] last stipulation was relaxed soon afterwards on the king ceding Diu as the price of the Portuguese alliance against the Moghals, but their passes had still to be taken and dues paid to them.[10] They were never however on such good terms with the Gujarát as with the Ahmadnagar kings, and there were frequent expeditions into their dominions, while in 1539 Bassein was besieged for some time by a Gujarát force.[11]

The Bijápur dominions in the Southern Konkan had during this time suffered from the marauding expeditions of the Portuguese quite as much as the Northern Konkan. In 1547 John de Castro made treaties both with Ahmadnagar and Bijnagar, that is

---

[1] Faria in Briggs, IV. 512. Bird says that this was in 1520, and the Mirát Ahmadi says that Chaul was plundered on this occasion. Bird, 237.

[2] Faria in Briggs, IV. 513 514.

[3] Faria in Kerr, VI. 210.

[4] DeBarros, VII. 217, 224.

[5] Hough, I. 156: Reg. I. of 1808.

[6] Cæsar Federick and Ralph Fitch in Hakluyt, II. 344, 384.

[7] Faria in Briggs, III. 531.

[8] DeBarros, VII. 501.

[9] DeBarros, VII. 531. This is not mentioned in the Mirát Ahmadi, which says that after 1536 the tribute from the ports held by the Europeans was not paid. Bird, 253.

[10] DeBarros, VIII. 69.

[11] Faria in Briggs, III. 516.

Vijayanagar, offensive and defensive, against Bijápur. The Portuguese were bound to defend the coast of the Ahmadnagar kingdom against pirates, in return for which they were to receive as payment sailors provisions and timber for their ships. The treaty with Bijnagar contained also many stipulations as to trade. Both stipulated against the ports of this coast being open to or any help being given to fleets or ships of the Turks.[1] Immediately after these treaties were concluded followed the Portuguese expedition of 1547-8, which seems to have exceeded all previous ones in cruelty and severity, for every place between Goa and Shrivardhan is said to have been burnt by the Portuguese, and the same thing was repeated in 1555 and 1557, Dábhol being always the first place to suffer. By 1548 however the Bijápur power had suffered so much as to find it necessary to cede ports to the Portuguese, and to accept the protection of their fleet; but for many years after the peace then made there were frequent hostilities in which the Southern Konkan suffered severely. In 1555 an expedition was sent from Goa which defeated the Bijápur troops at Áchra and on the Kárli river, both near Málvan.[2] Ferishta records a Musalmán success in 1571, which the Portuguese historians do not mention. A Portuguese force landed at Dábhol to destroy it in the usual manner but the Governor laid an ambush and killed 150 of the attacking party. It is evident however that by 1560 the Portuguese were entirely masters of this coast, and once established they never drew back. The Musalmán writers quite acknowledge the importance of the position of which they were thus deprived, and complain that nothing but an insignificant coasting trade was left to them.[3] The cruelties, which even the Portuguese historians admit, are of course put in a much stronger light by their victims.

It is easy to see that it was no part of the Portuguese plan to invade the inland parts of the country; in fact, the mere occupation of the ports would have caused too great a drain on the population of Portugal if Albuquerque had not provided his soldiers with wives from the women of Goa, baptised for the purpose, and given them grants of land in the Goa district.[4] He thus speedily raised up a race of half-caste Portuguese, who as Christians were entirely identified in interest with the Europeans. Such parts of the interior however as were productive and could be defended were not neglected by the Portuguese.[5] It does not appear indeed that they

[1] Annaes Maratimos e Colonials (1884), 69, 172.

[2] DeCoutto, VI. 77, 418; VII. 169, 198, 289.

[3] Tohfat al Mujahidin, 153.

[4] Gemelli in Churchill, IV. 202; Mickle, cxxv.

[5] The writer cannot forbear from entering a protest against a view of the Portuguese proceedings in India to which the name of the author who has adopted it and the character of his books may lend strength. Colonel Meadows Taylor in "The Student's Manual of Indian History" published in 1870 says: "The Portuguese were excellent sailors: but their never attempting military operations by land except in the defence of their own seaports either marks timidity or disinclination amidst opportunities which few others would have neglected during a period of more than a hundred years." The short sketch the writer has given of the objects of the Portuguese throughout Asia is sufficient to prove how unfair and superficial it is to ascribe

Section IV.

The Portuguese. 1500-1600.

possessed any territory between Bombay and Goa except the new town of Chaul, now called Revdanda; and in 1540, when they took the fortresses of Sáksa and Karnála, they speedily restored them to Ahmadnagar for an additional tribute.[1] They had however a factory at Dábhol, though it is very seldom mentioned, and it was apparently not established till after 1570.[2] In the Northern Konkan they seem from the first to have held the productive villages between Bassein and Agáshi, and this small district they then and afterwards called Casaba.[3] About 1556 they acquired the inland forts of Asheri and Manor[4] as giving them the command of a rich and productive district.[5] The fort of Asheri was considered almost impregnable, and was given up by the Abyssinian captain commanding the district on payment of Rs. 6500. A garrison of sixty soldiers was put in it and a church erected. This fort was always greatly valued by the Portuguese, and was described in 1818, after the Maráthás had had it for eighty years, as accessible only at one point, and of such natural strength that with a handful of men to defend it it may justly be considered impregnable. The latter part of the ascent is an almost perpendicular staircase (with a precipice of several hundred feet immediately below it) hewn out of the solid rock forty feet high, at the top of which is an iron door horizontally fixed, and from which the ascent is nearly as steep and of equal height to a second gateway.[6] Soon after the capture of Asheri and Manor, Daman, which the Portuguese had long coveted, was ceded to them, and with it apparently a good deal of the coast between Daman and Bassein. The Tárápur *pargana* is mentioned as the best and most prosperous of all the districts within the jurisdiction of Daman. In 1559 a body of Abyssinians made an attack on Sanján and Tárápur; at the latter place there was then only a stockaded fort (tranqueira) and forty men, but the Abyssinians after ravaging some villages were beaten off.[7] In 1569 there was an expedition against the Kolis which seems to have penetrated quite up to the foot of the Gháts, and a stockaded fort permanently held by the Portuguese is spoken of at Sáyván on the Vaitarna river. The Koli country was again ravaged in 1583, and on both occasions the Portuguese suffered considerable loss from the difficulty of the country and the activity of their enemy, whom

---

the want of activity of so small a nation in Gujarát and the Dakhan "to timidity or disinclination," while a comparison between their exploits and settlements in a hundred years and those of the English in the first hundred years after their coming to India can certainly not be unfavourable to the Portuguese. An historian of the first class may be properly, and the writer hopes conclusively, quoted against Colonel Taylor. Dr. Robertson says of the Portuguese conquests: "By the enterprising valour, military skill, and political sagacity of the officers who had supreme command in India, and who have a title to be ranked with persons most eminent for virtues or abilities in any age or nation, greater things were perhaps achieved than were ever accomplished in so short a time." Historical Disquisition, 150.

[1] DeCoutto, IV. 184, 201. [2] Milburn, I. 305; Bruce, I. 23; DeCoutto, X. 17.

[3] Gemelli in Churchill, IV. 190; O Chronista, I. 30.

[4] There is no trace of any fort at Manor, nor is there any commanding site near the present town.

[5] DeCoutto, VII. 229. [6] Dickenson's Manuscript Report. [7] DeCoutto, VIII. 28, 208.

Section IV.

The Portuguese, 1500-1600.

they described as jumping along from tree to tree like monkeys. The chief towns of the Kolis mentioned at this time are called Darila, possibly Darje Tavar and Vazen (perhaps Vásind). Tavar appears to have been to the north of Daman, but the other two in the Konkan, and Darila is described as a considerable town of great stone and tiled houses.[1]

In 1570 the kings of Bijápur and Ahmadnagar entered into an alliance against the Portuguese; and while the Bijápur troops in great force invaded the district around Goa, those of Ahmadnagar besieged Chaul, which was defended by Don Francisco de Mascarenhas, afterwards the first Viceroy under Philip II. of Spain.[2] This was one of the severest trials the Portuguese ever had to undergo, and the result covered them with glory. They estimated the troops of Ahmadnagar which invaded their territories at 42,000 cavalry and 120,000 infantry, a force which it is needless to say would have eaten up the Konkan ten times over. After the Musalmáns had several times unsuccessfully assaulted the fort a battle was fought outside, in which the Musalmáns were defeated, and soon after they made peace and retired.[3] All that the Muhammadan historian Ferishta says of this expedition is that the king Mortaza Nizám Sháh marched against the fort of Revdanda belonging to the Portuguese, but was obliged to raise the siege after a blockade of some months, as the enemy obtained provisions by sea, owing to the treachery of the Nizám Sháhi officers who were bribed by presents, particularly of wine.[4] While this was going on the Portuguese were able to make an attack from Bassein on Kalyán, which then belonged to Ahmadnagar. The suburbs were burnt and a considerable booty taken. Their fleet also destroyed Dábhol.[5] On the other hand 4000 Ahmadnagar cavalry marched along the Konkan north of Chaul to cut off reinforcements and supplies from Bassein, and the Portuguese were besieged in Karanja, where they had a small fort and forty men: they were however relieved from Sálsette.[6] The terms of the peace were altogether favourable to the Portuguese.

From the descriptions given of Chaul at the time of the two sieges[7] it appears that the main part of the fortifications were built between 1570 and 1592, and an inscription states that those along the beach were made in 1577.[8] It was later than this the extensive fortifications at Bassein were begun, though there had been a fort there since 1536.[9] In 1597 the new works having got on very slowly, Ayres de Silva de Mello was sent to superintend them.[10]

In 1592 there was again war with Ahmadnagar, as the king had determined to expel the Portuguese from the Chaul creek. It is

[1] DeCoutto, IX. 257 and XI. 346.
[2] DeCoutto, IX. 290.
[3] DeCoutto, IX. 453 and X. 17; Faria in Briggs, IV. 522.
[4] Briggs, III. 254. A very full account of the siege will be found in DaCunha's Chaul and Bassein, 47.
[5] DeCoutto, IX. 326, 427.
[6] DeCoutto, IX. 362.
[7] DeCoutto, IX. 290; XIII. 165.
[8] Hearn, III.
[9] DeBarros, VIII. 102.
[10] DeCoutto, XIV. 65.

Section IV.

The Portuguese, 1500-1600.

not clear whether the rock of Korlai, which commands the entrance of the creek, and which was called by the Portuguese and other Europeans Il Morro, had ever been in the possession of the Portuguese before this.[1] It was always looked upon by them as a position of the greatest value, and in 1557 they had determined to get possession of it somehow, but the king of Ahmadnagar on their asking for it temporised with them while he began to fortify it himself. The Portuguese had a cross at the extreme point which was miraculously preserved from the attempts the Musalmáns made to destroy it, while their fleet bombarded the rock, and prevented the Musalmáns from working at the fortifications. In the end an arrangement was come to, that no fort should be built on the rock by either people.[2] Nevertheless in 1592 when war broke out the Musalmáns were in possession of a fort there which is described as a wonder of strength and completeness, and Ferishta implies that it had only lately been built. They greatly harassed the Portuguese at Revdanda, having a considerable force outside the fort as well as within, and the latter after many skirmishes, being reinforced from Bassein and Sálsette, determined to beat up the enemy's camp, but without any idea of taking Korlai. On the night of September 4, 1594, fifteen hundred Portuguese crossed the river and attacked the Musalmán camp. The Musalmáns, though not altogether unprepared, fled to the fort, and the Portuguese following were able to enter with them through the first gateway being blocked by a wounded elephant. The resistance though brave was disorganised, and after about two hours the Portuguese got possession of the whole of the works, with a loss of only twenty-one killed and fifty wounded, the Musalmáns being said to have lost 10,000 men. The fort was destroyed, as the Portuguese could not afford men to garrison it, but they retained the battery commanding the entrance to the creek, and afterwards rebuilt the fort on the original plan.[3]

After this the Portuguese had full possession of the creek and the kingdoms both of Bijápur and Ahmadnagar were now too near extinction to give them serious trouble. Yet in 1609 the Musalmán governor in Chaul sent out a fleet of thirty prows to cruise against the Portuguese, and the latter could get no redress from the Ahmadnagar government.[4] This last event may be taken as illustrating the view of the Portuguese historians, that as the period up to 1560 was the infancy of their power in India, and from 1560 to 1600 its manhood, so from 1600 its decline began.[5] And as their rise had been rapid and their success marvellous, so their decline began early and was unchecked. After the beginning of the seventeenth century no more is heard of aggression or acquisition on their part,

[1] Gemelli says the Portuguese built a fort there in 1520 (Churchill, IV. 200), but this is not borne out by the accounts of their historians. [2] DeCoutto, VII. 370.

[3] DeCoutto, XIII; Briggs, IV. 284; Hearn, 42. Ferishta's account of these proceedings does not differ much from that given by the Portuguese historians, but he puts the Musalmán loss in the final assault at twelve thousand, and says that the Portuguese reduced the fort to ashes. Briggs, III. 284.

[4] Faria in Briggs, III. 528. [5] Hough. II. 213.

and they appear to have owed the retention of the territory they had to the forbearance or the dissensions of their neighbours. The few events in which they took part after this will be mentioned in the history of their struggles with the Dutch in the next section and in the account of the Maráthás. But it is necessary now to give some description of the way in which the Portuguese managed their possessions in the Konkan and of the causes which led to their decline and resulted in their losing this part of the coast.

SECTION V.

THE SYSTEM AND THE DECLINE OF THE PORTUGUESE.

Section V.

The Portuguese System.

In describing the system of government of the Portuguese in the Konkan it is, as may be expected, not possible to make a very accurate distinction between what would now be called the different departments. Although trade was the nominal object of the Portuguese settlements in India, the nature of their schemes, as already described, made it inevitable that at first the persons of the greatest influence should be the military governors. The trade being a royal monopoly, Albuquerque established custom-houses in every port, and later there were in every city factors (veadors) and treasurers.[1] At the same time magistrates (ouvidores) were appointed by Albuquerque, but only apparently at Goa Chaul and Bassein, and these decided all civil and criminal cases. They were subordinate however to the captains of the fortresses, "who often abused their powers and made the ouvidores decide as they liked. History is full of the arbitrary acts of these tyrants in their fortresses, who were nearly all Fidalgos of the highest class."[2] In case of disagreement between the ouvidor and the captain, the veador was called in, and the majority decided. The appeal from the judgments of this bench was in 1587 to the Supreme Court or Relação at Goa,[3] but later to the desembargadores or district judges, of whom there were six or eight, one being at Bassein.[4] These besides the appeals decided original civil and criminal cases of importance. The desembargador at Bassein in Gemelli's time was a gownsman (probably a doctor of laws), and Gemelli as a doctor of laws himself was asked to remain at Bassein as advocate for the various religious societies there, because the native pleaders in the courts were so ignorant.[5] The judicial establishment at Bassein in 1552 was one ouvidor, one officer of police (meirinho), one king's solicitor, two administrators of intestates, one sea-bailiff, and ten peons. At Chaul the establishment was smaller, but there was a jailor and presumably a jail,[6] neither of which are mentioned at Bassein at this time, although in 1674 Dellon, who had tried both, said that the jail at Bassein was larger than that at Daman and then contained a good number of prisoners of the Inquisition.[7]

---

[1] Mickle, cxii. and cxxiv. [2] Instituto, I. 117, 253. [3] Archivo, V. 1183.

[4] Gemelli in Churchill, IV. 192. The writer has quoted Gemelli Carreri as freely as any one else, and thinks it better therefore to mention here what Hallam says about him : "Carreri has been strongly suspected of fabrication, and even of having never seen the countries which he describes ; but his character, I know not with what justice, has been latterly vindicated." Literature of Europe. III. 603.

[5] Churchill, IV. 192. [6] Instituto, I. 253. [7] Dellon, 118.

Section V. The Portuguese System.

Very little is told of the arrangements for the collection of the revenue, but the lands of Sálsette and of the North Konkan generally were at a very early period parcelled out among the Portuguese settlers at a very small quit-rent, amounting it is said to not more than four to ten per cent of the ordinary rental.[1] Villages were also sometimes given to soldiers and others for their lives.[2] These large landholders were called fazendars, a name which still survives in Bombay and the neighbourhood, and their descendants lived on and managed their own estates, levying from the cultivators a fixed proportion of the produce in the manner usual under the Native Governments.[3] In the same way Bassein was said to owe a great part of its prosperity to the noblemen who lived there on the rents of their villages.[4] In Sálsette there were under the veadors, presumably for those lands not granted to the Portuguese, managers of the cultivation, called mhátarás[5] or elders, whose duties were similar to those of pátels under the Native Governments.[3] From an account supplied by the Government of Goa to that of Bombay in 1821 it appears that in 1688 the total revenue of the province of Bassein was about Rs. 1,30,000, and of this sum the quit-rents amounted to about half. The tobacco tax was farmed for Rs. 47,000. Twenty-one villages had to keep for the defence of the country one Arab horse each, and one village a country horse, and these obligations were commutable by a yearly payment of Rs. 132 and Rs. 88 respectively. Alienations of land and revenue to the Jesuits of different colleges and churches are mentioned.[6] It is expressly stated that the island of Sálsette was in a high state of prosperity under the Portuguese.[3] And the Factor of Bassein in 1728 wrote that the greater part of the establishments both in Goa and the Bassein district were supported by the Sálsette villages.[7] Yet it must be remembered that the grants of land on low quit-rents were confined to either Portuguese of European birth or to converts of high rank who adopted the names and style of living of their conquerors. The list of cesses at that time in addition to what would now be considered a heavy assessment on the land[8] would of itself raise doubts as to the prosperity of the island having extended to the lower classes. But an acute observer of the seventeenth century allows of no doubt on this point,[9] for he speaks of the native inhabitants as "poor wretched Gentiles Moors and Christians, worse than vassals to the lords of the villages." And in the articles of the cession of Bombay to the English[10] it is implied that their condition was that of slaves, for it was stipulated that "the Curumbies, Bandaries, or other inhabitants

---

1 East India House Records (1826), III. 774. 2 Gemelli in Churchill, IV. 198.

3 Reg. I. of 1808. This Regulation is the authority for many other statements throughout this work, and as these early regulations are but little known it may be stated that this one gives a complete and very interesting history of Sálsette as regards fiscal matters from the time of the Portuguese. There is reason to suppose that it was written by Mr. Jonathan Duncan Governor of Bombay.

4 DeCoutto, XI. 46.

5 Mhátára is still a very common surname in Sálsette and Bassein both among Christians and Hindus. 6 Manuscript Records.

7 O Chronista, I. 56. 8 Reg. I. of 1808. 9 Gemelli in Churchill, IV. 197.

10 Bom. Geo. Soc. Transactions for June 1839.

Section V.

The Portuguese System.

of the villages belonging to the Portuguese shall not be admitted into Bombay, and all such persons resorting there shall be immediately delivered up to their respective masters." There is in fact nothing whatever either in their own histories or in the accounts of travellers to show that the Portuguese ever took any trouble to protect or raise the condition of their native subjects as Shiváji did in the seventeenth century. With this fact may be mentioned their great establishments of domestic slaves brought in Portuguese ships from the African settlements and distributed at very low prices all over their Asiatic possessions.[1] In the treaty of peace after the fall of Bassein the negroes are specially mentioned in the stipulation for the release of prisoners.[2] To this institution of domestic slavery may no doubt be ascribed the strain of negro blood frequently perceptible in the Goanese.

The military establishments in the Konkan must be next mentioned. After the Viceroy and the great dignitaries of the Church there was no greater officer than the General of the North who resided at Bassein,[3] and after him came the captains of Bassein, Daman, Chaul, and Salsette. All these appointments were held for short terms of years. Bassein Daman and Chaul are said to have been the only fortresses (fortalezza) between Cambay and Goa, except one at Dábhol which was not in the possession of the Portuguese.[4] No fort is mentioned in Sálsette in 1634 except the small one at Vesáva (Madh). The Bassein district then extended from the Vaitarna to Karanja, and in this there were besides the captain of Bassein, fourteen captains of forts and tranqueiras, that is stockaded posts. The district of Daman extended from the Vaitarna to Párner and included the thánádáris of Sanján, Dáhánu, Tárápur, and Máhim. All along this part of the coast were many towers and fortified houses for protection against the pirates, as is apparent from the ruins still standing, and there were also the important inland forts of Asheri and Manor. But it does not appear that there was then anything so large or strong as the now ruined forts of Dáhánu and Tárápur must have been, and the garrisons were small and included but few Portuguese.[5] Bassein and Chaul were the two great places of arms, and were apparently considered sufficient for the protection of the whole coast. But in 1728 the Factor of Bassein made a detailed report[6] on the defences of the North Konkan, drawing particular attention to the insecure condition of the forts, and especially to the want of protection in Sálsette against the Maráthás. There was no fort at Thána but only the three small towers commanding the creek, and containing three or four men each. Bassein had ninety pieces of artillery, the largest being twenty-four pounders, Chaul fifty-eight, and a fortified camp outside the walls nineteen

---

[1] Baldæus in Churchill, III. 546 and Gemelli in Churchill, IV. 203.

[2] Jervis, 130. [3] Gemelli in Churchill, IV. 190.

[4] Linschotten also says that in 1598 the Portuguese did not hold Dábhol, having been dispossessed of it some years before. Histoire, 20.

[5] O Chronista, III. 149, 198, 218, 244. [6] O Chronista, I. 29.

Section V. The Portuguese System.

more. The rock of Korlai opposite Chaul, which had been considered so great an acquisition, had thirty cannon, but many of them unserviceable. Asheri was in very bad condition, Manor not worthy to be called a fort. Thus though the military power and spirit of the Portuguese had in 1634 greatly degenerated from the days when Bassein was ready at any moment to send out an expedition against the king of Gujarát, or help to any of the smaller posts that might be attacked, yet in 1728 affairs were infinitely worse all over the district, and Sálsette notwithstanding its great value was quite indefensible. The recommendation to protect it by making a great place of arms at Thána was followed, but with too little vigour, for the fatal year 1739 arrived before the fort was finished.[1]

It has been already stated that Albuquerque gave his soldiers wives from the native women whom he caused to be baptised, and land on which they might settle and support families. This was probably the origin of the division of the military forces in India into soldados and cazados, the latter word meaning simply 'Married.' Many of the soldados were convicts sent from Portugal for a term of years, and kept in the forts: others were boys enlisted in Lisbon and on their arrival allotted to Fidalgos as pages, but obliged after reaching manhood to do seven years' service in the army. But all the single men not ecclesiastics in India were liable to military duty and were called soldados, otherwise men of the sword to distinguish them from churchmen. The cazados wore the cloak which the soldados were not allowed to do, and were not generally sent away from their homes for service.[2] They were in fact a sort of first class reserve and were held in considerable estimation, and the quarters of the cazados within or without the walls are always mentioned in the description of forts. Native soldiers in the Portuguese service are mentioned under the name of Piaes as early as 1534,[3] but it is evident that their system made them much less dependent on sepoys as time went on than they would have been under a system more like ours.

While the military spirit of the Portuguese steadily declined after the end of the sixteenth century the ecclesiastical power went on ever increasing. Goa was created an episcopal see in 1534,[4] and by this time numbers of priests had come out from Portugal and established themselves in various places, the Franciscans being the first to arrive, and the Dominicans soon following. The time when the work of conversion was seriously begun is a point of dispute,[5] some writers believing that from the first the propagation of Christianity had been as great an object with the Portuguese monarchs as the extension of their dominions, others and even some Catholics acknowledging that there was no great zeal until the establishment

---

[1] Grant Duff, 237. [2] Pyrard, II. 106. [3] DeCoutto, IV. 96.

[4] In the "Three Voyages of Vasco da Gama" (page 391) mention is made of a Bishop at Goa in 1524, but the bull of Pope Paul III. creating the Bishopric is dated November 3, 1534.

[5] Murray, II. 72: Hough, I. 158: Gemelli in Churchill, IV. 208.

Section V.

The Portuguese System.

of the Inquisition. But the account given of the state of public morals at Goa when Xavier arrived in 1544[1] is sufficient to prove that so far from any missionary spirit existing there was then scarcely any practice of Christianity at all. Two years later the King, after regretting that the worship of idols was allowed even in Goa, mentioned among other objectionable practices that of the Portuguese buying slaves cheap and selling them to Musalmáns and other heathens.[2] Xavier, however, though he spent but a very small part of his time at Goa, or any place north of it, was able to change the whole aspect of affairs in respect of Christian observances: he established a Jesuit seminary at Bassein in 1548, and in 1552 sent missionaries there as well as to Thána and Chaul. But he refused to establish a college at Chaul because there were still so many forts and stations without a single missionary. The visits of so great a man are sufficient to distinguish any district, and it is recorded that he was at Bassein at least three times, first at the end of 1544, again in 1548 when the great Viceroy John de Castro was there, and lastly in 1552. He also visited Chaul on more than one occasion, and Khárepátan once.[3] After his death he was made patron saint of both Bassein and Chaul.[4]

In 1560 Goa was made an archbishopric, and Inquisitors were sent out from Europe, and from this time the work of the Church was carried on with great vigour. The power of the ecclesiastics in the State was well shown soon afterwards, when the tooth of Buddha having come into the possession of the Portuguese during their wars in Pegu they were offered an enormous sum if they would return it. This the Viceroy was anxious to do, but the Archbishop opposing the ransom as an encouragement of idolatry, not only carried his point, but also persuaded the Viceroy to join in a great auto-da-fé, in the course of which the Archbishop publicly pounded up the tooth in a mortar. Not long after this the Franciscan Fathers took possession of the caves of Kánheri and Mandapeshvar,[5] expelled the *jogis* who occupied them, and did their best to destroy the sculptures, as at Elphanta, on account of the superstitious feelings of the natives with respect to them.[6] Over the caves at Mandapeshvar were built a church and the Royal College of Sálsette for the education of the children of the converts, and this received from the King all the endowments which the caves had enjoyed.[7]

The Jesuits, commonly called Paulistines,[8] gradually established themselves in every town and village;[9] but in 1585 the Franciscans

---

[1] Bohours, 74; Vida de Xavier, 18. [2] Vida de J. de Castro, 50.

[3] Vida de J. de Castro, 110, 120, 179. Bohours mentions a visit to Bassein in 1549, after the death of John de Castro, but does not give that of 1552.

[4] Inscriptions. [5] DeCoutto, VII. 245, VIII. 335, 429. [6] Fryer, 73.

[7] DeCoutto, VII. 247. An inscription gives 1623 as the date of the college being built, but this probably refers to some particular part of it. Bom. Geo. Soc. Transactions, VII. 149.

[8] This name is explained, firstly, by the Jesuits' college at Goa having been dedicated by Xavier to St. Paul, and, secondly, by all their churches in India being called after the same saint. De la Valle, III. 135; Hough, I. 57.

[9] De la Valle, III. 360.

Section V.

The Portuguese System.

received charge of Mandapeshvar, Máhim, Bombay, Karanja, Mount Calvary, and Agáshi, in each of which places there was an official called "O Pay dos Christaõs" paid by the State.[1] Gradually all power fell into the hands of the ecclesiastics, and the Church was said to have a larger revenue in India than the King himself.[2] One writer says[3] that "Few men can enjoy very peaceable lives who have any fair possessions near the convents of the Jesuits: a pleasant seat and a fruitful plantation can hardly escape their gaining", and another that at the end of the seventeenth century the General of the North at Bassein had both an uneasy and precarious government because of the superintendence of the Church.[4] Goa was said to equal any city in the world in the number and grandeur of its religious processions.[5] The Jesuit college there conferred degrees, and while one Englishman at the end of the seventeenth century says that at Bándra their college "was not inferior as to the building nor much unlike those of our universities," and that the Fathers "lived sumptuously, the greater part of the island Sálsette being theirs,"[6] another about the same time reports the income of the chief church there to be of the value of a pound of gold a day. In 1598 a Father who had come from Europe to visit all the houses and colleges of the Society in India, was received at Bándra with great rejoicing, and entertained with a sham sea fight at the mouth of the river. The Father left four Panjábi converts to be educated at Bándra whom he had fallen in with at Chaul, and then visited the house at Thána, and all the churches in Sálsette (not named), founding the church of St. Cecilia at Ponçar (probably Poisar). He then went on to Bassein where he established a seminary called the College of the Purification, in which noble children, natives of those parts, might be brought up as missionaries. From Bassein he went on direct to Daman, from which the inference seems to be that there were no Jesuit houses between these two places.[7]

When Bombay was made over to the English, the Bándra College claimed much land and various rights in the island,[8] and these not being acknowledged, the Fathers in 1667 received and assisted a dismissed English officer, who attempted to raise a force for the capture of Bombay.[9] In 1720 and 1722 there were again disagreements and skirmishes between the English in Bombay and the Portuguese at Bándra, where the Fathers had some great guns mounted.[4] At Thána in Fryer's time (1673-75) there were seven churches and colleges; at Bassein six churches, four colleges, and two convents.[6] There was in 1623 no Bishop down the coast nearer than Cochin, all being subject directly to the Archbishop of Goa,[10] but in the account of the district given in 1634 Thána is mentioned as having a cathedral church.[11] The Inquisition at Goa had jurisdiction over all countries east of the Cape of Good Hope: it extended its

---

[1] Archivo, V. 1083. [2] Gemelli in Churchill, IV. 198. [3] Ovington, 156.
[4] Hamilton in Pinkerton, VIII. 327, 328. [5] De la Valle, III. 377.
[6] Fryer, 70, 73, 75. [7] Du Jarric, 3, 9, 12.
[8] Bom. Geo. Soc. Trans. for June 1839. [9] Bruce, II. 213.
[10] De la Valle, III. 134. [11] O Chronista, III. 245.

Section V.
The Portuguese System.

operations all over the Portuguese possessions, and had commissaries at Daman, at Bassein, and doubtless at other large towns.[1] The Grand Inquisitor was appointed by the King and confirmed by the Pope, and had authority over all persons clerical and lay, except the Archbishop, his grand vicar, and the Viceroy ; but even these the Inquisition might arrest after advising the Court of Lisbon and receiving orders from the great Council of the Inquisition there.[2] Thus Dellon[3] seems justified in saying that people had much more respect for the great Inquisitor than for the Archbishop or the Viceroy. Pyrard says that the Inquisition in Goa was much more severe than in Portugal, and its administration of justice the most curel and pitiless in the world. "Sometimes the converts are accused of putting crucifixes under the cushions on which they sit or kneel, sometimes of whipping their images or of not eating pork, or in some other way respecting their old faith, while they outwardly conformed as Christians".[4] The auto-da-fé at Goa usually took place only once in two or three years, and as this was the only gaol delivery for spiritual offenders that there was, it followed that if any one was arrested soon after an auto-da-fé he had to undergo a long imprisonment, as Dellon had.

Now as to the work of converting the natives, DeCoutto at the end of the sixteenth century speaks of this whole coast "as a great fishing ground for the Fathers of the company," and estimates their converts at 60,000.[5] As to the extent to which this was assisted by the State it must be noticed that its action was very different under different Viceroys, some of the greatest of whom expressly tolerated and protected the religions of the natives.[6] Thus Albuquerque endeavoured to conciliate the goodwill of the natives, and to live in friendship with all the Indian princes, most of whom were better pleased to have the Portuguese as governed by him for neighbours than the Moors. So also Nuno da Cunha prohibited the priests from persecuting the Hindus for not being Catholics, and he administered justice to all persons, whether Portuguese Hindus or Moors. But others (and the policy of these eventually prevailed) went as far as they possibly could in destroying the temples of the heathen and even slaughtering the worshippers. In 1546 the King wrote to the Viceroy John de Castro,[7] complaining that idols were worshipped, not only in other places subject to Portugal but even in Goa itself. He therefore commanded that search should be made and all idols broken to pieces. Any one who should venture to make them was to be severely punished, as well as all who should publicly or

---

[1] Hough, I. 214 ; Dellon, 118, 339. [2] Dellon, 192.

[3] Dellon was a French doctor and when living at Daman was arrested by orders of the Inquisition and taken to Goa. After a long imprisonment he had the good fortune to escape with his life, and afterwards published a most interesting account of his experiences, a good summary of which is given by Dr. Rule in his "History of the Inquisition." [4] Pyrard, II. 80.

[5] DeCoutto, XI. 49. This expression is probably due to the fact that by the early Portuguese writers the coast between Cape Comorin and the Isle of Manár was called the "Coast of Fishery." Bohours, 81.

[6] Mickle, clix. [7] Vida de J. de Castro, 48.

Section V. The Portuguese System.

privately celebrate any games of a heathen sort, or should help or conceal Bráhmans, " those pestilent enemies of the Christian name." And since it was intolerable that images of Christ or his saints should be made by heathen hands, any person making or selling such was to be fined and to receive two hundred lashes. The Musalmán mosques in the Portuguese territories were to pay tribute to the Church to the amount of Rs. 3000 a year. Converts were to have various privileges, and to be exempt from forced labour on board ship, to which other Indians were liable. His biographer is careful to state that John de Castro did not carry out these orders, not from any want of zeal in the service of God, but because the continual wars in which he was engaged prevented him,[1] but those who prefer it may be allowed to suppose that this great Viceroy thought with Albuquerque and Nuno daCunha rather than with the clerical party and his royal master. Four or five years later the King communicated to the Pope his intention of founding many colleges for the Society of Jesus, so that the East might be filled with apostolical labourers: and in the meantime ordered all the seminaries established in the Indies for the education of youth to be made over to the society, and all the charges of the missioners in all their voyages to be defrayed by the Viceroy and the captains of the fortresses.[2] And in 1555 the then Viceroy, who was near enough to see that his orders were obeyed, prohibited private as well as public temples throughout the territories of Bassein, and also feasts, ceremonies, preaching by Bráhmans, ablutions, and burnings. Houses were to be searched for idols, and if any were found or forbidden practices discovered, the offender was to be sent to the galleys, and all his property forfeited, half to the informer and half to the church. In 1581 new converts were encouraged by a proclamation excusing them from payment of tithes and first-fruits for fifteen years, and at the same time the issue of licenses for the performance of heathen rites and festivals, by which it may be assumed the previous orders had been evaded, was prohibited throughout the Portuguese dominions.

In 1591 the desembargadores and other lawyers were forbidden in the interests of God and the King to have anything to do with Bráhmans or other Hindus in the way of business, even through third persons. The officer offending was to be suspended, and the Hindu compromised to be condemned to the galleys for life.[3] In 1594 an order arrived from the Pope and the King to convert the natives by force. This was in fact a general commission to murder and plunder, and the pagodas and temples hitherto respected were now despoiled of their accumulated riches.[4] In 1600 the " Visitor of the Jesuits already mentioned rejoiced specially over the children of heathen parents snatched from them by the church as roses from among the thorns.[5]"

In Gemelli's time the natives at Goa "lived apart and without

---

[1] Vida, 53. [2] Bohours, 402. [3] Archivo, V. 1369. [4] Macpherson, 33. [5] Du Jarric, 5.

Section V.

The Portuguese System.

any public practice of their religion," while all the monasteries throughout India were subsidised by the State.[1] Linschotten says that the people of India had liberty of religion, but with these rather large exceptions, that they were not allowed to burn their dead nor to perform marriage ceremonies or other diabolical superstitions (over which the Bishop had supervision,) for fear that scandal might be caused to the converts; so also Musalmáns and Jews might not publicly exercise their religion in the towns under pain of death, but outside the towns might do so.[2] Dellon says that although the King allowed liberty of conscience, yet the Holy Office interpreted this to mean that heathens might live in their religion but would be punished if caught in the exercise of it.[3] Finally after all these Christian writers, both Roman Catholic and Protestant, the Musalmán historian Kháfi Khán may be quoted, who after praising the Portuguese system of government, called it an act of great tyranny that if one of their subjects should die leaving young children only they were considered wards of the State and brought up as Christians, whether they were Syeds or Bráhmans.[4] And in a recently published work by a Hindu[5] it is stated that the Portuguese utterly disregarded difference of caste, and exacted the same service from Bráhmans as from Kolis. Several Prabhus were employed in high positions under the Portuguese Government, and even these could only perform their religious duties secretly and by night, while some were forcibly converted to Christianity, whose descendants are still to be found in Sálsette and Bassein.

The jealous and rigorous system of the Portuguese in matters of religion may be pretty well understood from the above extracts. Yet there is one more fact to be noticed which shows in an even stronger light the pressure under which their native subjects lived. It has been already mentioned that the Dominicans sent missionaries to India before the Jesuits did, and it must be noticed that between these two orders there was always a great jealousy, and that while the Jesuits were particularly given to the work of conversion, the work of the Inquisition was chiefly done by the Dominicans. "In India and China the Inquisition and the Jesuits could the less easily agree because their action was entirely different. The Jesuits thought it expedient to pursue a policy of extreme concession, surrendering the distinctive truths of Christianity and keeping out of sight the discipline and ritual of their own church, if they could thereby win over the heathen to their side rather than lead them to Christ. The Inquisitors on the other hand pretended perfect orthodoxy, assumed an air of intense anxiety to preserve the integrity of the Romish faith, and so far as the power of Portugal extended and they could avail themselves of military force, they had the power of life and death in their hands, and could impress the natives with dread, and overawe their own clergy too. Hence it came to pass that not only the Jesuits but the bishops and the

---

1 Churchill, IV. 203. 2 Linschotten, 156. 3 Dellon, 186.
4 Sir H. Elliot, VII. 345. 5 History of Pathana Prabhus, 69, 81.

Section V.

The Portuguese System.

priests regarded them with dread and jealousy and appealed to Rome against their violence." In 1673 Clement X. ordered that all Vicars Apostolic and their missioners in the East were to be altogether free from the jurisdiction of the Inquisition of Goa in those regions which were not under the temporal government of the king of Portugal.[1] But this of course did not touch their power in the Konkan, and it is pretty certain that between the Jesuits who armed with all the power of the State sought to convert the heathen, and the Inquisitors who so carefully guarded the faith of the new converts, the native subjects of the Portuguese must have had a hard time of it. The absence of high-caste Hindus in the Bassein district at the time of its conquest by the Maráthás is ascribed to these severities.[2] And it is even said that the expulsion of the Portuguese from the Konkan was chiefly due to the tyranny of the Jesuits and the Inquisition.[3] It is also a significant fact that the Inquisition in India was abolished by the king of Portugal in 1775, that is just at the time that it was decided to make a great effort for the recovery of the Portuguese power on this coast. But in 1779 the Inquisition was re-established.

The trade in this country was at first, as has already been stated, a royal monopoly. The Portuguese had gradually obliged all trading vessels to take out their passes; but as early as 1570 the Malabár pirates, who Gemelli says[4] were composed of Moors Gentiles Jews and Christians, began to give trouble,[5] and a little later the Arabs followed their example, so that after this there were always two fleets sent out from Goa, called the fleet of the North and the fleet of the South,[6] occupied nominally in protecting the Portuguese ships and possessions from the pirates. In 1598 six small vessels were built and fitted out at Thána and had great success against the pirates.[7] But the Musalmán historians, and even some European writers,[8] put the case of the Portuguese and of the so-called pirates in a very different light. They describe the Malabár and Arab mariners as honest traders who only wished to carry on in peace the traffic which their fathers had enjoyed for centuries, but who were constantly harried and plundered by the Portuguese unless they consented to pay them tribute. The free-traders, as they were called, who were generally discharged or deserted Portuguese soldiers,[9] deprived the natives of even that part of the coasting trade which the Government of Goa had left them, and it is acknowledged by all that these free-traders, like the Interlopers who gave the English East India Company so much trouble,[10] were little, if at all, better than pirates. "They infested every creek on the coast in the double capacity of pirates and merchants," and caused a perpetual petty but sanguinary war. "They seldom scrupled to defraud those who traded with them if

---

[1] Rule, II. 100, 112. [2] Bom. Geo. Soc. Trans. VII. 111.
[3] Reg. I. of 1808. [4] Churchill, IV. 201. [5] DeCoutto, IX. 110.
[6] De la Valle, III. 131, 418. [7] DeCoutto, XIV. 163.
[8] Tohfat al Mujahidin, 157; Mickle, cxiv. [9] Mickle, clxviii.
[10] Bruce, III. 210.

Section V.

The Portuguese System.

they felt themselves strong enough to do it with impunity, and frequently they procured their cargoes entirely by plunder. By such acts of piracy they brought disgrace upon their country and became a principal cause of the downfall of the Portuguese empire in India."[1] The army and other departments of the Government service were deserted for this illicit trade, while Portuguese sailors after coming to India despised any places but those of captain or officer, so that the merchantmen were chiefly manned by Arab and Abyssinian sailors, who were cheap and docile.[2] Both on account of these inconveniences and for the sake of the profits of the Government monopoly the Portuguese Governors did all they could to put down this private trade, but with little effect. The universal practice of illicit trading, in which all the servants of Government from the Viceroy down to the private soldier indulged,[3] was of course another hindrance to the King's Government getting the fair profits of the trade. Linschotten says that even before the end of the sixteenth century all the officials from the Viceroy downwards thought of nothing but enriching themselves, and he ascribes this in great measure to the fact that all appointments were held for three years only.[4] The result of all this was that in 1586 the monopoly of the trade was made over by Government to the Portuguese East India Company. But the private trade was never stopped.[5]

Up to 1565 the chief trade of the Portuguese was with the kingdom of Bijnagar or Vijayanagar. They took horses, velvets, and satins there and brought back linens and muslins, which were sent to Europe by way of Ormuz as well as round the Cape.[6] John de Castro made a treaty with Bijnagar in 1547 for mutual defence against Bijápur, and in this there were many stipulations as to trade. Besides the articles given above coral and silk from China and Ormuz are mentioned in this treaty as being taken to Bijnagar, and saltpetre and iron as coming from there. The fall of Bijnagar therefore is mentioned as a calamity to the Portuguese, but it is not stated why no effort was made to save the kingdom.

The exports of Chaul were indigo, opium, cotton, silk of every sort, with great store of iron and corn; and the imports came from Mecca and China as well as from Europe.[7] Ships laden with fine stuffs used to come to Goa from Sindh.[8] But with the seventeenth century the European rivals of the Portuguese began to trouble them as well as the Malabár and Arab pirates. In 1615 the chief points in the treaty made between the Emperor Jahángir and the Portuguese expressed their mutual enmity to the English and Dutch and the necessity of destroying the Malabár pirates.[9] The entry

---

[1] Macpherson, 26, 30, 32. [2] Linschotten, 78.

[3] In Chiverius's Geography published at Amsterdam in 1697 there is no mention of the Dutch on the west coast of India, nor is Vengurla marked on the map. The name of the district is given in the map as 'Cuncam,' and in a note it is called 'Decan sive cuncang', Decan being also given as a city.

[4] Linschotten, 62, 66. [5] Mickle, exc.; Macpherson, 32.

[6] DeCoutto, IX. 93. [7] Cæsar Frederic in Hakluyt, II. 384.

[8] DeCoutto, XIV. 59. [9] O Chronista, III 269.

Section V. The Portuguese System.

of other Europeans into the Indian seas was looked on as so much of a calamity that De la Valle[1] calls it one of the signs of the decay of the Portuguese that English and Dutch ships frequent the ports of Dábhol Chaul and Bassein without hindrance and without acknowledging the Portuguese supremacy, though the latter still prevented native vessels from sailing in these seas without their permission.[2] So late as 1624 no one could go to Europe by way of Persia and Turkey without obtaining leave from the authorities of Goa.[1]

The Dutch found it easier to conquer the Portuguese on the Malabár coast than to make new settlements for themselves, and they were everywhere assisted by the hatred which the natives now had for the Portuguese. The Dutch blockaded Goa from 1639 to 1642; and in the last-mentioned year took some ships trying to enter the port.[3] A cessation of arms for ten years had been concluded in Europe between the Portuguese and Dutch in 1641, and this extended to Asia in the following year, but in 1649 the war was again going on. The Dutch had built a fortified factory at Vengurla previous to 1641.[4] But it does not appear that they ever cared much about establishing themselves in the Konkan, as at that time they refused an invitation from the king of Bijápur to winter their ships in Dábhol, Ortzery (A'chra?), or other of his harbours.[5] They were however for many years the strongest of the European powers in the East, and in 1660 their fleet was again blockading the harbour of Goa, but could not get close enough to take it.[5] In 1661 when Bombay was ceded to England the object was said to be that King Charles might be "better able to assist and protect the subjects of the King of Portugal in those parts from the power and invasion of the States of the United Provinces."[6] But it does not appear that any thing was ever done to carry this into effect, probably because when the English troops came to take possession, a dispute arose as to whether Sálsette was or was not included in the cession.[7] This so-called claim of the English may

---

[1] De la Valle, III. 402, 406. [2] Gemelli in Churchill, IV. 208.
[3] Mickle, cciii.; Baldæus in Churchill, III. 546, 548. [4] Stavorinus, III. 107.
[5] Nieuhoff in Knox, II. 452; Hamilton in Pinkerton, VIII. 356. At that time the following description is given of an event at Vengurla in which the Dutch took part: "The Bantam yachts were waiting to transport the Queen of Golkonda from Vengurla to Mokha on her way to the tomb of Muhammad. Her guards who had conducted her eighty leagues were 4000 cavalry with long coats of mail, the shoulders whereof were embroidered with serpents' heads like the ancient Romans, they had bright polished helmets, were armed with bows and arrows, wore long beards, and were mounted on very fine Persian horses. On each side of every man of quality who attended her was a footman holding the bridle: the queen and all her ladies were carried in close litters concealed from public view, and they were preceded by several camels covered with rich furniture, on one whereof was mounted a kettle drummer, who performed with great dexterity. The Commodore and the Director of the Dutch East India Company met her two leagues from the town, in which while she stayed she dictated to her Secretaries in several different languages. There was a magnificent tent erected for her on the sea-shore, the passage from whence to the shallop which was to carry her on board the yacht was covered with calico." Nieuhoff in Knox, II. 452. Vengurla is described as a large village on the sea-shore where most ships for Persia are obliged to touch for wood and water. This is to be understood of Dutch ships. [6] Bom. Gov. Records, X. 347. [7] Mill, I. 95.

Section V.

The Portuguese System.

have influenced them as long as the Portuguese were in possession, for as early as 1686 the conquest of Sálsette was proposed on a sufficient force coming from England, and the same course was suggested from home, and apparently only abandoned from doubts as to the complications that might ensue.[1] It must be evident that after the European trade with India had been turned into the route of the Cape of Good Hope the Malabár ports were of far greater value than those of the Konkan or Gujarát, which had their day when the line of traffic was by the Persian gulf and the Red Sea. The capture of Ormuz by the English in 1622 and of Cochin by the Dutch in 1663 deprived the Portuguese of commercial superiority and prestige on both routes, and in 1664 when peace was concluded the claim of the Portuguese to the monopoly of the trade was finally abandoned.[2] The Dutch gradually succumbed to the English, and never made any other settlement in the Konkan than Vengurla, though they are said in the eighteenth century to have greatly wished to establish a factory at Bassein.[3]

One cause of the decline of the Portuguese power remains to be mentioned, the indifference of the kings of Portugal, and the small value they set on their Eastern possessions. This was due partly to their thinking so much more of their Brazilian colonies and partly to the Indian settlements being so expensive. Their disregard of this country was particularly great during the subjection of Portugal to Spain,[4] when the Court of Madrid ordered that to meet the expenses of Government all employments and offices in India should be sold publicly to the highest bidder. On the restoration of the national dynasty of Portugal in 1640 more interest began to be shown in the Indian colonies,[5] but the Dutch were by this time too strong to be opposed, and the English after the civil war soon became so. By the end of the century India was again neglected, and so remained till the catastrophe of 1739.

This sketch of the Portuguese Government of the Konkan has rather exceeded the proper limits, but the subject is an interesting one, and no connected account of it can be got from books readily obtainable. It only remains to add that the Portuguese during the period of their supremacy and for many years afterwards lived in India with considerable magnificence. Fryer speaks of the "stately aldeas and dwellings on both sides of the Thána creek, and the delicate country mansions of the Fidalgos who all over the island live like petty monarchs." The mansion of John de Mello, three miles from Thána, was "curiously built with a terraced descent and walks and gardens extending half a mile down to a stately banqueting house over the water with stone steps for landing." And a mile further stood "Grebondel, a large neat built town of Martin Alfonso's, with his house fort and church of as stately architecture as India can afford, he being the richest Don on

---

[1] Bruce, II. 577, 626, 635. [2] Hough, II. 381. [3] Stavorinus, III. 107.
[4] Gemelli in Churchill, IV. 208; Mickle, cxv.
[5] Mickle, ccix. ccxii.; Macpherson, 35, 37.

this side Goa." The Fidalgos at Bassein had "stately dwellings graced with covered balconies and large windows two stories high with panes of oyster shell or latticed."[1] Gemelli speaks of the pleasure-houses of the Portuguese gentry near Bassein in the same way.[2] Of these lordly mansions there is now nothing to be seen but a few ruined walls, though foundations may here and there be traced of sufficient extent to prove the truth of these accounts.

Section V.

The Portuguese System.

The chief remains of the Portuguese are at Bassein and lower Chaul, now known by its old Hindu name of Revdanda. These are large walled towns, but the fortifications generally have little appearance of strength. At Bassein the line of the streets can be traced, and many lofty buildings, principally churches, remain. These are "of considerable size but mean architecture, though they are striking from the lofty proportions usual in Roman Catholic places of worship, and from the singularity of Christian and European ruins in India."[3] There is now a high road through the middle of the city which prevents it from being utterly desolate; on the north side there is a large space without any ruins, owing no doubt to the plague which towards the end of the seventeenth century is said to have unpeopled one-third of the city on that side.[2] The ruins of Revdanda are similar but on a smaller scale, and from the space within the walls being entirely occupied by cocoanut gardens they can be seen less favourably than the Bassein ruins. The main walls are nearly entire, those on the north side being far the strongest, and having been protected, in its whole length apparently, by an outwork which has now mostly fallen into the sea. The present main entrance facing nearly south and with the citadel just inside it is probably the original entrance.[4]

All over Sálsette and in the neighbourhood of Bassein are parish churches still in use; but though some of these, for instance those of Thána and Remedi near Bassein (originally Nossa Senhora dos Remedios),[5] are large and respectable, and appear to be in the same state as when first built, there is nothing very striking in any of them. Deserted churches and convents more or less ruined are found at many places, especially in Sálsetté. The ruins at Marol have been already mentioned.[6] At Mándvi on the Vaitarna there is a picturesque ruin of a conventual building, and at Yerangal, ten miles north of Bándra, a large church stands in a very pretty little bay close to the sea but distant from anything like a town. This is dedicated to St. Bonaventura, and is still used on the feast of the Epiphany. The outline of the church at Kelva-Máhím is now barely traceable, but the buildings there were certainly of considerable size. These convents were very frequently either themselves fortified as that at Yerangal or built close to a fort: thus the College at Bándra had "seven guns mounted in front of it and a good store of small

[1] Fryer, 74-75; Churchill, IV. 190. [2] Gemelli in Churchill, IV. 190.
[3] Heber, II. 130.
[4] Detailed descriptions of the ruins of Bassein and Chaul with many particulars as to their history will be found in Dr. DaCunha's Chaul and Bassein.
[5] DeBarros, VII. 244. [6] Section II near the end

Section V.

The Portuguese System.

arms,"[1] and took toll from all vessels going up the creek.[2] The greatest in extent of these ecclesiastical ruins is at Mandapeshvar or Mont Pezier already described, and this part of Sálsette must have been a favourite one, as within a mile of this there were the two large churches of Mágáthan and Poisar standing within a stone's throw of each other, and within four miles on the other side is Ghodbandar. The buildings at this delightful place included a fort, a monastery, and a large church. The latter, dedicated to St. John,[3] is the present bungalow, but many of its features make it appear to have been originally a Musalmán rather than a Christian building.

There are two forts which show that the Portuguese were scarcely inferior in the art of fort-building to the Maráthás. One of these is Thána, the size and strength of which can still be seen after all the alterations it has undergone, and which seems to owe nothing to the Maráthás. The other is the fort of Korlai opposite to Chaul, which is perhaps the most interesting of any Portuguese building remaining in the Konkan. The plan, however, which is very striking and unlike anything else in the district, is Musalmán,[4] the Portuguese having destroyed the first fortress and afterwards rebuilt it on the same plan. It stands on a very narrow ridge which stretches far across the mouth of the river, and which is completely surrounded by a strong wall. Inside this are two walls crossing the ridge at the top, and as each was strongly protected by towers and bastions there were virtually three fortresses. On the north side the hill slopes gently down to the water's edge, and this slope, being enclosed like the rest of the hill by the fortified wall, formed a broad way, which also was crossed by walls and bastions and ended at the bottom in a wide level space. Here apparently were the quarters of the garrison and a strong battery commanding the entrance of the river. On the most prominent point of this stood a large cross, and the bastions and gateways all over the fort were dedicated to saints whose names are engraved on them.

There were numbers of other forts all along the coast, of which Tárápur and Dáhánu appear to have been the chief. Others may be traced which were little more than fortified outposts. At the time of the expulsion of the Portuguese, Bándra and Vesáva (probably Madh) were the most important forts in Sálsette after Thána.[5] Scarcely anything remains of the fortifications at Bándra, and Vesáva appears to have been so rebuilt and enlarged by the Maráthás that it is difficult to trace the Portuguese work. Finally there are a number of round watch-towers on promontories and rocky islands, the use of which is said to have been to give notice of the approach of Arab pirates. The most southerly of these which is on a small rocky island with four palmyra trees towering above it, is visible from Malabár Hill on a clear day.

---

[1] Fryer, 70. [2] O Chronista, II. 71. [3] Macleod's Manuscript Account of Sálsette.
[4] DeCoutto, XIII, 165. [5] Grant Duff, 242.

SECTION VI.

SHIVA'JI.

1648 TO 1680.

Section VI.

Shivaji.

THE state of the powers who ruled the Konkan in the middle of the seventeenth century may be thus described. The Portuguese had lost their prestige, and could scarcely hope ever to regain it. The Bijápur kings had seen and profited by the fall of their ancient rivals of Ahmadnagar, but had now begun to feel the power of the Emperors of Delhi. In the north the Jawhár state and in the south the Maráthás of Sávantvádi had become stronger through the weakness of the greater powers, and there were no doubt other and less important Hindu chiefs who still exercised local authority. It was under these circumstances that the founder of the Marátha empire arose. Under him the Konkan attained its greatest importance and we have in his time more historical mention of the province than at any other, for, though not a Konkani himself, he soon found that the wild and strong country just above and below the Gháts was the best field for his operations.

In Section III. mention has been made of the raids of Sháhji Bhonsla in the Konkan and of Shivájí his famous son. It was in 1648, when he was little more than twenty, that Shiváji extended his operations to the Konkan.[1] He at first avoided those parts which were in the possession of the Moghals, but as the whole of the Konkan south of Kalyán was at this time subject to Bijápur there was abundant room for his energy. And he began operations in that part which having until a few years before belonged to Ahmadnagar and having then for some years been overrun by his father[2] was probably held less firmly than the rest of the Bijápur possessions. At the very beginning he appears to have surprised Káiri, which was afterwards his capital under the name of Ráygad, and after plundering other towns he got possession of Kalyán, and immediately began to arrange for the revenue management of the province as if he meant to keep it. The first forts in the Konkan which he built were Birvádi and Lingána, both near Ráygad. He seems to have kept possession of what he had gained by playing off the Moghals against Bijápur, and he lived for four or five years in comparative quiet, spending much of his time at Mahád. In 1656 he built the fort of Pratápgad and thus by gaining command of the pass leading from the Dakhan to Mahád he secured to himself the means of safely retreating to the Konkan whenever he might find the Dakhan

---

[1] Grant Duff, 64.

[2] Grant Duff, 50, 65, 68, 74, 75.

Section VI.

Shivaji.

too hot to hold him. In 1658 he got permission from Aurangzeb to take possession of the whole Konkan, and the first use he made of this was to occupy some of the neglected strongholds of the coast, and to invade the Sidi's districts.[1] But now as afterwards the conquest of the Sidi was too great a task for his power. The Sávants were of the Bhonsla family as Shiváji was, and were anciently known as the Sardesáis of Kudál, under which title they entered into engagements and treaties with the Bombay Government as late as 1838.[1] At this time they made a temporary alliance with Shiváji, but soon afterwards returned to their fealty to Bijápur.[2]

In 1660, after the murder of Afzul Khán, Shiváji carried the war into the oldest of the Bijápur possessions by plundering Rájápur and burning Dábhol; and the three powers of the Southern Konkan—Bijápur, the Sidi, and the Sávants—then united against the invader. Early in the following year, 1661, Shiváji again plundered Rájápur and captured Dánda-Rájápur, though neither now or at any subsequent period did he succeed against Janjira. He was however to a great extent successful during this campaign and the Sávants having submitted to him,[3] that part of the Konkan south of Sálshi Mahál (that is the whole of the present Málvan sub-division and a part of the Vádi districts) was left under their exclusive management, and the revenue system there remained unchanged.[3] At this time Shiváji caused a survey to be made of the coast, and having fixed on Málvan as the best protection for his vessels and the likeliest place for a stronghold, he built forts there, rebuilt and strengthened Suvarndurg, Ratnágiri, Jaygad, Anjanvel, Vijaydurg, and Kolába, and prepared vessels at all these places. But in the meantime the Moghals had taken Kalyán, and Shiváji did not then find it convenient to oppose them or to attempt to retake it. His position in the Southern Konkan was now however very strong, and he removed his capital to Ráiri, henceforward to be called Ráygad, and for some years after this bestowed much labour both on the fortifications and the public buildings of that mountain, which Grant Duff calls the Gibraltar of the East.[4]

In 1663 little was done in the Konkan till late in the year, when Shiváji collected a force near Kalyán and another near Dánda-Rajápur.[6] Four thousand horse from Kalyán marched secretly to Surat, and after plundering it brought the booty to Ráygad.[7] In the following year, 1664, the Bijápur troops made a strong attempt to recover the southern part of the Konkan, but Shiváji came upon them suddenly, and completely defeated them. He burnt Vengurla which he believed to be hostile to him, and then collecting a fleet at Málvan made a plundering expedition as far as Barcelor. This was romarkable as the only maritime expedition in which

[1] Aitchison's Treaties, VI. 119. [2] Grant Duff, 50, 65, 68, 74, 75.
[3] Grant Duff, 80, 83, 84. [4] Jervis, 101. [5] Grant Duff, 85. 86; Hutchinson, 155.
[6] Grant Duff, 89. Orme says the two camps were at Chaul and Bassein. Fragments, 12. [7] Orme's Fragments, 12: Grant Duff, 89.

Shiváji himself took part, and perhaps the adverse winds which delayed him on his return, as they usually do all voyagers up the coast during the latter part of the cold weather, had something to do with his not repeating the experience. Immediately after his return to Ráygad a most formidable Moghal force attacked his possessions in the Dakhan, and Shiváji, having resolved to yield, left Ráygad and went up the Gháts. There he gave up all the forts and territory he had taken from the Moghals, but some were returned to him, and his possession of the South Konkan was not interfered with. He did not return to Ráygad till December 1666, having in the interval been to and escaped from Delhi.[1] During his absence, Annáji Dattu, who was *deshpándya* of Sangameshvar, had charge of the Dábhol *subha*, Moro Pingla the Peshwa of Rájpuri and Ráygad, and A'báji Sondev of the Kalyán province.[2] On his return Shiváji immediately recommenced hostilities against the Moghals, who were once more and very speedily driven out of the greater part of the province of Kalyán, the forts being occupied and repaired by Shiváji's troops. In 1668 he attempted to complete his power in the Southern Konkan by the conquest of Goa and Janjira, but was unsuccessful in both attempts.[1] Soon afterwards he visited Málvan, and built the Sarjekot fort commanding a river two miles north of Málvan, which was then navigable for some distance.[3]

The Moghals had continued to hold the ports of Máhuli and Karnála, two of the most famous in the Konkan; but in 1670 when after nearly three years' truce open hostilities again broke out, these two forts were besieged, and the latter taken without much trouble. At Máhuli however Moro Pant was at first repulsed with a loss, it is said, of a thousand men, but after a second repulse and a siege of two months the place surrendered, and the whole province of Kalyán was taken before the rains.[4] During this time proceedings were going on in the Konkan with a view to the capture of Janjira. The historian Kháfi Khán was then in that district and has given a long account of what took place, but it need only here be said that Shiváji was himself present in this year, and that Fateh Khán the Sidi who was in the Bijápur interest, abandoned Dánda-Rájápur and took refuge in Janjira, and was willing to surrender even that. But three of the other Sidis prevented this, and having deposed Fateh Khán put themselves and the state under the protection of the Moghals. Khán Jahán the Imperial general sent ships to assist them, and during this year and the next there were frequent naval fights between these and Shiváji's fleet, in which the Moghals and Abyssinians were often victorious.[5] At the end of 1670 Shiváji sent a large fleet up the coast, of which the Portuguese captured twelve vessels and took them into Bassein. The Marátha fleet, however, took a large Portuguese ship and brought her in triumph to Dábhol.[6] The Sidis were now as anxious to take Dánda-Rájápur as Shiváji was to get

[1] Grant Duff, 90, 94, 97. [2] Jervis, 92. [3] Hutchinson, 156.
[4] Grant Duff, 110. [5] Sir H. Elliot, VII, 289. [6] Grant Duff, 111.

Section VI.

Shivaji.

Janjira, and on one occasion, apparently the Holi of 1672, took advantage of Shiváji's absence to land and destroy the fortifications. At the same time the Sidi took several forts in the neighbourhood, one of which held out for a week, after which it surrendered on the promise of quarter. But when seven hundred people had come out the Sidi put the men to death, made slaves of the children and pretty women, and released only the old and ugly. For these services he was well rewarded by the Emperor.[1] While this was going on Shiváji twice brought troops down from Ráygad to retaliate, and sent a force under Moro Pandit to burn the Moghal ships at Surat, but in this he did not succeed.[2] He however took possession of various places (in the Bassein and Dahánu sub-divisions apparently) which had hitherto belonged to Koli Rájás. He made an attempt on the fort at Ghodbandar, then with the rest of Sálsette belonging to the Portuguese, but was repulsed.[3] In November 1672 he marched from Ráygad with ten thousand men, levied a large contribution from the Dakhan, and returned to Ráygad without interruption.[4]

In 1673 the Sidi's fleet blockaded the Karanja river, and built a small fort to command its mouth.[5] In October the troops from the Sidi's and the Moghal's ships landed in the Nágothna river, laid the villages waste with great cruelty, and carried away many of the inhabitants as slaves, but troops arrived unexpectedly from Ráygad and inflicted a defeat on the Sidi.[6] Shiváji in April 1674 returned to Ráygad, and in June was crowned there with great pomp.[7] After the rains Moro Pandit came down to Kalyán with 10,000 men, and sent to Bassein to demand *chauth* from the Portuguese. At the same time a fleet from Muskat appeared before Bassein and landed 600 Arabs, who plundered villages and churches and behaved with great cruelty, the garrison of Bassein not attempting to molest them. At the end of the year Shiváji with reinforcements having joined Moro Pant, the whole army marched up the Gháts towards Junnar, but after ravaging the country they returned to Ráygad in February 1675.[8]

The siege of Janjira was continued as it had been every year since 1661,[9] and an expedition at the same time went against Phonda on the Goa frontier, and on his way there Shiváji visited Rájápur, where he kept great quantities of warlike stores. After the rains of 1675 a large Moghal fleet came from Surat to Bombay and proceeded down the coast as far as Vengurla, which they burnt. By this time Shiváji's fleet, now increased to fifty-seven sail, was considered fit to meet the Moghal's, and it put to sea from Vijaydurg and Rájápur, but did not fall in with the enemy. A Moghal force at the same time came down to Kalyán, and threatened the districts south of Bombay, but soon after returned above the Gháts. On this Shiváji's troops returned to Kalyán, and began to build a fort

---

[1] There is some confusion in Kháfi Khan as to the exact year in which some of these occurrences took place.

[2] Orme, 28. [3] Grant Duff, 113. [4] Orme, 30. [5] Bruce, II. 340.

[6] Orme 38 - 39. [7] Grant Duff, 117; Orme, 40; Fryer, 77. [8] Orme, 38, 45, 46.

[9] Orme says since 1665, Fragments, 24.

near Sáyván on the Vaitarna river, within the territory of the Portuguese, who of course resented the encroachment, but ineffectually.[1] From the end of 1675 to July 1676 Shiváji was at Sátára or Ráygad,[2] and this is stated to have been the longest rest of his life. He then made a rapid excursion to the Dakhan and returned with his plunder to Ráygad in September, but immediately afterwards set off with a still larger force on his expedition to the Karnátak. From this he did not return to the Konkan till April 1678,[3] and in the meantime Annáji Datta, the Pant Sachiv, was left in charge of the Konkan from Kalyán to Phonda,[4] and he, besides appointing officers to every district, is said to have made a survey and assessment of the land on fair and equitable principles.[5]

The usual operations on the coast were continued notwithstanding Shiváji's absence. Moro Pant took 10,000 men against Janjira in August, and in October Sidi Sambhal set out on a cruise of retaliation. He burnt Jaytápur at the mouth of the Rájápur river in December 1676, but Rájápur itself was too well defended to be attacked, and in the meantime Moro Pant's attack on Janjira had been beaten off. In the following season, 1677-78, the Sidi's fleet plundered on the coast as usual, and finding little other pillage carried off numbers of the inhabitants as slaves. In revenge for this Shiváji on his return to the Konkan sent down ships and men in July 1678 to Panvel in order to burn the Musalmán fleets then in Bombay harbour, but not being able to get boats to cross they went up to Kalyán with the intention of passing by Thána into Bombay. This alarmed all parties, and the Portuguese Governor of the Bassein district anchored forty armed boats off Thána, which prevented any attempt being made there. The Maráthás thus baffled burnt some Portuguese villages, but were soon recalled to Ráygad. This complication was followed by a rupture between Shiváji's *subhedár* of Chaul and the Bombay Government, for the *subhedár* seized thirty Bombay boats in the Panvel and Nágothna rivers, most of which were retaken by some Europeans from Bombay. Shiváji however did not find it convenient to support his officer. While this had been going on, an attack on a larger scale than usual had been in progress at Janjira, but with the usual want of success.[6]

Early in 1679 Sambháji deserted his father's cause and leaving Ráygad joined Sultán Mauzim, Aurungzeb's son, at Aurangabad.[7] In return Shiváji ravaged the Musalmán territories up to near Surat. He also in the middle of the rains took possession of Khánderi or Kennery, which until now had been uninhabited, and

---

[1] Orme, 51, 54. [2] Grant Duff (page 120) says Sátára; Orme (page 58) Ráygad.
[3] Orme, 60, 69. [4] Grant Duff, 123.
[5] Jervis, 93. Jervis states (page 68) that Dádáji Konddev's assessment had extended very partially through the Dábhol *subhedári*. This is not consistent with Grant Duff's account of Dádáji's government, which does not seem to have extended into the Konkan at all, nor does Sháhji at that time appear to have had any possessions in the Konkan. Grant Duff, 56-57. [6] Orme, 64, 70-72; Grant Duff, 128.
[7] Grant Duff (page 130) says it was the commander-in-chief Dilávar Khán to whom Sambháji deserted. The difference is not material.

Section VI.
Shivaji.

fortified it, on which both the English and the Portuguese claimed the island.[1] On October 15 Daulat Khán, Shiváji's Musalmán admiral, brought his fleet to engage the English vessels which were watching Khándori. The *Revenge* a sixteen-gun frigate, beat them off singlehanded, and they sailed off to the Nágothna river. Boats and troops however managed to get over to Khánderi a few at a time, notwithstanding the watch kept by the English vessels, and 5000 of Shiváji's troops came down to Kalyán to be ready to take advantage of any opening. The Sidi was now in open alliance with the English, as he had been in reality though in rather an arrogant way for several years: but after working with them for some time in the blockade of Khánderi he in January 1680 suddenly and secretly took possession of the neighbouring island of Underi or *Hennery* and began to fortify it, a proceeding which was scarcely more agreeable to his allies than to his enemies. Two engagements between the Sidi and Daulat Khán's ships followed, in the last of which the Maráthás lost 500 men, and were so much damaged that they sailed away to Rájápur to refit. The Sidi then sailed up the Panvel river, and burnt and pillaged without mercy. The English however now made a treaty with Shiváji, and being heartily tired of the Sidi's alliance, agreed to exclude him from Bombay harbour for the future.[2] This, as far as this district is concerned, may be considered the last event of Shiváji's life. After returning from an expedition into the Dakhan he died at Ráygad on April 5, 1680.[3]

It cannot of course be supposed that the general condition of the Konkan during the reign of Shiváji was prosperous according to our present understanding of the word. Fryer[4] speaks of both Kalyán and Chaul as utterly ruined in 1672, the Moghals having been expelled from both at the time of his visit. Dábhol had been burnt so often since 1508 that but little could have been left in Shiváji's time, and it is then described as much ruined by the wars and decrease in trade.[5] A curious proof of its desolation is that, a few years after this, this once great city was granted to the Shirké family.[6] There would thus remain of the old marts of the Konkan only Bassein in the north, and this, as has been shown was gradually declining, and Rájápur in the south, which Baldæus[7] calls one of the cities of note of the Bijápur kingdom, and which alone of the older towns had prospered under Shiváji. On the other hand Mahád had no doubt increased and flourished from its neighbourhood to Ráygad, and Ráygad itself was of course a small centre of prosperity. At the same time it is clear from what has gone before, that the great ravages of war had fallen on the district between Kalyán and Ráygad. The coast of the Northern Konkan had felt them but little; but on the other hand the Portuguese could no longer pretend to be a match for the Arab pirates.

---

[1] Orme, 78; Bruce, II. 442. [2] Orme, 80-88. [3] Orme, 90; Grant Duff, 133.
[4] Travels, 124. [5] Ogilby, Vol. 5; Sir Thomas Herbert, 349; Mandelslo, 75.
[6] Grant Duff, 17. [7] Churchill, III. 541.

In the Southern Konkan, except on the coast where alone Shiváji was much opposed, there was perhaps not much to complain of. His revenue system was a great improvement on any that had been previously known in the Konkan, the cultivators were protected, and all classes of the population, except perhaps the outcastes, had the opportunity of entering and rising in the military service. The Hetkaris[1] (Maráthás from Málvan) had very early been among Shiváji's favourite troops, and the Maráthás all along the Gháts, or Mávalis as they were then called, have always been inclined to military service. Besides this, the establishment of the Gadkaris,[2] or sepoys holding land round the forts on condition of serving in them when necessary, must have provided for a considerable proportion of the population in a district where forts were so numerous. And the mere re-building of the great forts on the coast must have given subsistence at least to great numbers and for many years. Shiváji's system of government and revenue administration is described at length by Grant Duff,[3] and must have been more systematic than any thing that the Konkan had known previously. The Musalmán historian Kháfi Khán, who, as already mentioned, spent some time in the Konkan, abuses Shiváji as an infidel and a rebel, and is particularly proud of a chronogram which he made on the date of his death, "Káfir bajahannam raft," that is "the infidel goes to hell." But he says in favour that he always strove to maintain the honour of the people in his territories: he persevered in rebellion, in plundering caravans, and in troubling mankind, but entirely abstained from other disgraceful acts, and was particularly careful as to the honour of the women who fell into his hands, and would not allow any dishonour to be done to mosques or to the Korán. In short this historian dignifies him with the title of a wise man.[4] It is necessary to remember the cruelties and hardships which the Portuguese in the name of religion and civilization had inflicted on the inhabitants of the Konkan, and the atrocities of the Musalmáns during their wars with Shiváji, and in particular the death which Aurungzeb himself inflicted on Shiváji's son and successor. In view of these things we certainly cannot say that Shiváji, barbarian as he was in many respects and without pretence to culture of any sort, was the inferior of those of his contemporaries either Christian or Musalmán, with whom he was brought in contact on this coast. And altogether it is possible to believe that notwithstanding "the clamour of continual war," the greater part of the Konkan in his time enjoyed more prosperity than at most periods of its history.

The great forts, both on the coast of the Southern Konkan and inland, are so entirely associated with Shiváji that this seems the most fitting place to describe them. There is scarcely an instance of one of these standing on level and open ground: they are all built on some natural post of advantage. If on the coast, on a cliff

[1] *Het* or *hed*, said to be originally a Gujaráti word, is very commonly used in the Southern Konkan to signify "down the coast."

[2] Grant Duff, 100, 103. [3] History, 104 to 106. [4] Sir H. Elliot, VII. 260, 305, 341.

Section VI.

Shivaji.

or a spit of land more than half surrounded by the sea; if in the low country, on some steep hill commanding a river or a pass; if on the Gháts, on some projecting spur or rock, or above a great natural scarp. The construction of all is on the same principle, the whole top of the hill or the end of the promontory is surrounded by a wall relieved by numerous bastions. If there is any slope or place likely to invite approach, an outwork is projected and connected with the main fort by a passage between a double wall. There is seldom more than one entrance to the fort, and this is generally the strongest part and the most noticeable. The outer gateway is thrown forward and protected by a bastion on each side and often by a tower above; entering this a narrow passage winding between two high walls leads to the inner gate, which is in the face of the main wall, and defended by bastions which command the approach. This arrangement in a time when guns could not compete with stone walls rendered the approach to the gates very hazardous. Inside the main wall there was generally an inner fortress or citadel, and surrounding this were the various buildings required for the accommodation of the troops, and also magazines tanks and wells. In many of the greater forts living houses for the commandant or massive round towers were built upon the wall of the main works on the least accessible side. The larger forts had generally a town or *petha* clustered about the base of the hill on which the fort stood. Finally may be mentioned, as one of the invariable features of Shiváji's forts, a small shrine with an image of Hanumán the monkey god, standing just inside the main gate.

This general plan was of course subject to many modifications, due to the greater or less size of the site and also to the consideration of the fort being required only as a place of arms or also as the residence of a chief. The greatest forts answered both purposes, and perhaps Vijaydurg

> "Broad, massive, high, and stretching far,
> And held impregnable in war"

is the most perfect example of a great coast fortress, which was also as much of a palace as the Marátha chiefs allowed themselves. This stands on a spit of land projecting into the broad estuary of a noble river, and communication with the continent was cut off by a ditch which extended across the spit. The outer walls are washed by the sea round the greatest part of their extent, and wherever that is not the case out-works are thrown forward down to the shore. The citadel is of great size, and the walls both of it and of the main works are immensely massive and lofty, and thus looking up from the landing place a triple line of most formidable defences is seen. On one side a great round tower and other buildings rise from the highest part of the main wall, and from these the view is lovely and varied. In front the open sea, on one side the broad estuary, and on the other one of those little coves of white sand bounded by black rocky promontories which are so common through the Southern Konkan. Behind the river stretches away to the blue line of the distant Gháts.

The island forts or Janjiras deserve separate notice. Suvarndurg (the fort of gold) is perhaps the most striking, as the walls remarkable for their loftiness seem to rise straight out of the sea, and are now so well covered with trees and shrubs as to be very picturesque. But the forts of Málvan are in other respects more interesting. They consist of a fort on the mainland and two fortified islands about a quarter of a mile from the shore lying in a bay which is so studded with rocks and reefs that at low water it looks as if nothing larger than a rowing boat could enter. The largest of these islands, Sindhudurg (the ocean fort), is of considerable extent, but being no more than a sand-bank and the walls neither massive nor very lofty, it is not so striking as Suvarndurg. The fort seems to have been very full of buildings, and though there is no record of Shiváji ever having spent any long time there, it is impossible to resist the belief that he meant it, partly at least, as a place of refuge in case he should ever be too hard pressed to be safe on the mainland.[1] He is said to have worked at the walls of this fort himself, and what is called a print of his hand and foot in the stone is shown and reverenced. He himself is enshrined in a temple as a deity or an *avatár* according to the taste of the worshipper, and the idol which represents him has a silver mask for common use and a gold one for festivals, both bearing the semblance of an ordinary Marátha face. The second island is called Padmagad, and is said to have contained Shiváji's ship-building establishments. This is now the most pleasing point in the scene, being half reef and half sand-bank and adorned with ruins and cocoanut trees just sufficient to make it picturesque.

The only entrance to the bay at Málvan is by a narrow channel through the rocks, and the passage from the land to the island is equally intricate. From the landing place the approach to the fort is even narrower than usual, and altogether the choice of this place in preference to the many good bays and harbours all about seems to prove that a convenient naval station was not the chief object. But it would seem that Shiváji's idea of a good harbour was a place that could not easily be got into, for Kolába, which Grant Duff says was his naval head-quarters previous to his fixing on Málvan, is nearly as much hemmed in by rocks and reefs as the latter, and much more so than any other port south of Bombay. And when it is considered that he might have chosen Vijaydurg with its noble river, easy entrance and safe anchorage, or Jaygad being similar in position and but little inferior in advantages, or Devgad with a narrow but safe channel opening into a large and perfectly land-locked harbour with deeper water than any of Shiváji's ships could ever have required, the preference shown to Málvan and Kolába seems only to be explained as above.

Of the inland fortresses it seems unnecessary to give any particular description, since though many of these, as Ráygad and Vishálgad, are both grand and celebrated, they do not differ much from hill-forts in the Dakhan and other parts of the country.

[1] This is hinted at by Hutchinson, but the writer has seen it nowhere else mentioned.

SECTION VII.

THE MARÁTHÁS FROM THE DEATH OF SHIVAJI TO THE EXPULSION OF THE PORTUGUESE.

1680 TO 1739.

ON the death of Shivája there was for some months every prospect of a war between the adherents of his two sons. Rájárám, the younger, was at Ráygad, and the army there and in the neighbourhood was greatly strengthened in his interest. Sambhájí was at Panhála, and the conspiracy against him at first seemed formidable and Phond Sávant took the opportunity of recovering the territory south of the Karlai river. But by the end of June the opposition had lost all its strength, and Sambhájí escorted by 5000 horse entered Ráygad in July. He there punished with great rigour those who had led the opposition against him, and Annáji Dattu, the late governor of the Konkan, was one of the first who was imprisoned, and soon afterwards put to death.[1] His place was taken by the notorious Kalusha, who having at first put additional cesses and exactions on the mild and equal assessment which Annáji Dattu had imposed, eventually displaced the regular revenue officers and farmed out the districts.[2] The struggle between Sambhájí and the Sidi for the possession of the islands of Underi and Khánderi was renewed but without any decided result, and the fleets did little more than threaten one another.[1] The English were equally anxious to get rid of both parties, but were not able. In May 1681 Sultán Akbar, the fourth son of Aurangzeb, having been in rebellion against his father, fled with 400 Rajputs to Sambhájí, and arrived at Páli[3] near Nágothna on July 1st, where he remained and was treated with great respect till Sambhájí came down in September, and they returned together to Ráygad.[4] Sambhájí gave him a house three *kos* from Ráygad and a fixed allowance but after a time began to treat him with less respect.[5] This alliance increased Aurangzeb's hostility to the Maráthás, and his ships were again ordered to ravage the coast. In July 4000 of Sambhájí's troops had come from Ráygad to Nágothna, and from there made an attack on Underi, but were beaten off, and the Sidi retaliated as usual on the inhabitants of the opposite coast. In particular the town of Apta was burnt as it had been in 1673.[4] In January 1682 Sultán Akbar

[1] Orme's Fragments. 96, 97; Grant Duff, 134-137. [2] Jervis, 108.
[3] Grant Duff says (page 136) that Dodsa was his place of residence. This however is close to Páli. [4] Orme, 105, 107. [5] Elliot, VII. 309, 312.

Section VII.

The Marathas, 1680-1739.

accompanied Sambháji to the siege of Janjira, which was carried on this year on an unusual scale, the fortifications first being levelled by cannonading, and the arduous work of filling up the channel between the mainland and the island then entered on.[1] The siege was continued till August, and then abandoned after a storming party had been repulsed with a loss of 200 men[2]; but Sambháji had been called away in February by a raid of the Moghals in the Kalyán district, 20,000 horse and 15,000 foot having come down the Gháts from Junnar. These he successfully opposed with a large army, and he also this year built the fort of Belápur[3] to protect that neighbourhood from the irruptions of the Sidis. But the latter who again kept their ships during the rains in Bombay harbour, made raids into the Marátha territory even as far as Mahád, and Sambháji's fleet at Nágothna and Khánderi could do little. In October the fleets of Sambháji and the Sidi were engaged in Bombay harbour, and the Maráthás, who on this occasion were also commanded by a Sidi, were defeated after a fight of four hours, on which Sambháji plundered a few Portuguese villages in disgust and prepared to fortify Elephanta.[4]

In the beginning of 1683 the Company's ship *President* on her voyage up the coast was attacked off the Sangameshvar river by some Arab vessels which were afterwards found to be in Sambháji's pay. The *President* lost eleven men killed and thirty-five wounded. The Moghals this year again ravaged the country about Kalyán and the war between Sambháji and the Portuguese was carried on with great vigour on both sides. Sambháji in June brought 30,000 men to besiege Chaul, but was repulsed. He however succeeded in taking Karanja where the Portuguese had some vessels and he destroyed some places on the coast north of Bassein.[5] The Viceroy invaded the Marátha territories, but had to retreat with loss, and the Portuguese were fallen so low as to be obliged to make overtures for peace, which however were not successful. At this time Sultán Akbar went to the Dutch factory at Vengurla with the intention of leaving the country, but was prevailed on to return.[6]

The Northern Konkan again suffered in 1684, when Bahádur Khán Ranmast entered the Konkan by the pass of Mhajah (Mándha?), and shortly afterwards Aurangzeb sent his son Sultán Mauzim (afterwards the Emperor Bahádur Sháh) with a larger army, said by Orme to have numbered 40,000 cavalry, to subdue the fortresses on the coast. Sultán Mauzim was accompanied by his son Muizuddin, and came down the Ambadári Ghát, and finding the province of Kalyán already ravaged, passed on to the neighbourhood of Ráygad, and is said to have plundered and burnt the villages from there to Vengurla.[7] This town he sacked as a punishment for its former protection of Sultán Akbar, but the Dutch successfully

[1] The remains of the stone mole built for this purpose may still be seen below the surface of the water.

[2] Orme, 110; Grant Duff, 138.

[3] Hamilton says Panwel, II. 151.

[4] Grant Duff, 139; Orme, 113.

[5] Orme, 120, 122; Grant Duff, 140.

[6] Orme, 125.

[7] Scott, II. 60; Orme, 132; Grant Duff, 144.

Section VII. The Marathas, 1680-1739.

defended themselves in their fortified factory.[1] This was one of the greatest military expeditions ever made in the Southern Konkan, and was on too large a scale for Sambháji to resist: so after putting garrisons into the forts he retired to Vishálgad with Sultán Akbar and watched his opportunity. The country no doubt suffered very severely. The Moghals however made no attempt on the hill-forts, and by the time they got near Goa they had, although unopposed, lost almost the whole of their horses and cattle, and even the men began to suffer from scarcity. The Maráthás then came down on them and harassed their retreat. "The enemy swarmed around on every side and cut off the supplies. On one side was the sea and on two other sides mountains full of poisonous trees and serpents. The enemy cut down the grass which caused great distress to man and beast. They had no food but cocoanuts and the grain called kudu, which acted like poison upon them.[2]" Numbers of vessels containing supplies for the Moghals were sent off from Surat, but most of them were taken by the Marátha cruisers, and at last Sultán Mauzim was obliged to retreat with the remainder of his force up the Amba Ghát. In the meantime Sháhábuddin Khán had brought a force nearly as far as Ráygad, and defeated Sambháji in an unimportant action at Nizámpur,[3] after which he returned to the Dakhan.[4] The country being thus abandoned, Sambháji took possession of it without opposition and returned to Ráygad. After the rains the Portuguese re-took Karanja and also the hills of Santa Cruz and Asheri.[5] Sultán Akbar and Sambháji came to Kalyán, and after ravaging the Portuguese territory invested Bassein,[6] but were called away by a reported invasion of the Musalmáns. The chances of war on land appear thus to have fallen pretty equally, but Sambháji's ships at Rájápur were at this time more than a match for the Goa fleet.[7]

For the next three or four years nothing of importance is recorded in the Konkan, the war between the Maráthás and Aurangzeb being carried on chiefly in the Dakhan. The Bijápur kingdom had ceased to exist, and though the Moghals had succeeded to its possession yet they had no reason for valuing the Southern Konkan so highly as the Ádil Sháhi dynasty had done. Sambháji spent his time between Panhála Vishalgad and Sangameshvar, and being given up to sensual pleasures was at last abandoned by Sultán Akbar, who in October 1688 found at Rájápur a ship commanded by an Englishman, and sailed in her to Persia about the middle of 1689.[6] A small party of Moghal cavalry set off from Kolhápur and having got close to Sangameshvar before the alarm was given, succeeded in capturing Sambháji. Kháfi Khán says that he had two or three thousand horse with him, and was told of the approach of the hostile force, which consisted of two thousand horse and a thousand foot, but would not

---

[1] Baldæus, 152.

[2] Kháfi Khán in Elliot, VII. 314. In this account Kháfi Khán calls the Konkan (or the part of it ravaged) Rám-darrá, which is not explained.

[3] This is not mentioned by Orme.

[4] Elphinstone, 575; Grant, Duff, 145; Scott, II. 61.

[5] Orme, 134, 141; Kloguen, 48. [6] Grant Duff, 155. [7] Orme, 141-145: Bruce, II. 63.

believe it.[1] Only two or three hundred of them surprised Sambháji, and Kalusha with a party of Maráthás tried to save him, and was himself wounded, while Sambháji hid himself in a temple. When found he was immediately carried off to the Emperor's camp above the Gháts, and there put to death a few days afterwards.[2]

During the reign of Sambháji his family had lived at Ráygad, and his half-brother Rájárám had been detained there in easy captivity. The chief Marátha leaders met at Ráygad as soon as Sambháji's death was announced, and came to a decision which showed great wisdom. As the Moghals were then in force above the Gháts, and as the Marátha state had in the last few years lost most of its power, they agreed to act on the defensive and to trust to the forts, which they put in preparation for attack. Rájárám went about the country as occasion required, and his family were sent to Vishálgad, but Sambháji's widow and child remained at Ráygad. Immediately after the rains of 1689 the Moghal force came down into the Konkan and took Ráygad after several months' siege. Sháhu, then a child, was taken prisoner with his mother,[3] and there is no record of his ever having returned to the Konkan. And from this time Ráygad lost its importance, because the degeneracy of the descendants of Shiváji prevented their making use of the forts in the same way as he and Sambháji had done.

Aurangzeb now gave the Sidi a *sanad* for some of the territories which he had held previous to the rise of Shiváji, and armed with this authority he took the districts of Suvarndurg and Anjanvel and in 1699 the forts of Rájpuri and Ráygad.[4] The Maráthás still retained command of many of the forts, and kept up their fleet, and so harassed the Sidi and retained some power on the coast. The Moghals did not interfere much with them in the Southern Konkan, and the most southern districts were practically independent. The province of Sálshi was divided among three different claimants, two-fifths of the revenue going to the Sávants, three-tenths to the Pant of Bávda, and three-tenths to Ángria, while a payment had also to be made to the Killedár of Málvan. About 1700 Phond Sávant built the fort of Bharatgad, only three or four miles from Málvan, and immediately afterwards the Pant of Rávda built Bhagvantgad on the other side of the river.[5] In 1698 Mánkoji Ángria succeeded to the command of the Marátha fleet, and with it of the coast. The principal place of arms was Kolába, and there were depôts also at Suvarndurg and Vijaydurg[6] and by this time the Maráthás were the strongest naval power on the coast and attacked the vessels of all nations. The only expedition which in the latter years of his life Aurangzeb appears to have sent to the Southern Konkan was

---

[1] This may be true and yet they may have been quite unavailable for help, as Sangameshvar is so closely hemmed in between hills and the creek that in the supposed absence of danger the guard would probably be at some distance.

[2] Grant Duff, 159; Elliot, VII. 338. Orme (pages 163, 305) gives the neighbourhood of Panhála as the scene of the capture, and relates the circumstances differently.

[3] Grant Duff, 162.

[4] Grant Duff, 231; Jervis, 109.

[5] Hutchinson, 156.

[6] Grant Duff, 172.

Section VII. The Marathas, 1680-1739.

against Vishálgad in 1700-1. The Amba Ghát was blockaded in order to prevent supplies getting in by that route, and to keep the road open for the Vanjáris of the royal army. The villages were burnt, the cattle carried off, and the people generally so harried that no sign of cultivation or the name or trace of a Marátha was to be found. The siege works were pushed on till a mine was carried near the gate. For raising the earth-works camel saddles and baskets innumerable were used full of earth and rubbish and litter heads of men and feet of quadrupeds, and these were advanced so far that the garrison were intimidated.[1] Negotiations for surrender went on for a long time and at length in June 1701 after a six months' siege Parashrám the commandant hoisted the imperial flag over the fortress. He and his family went off the same night, and the rest of the garrison were allowed to leave the fort next day. Its name was then changed to Sakhkharalana.[2]

The only events recorded during this time in the Northern Konkan, where the Moghals still retained their power, come under the general description of rapine and anarchy. About 1690 a multitude of outlaws with 4000 soldiers, all under the command of a ruffian named Kákáji, went about plundering and burning villages, and even burnt the church of Remedi close to Bassein.[3] In 1692 the Sidi attacked Bassein and threatened Sálsette, and for two or three years his troops ravaged the country.[4] About this period he is stated to have been in alliance with the chief of the Jesuits at Bándra for the extermination of the English.[5] Then in 1694 Aurangzeb declared war against the Portuguese. In that year and the following he treated their subjects with great cruelty, and numbers were obliged to take refuge in the forts of Damau and Bassein:[6] but fortunately for the Portuguese Aurangzeb was persuaded to make peace with them with a view to obtaining cannon for the reduction of the Marátha forts. About the same time the Muskat Arabs made a descent on Sálsette, burnt many villages and churches, killed the priests, and carried off about 1400 captives into slavery.[7] The Portuguese in 1695 succeeded in burning three of the Marátha ships in the Rájápur river, the largest said to carry thirty-two guns and more than 300 men: the Portuguese lost six men killed and thirty-four wounded,[8] and the triumphant tone they adopted on this occasion shows how little they were now accustomed to victory.

It was just at this time, 1697, when the whole coast was so given up to piracy that the notorious English pirate Captain Kidd appeared in these seas to add to the general terror. On one occasion he escaped from a Dutch and English squadron and got to Rájápur, and off that port plundered a Bombay vessel. His ship was the

---

[1] Those who have seen Vishálgad will understand that all this was done to raise the two narrow necks of land across which alone access can be had to the fort, to the level of it.
[2] Kháfi Khán in Elliot, VIII. 370; Grant Duff, 177.
[3] Gemelli in Churchill, III. 192.
[4] Bruce, III. 124.
[5] Ovington, 155.
[6] Grant Duff, 168.
[7] Hamilton in Pinkerton, VIII. 353.
[8] O Chronista, II. 201.

Section VII.

The Marathas, 1680-1739.

Adventure galley of thirty guns and thirty oars, and with a crew of 200 Europeans.[1]

It cannot be doubted that in the twenty-seven years which elapsed between the death of Shiváji and that of Aurangzeb the condition of the Konkan had greatly altered for the worse. Both the military and the revenue system of Shiváji fell much into decay under Sambháji, who, Kháfi Khán says, so oppressed the rayats that they fled from his country to that of the Feringis.[2] Although Rájárám tried to return to the old ways yet the success of the Sidi and A'ngria and the generally unsettled state of the country prevented any great measure of reform. The frequent ravaging expeditions of the Moghals and the Sidi in the Northern Konkan, with the fewer but more regular campaigns in the south, must have caused great misery. The Portuguese were utterly unable to protect their possessions. The districts owned by the Sidi were less exposed to external aggression than any other part, yet his was a government that never paid much attention to the wants or the miseries of its native subjects, and his system of revenue exactions was, if more certain, scarcely less oppressive than that of Kalusha. The divisions of authority in the Málvan district already mentioned must have kept the people in a perpetual fever of civil war. Trade of course could not have flourished under these circumstances, and almost the only mention of it that can be found at this time is that on exports from Bombay duties of five per cent were levied by the East India Company, eight per cent by the Portuguese at Thána, and arbitrary exactions by the Moghals at Kalyán.[3]

The civil war amongst the Maráthás which followed almost immediately on the death of Aurangzeb and the release of Sháhu from captivity were not likely to improve the condition of any part of the country, and from this time the Konkan chiefly suffered from the divisions among the Maráthás themselves. Sháhu advanced as far as Rángna, south of the Phonda Ghát, and laid siege to the fort, and Tárábái, widow of Rájárám, fled to Málvan. Sháhu did not however descend into the Konkan, and Tárábái in 1710, having collected a force and being supported by the Sávants, again went up the Gháts and established herself at Kolhápur. In the discords that thus arose between Shiváji's descendants Kánhoji Ángria became the greatest power in the Konkan, having possession of the coast from Sávantvádi to Bombay, and extending his authority into the province of Kalyán.[4] Orme says that Kánhoji held Suvarndurg against Sháhu and that the latter built the Harnai forts in order to reduce him to obedience, but Kánhoji took them.[5] This must probably have happened between 1707 and 1713. The Maráthás in 1707 equipped a fleet of sixty vessels under a leader independent of Ángria to cruise between Bombay and Goa, partly to make what they could by piracy themselves and partly to oppose

1 Bruce, III. 237, 271. 2 Elliot, VII. 342. 3 Bruce, III. 239. 4 Grant Duff, 187, 192. 5 History, 407.

Section VII. The Marathas, 1680-1739.

the Arab pirates, who were now thoroughly organised and had ships carrying from thirty to fifty guns.[1] Between 1712 and 1720 four actions are recorded between the Portuguese and the Arabs, the first of which was at the mouth of the Rájpuri river. In the last three the Portuguese are said to have been successful, but these successes are spoken of in terms which show the strength and position of the pirates.[2]

In 1713 Kánhoji Angria went over to Sháhu and the concessions then granted were such as to make him practically independent. He received all the great forts on the coast from Khánderi to Vijaydurg, and many inland, including Avchitgad Rájápur and Khárepátan. Báláji Vishvanáth, a Chitpáwan of the family of Bhat and town of Shrivardhan a little north of Bánkot, was the chief agent in the negotiations which led to this arrangement, and this was the first important service of this great man, who was soon afterwards appointed Peshwa, and whose successors so soon eclipsed the Marátha dynasty. The first consequence of the new alliance was the taking from the Sidi of some places which he had held for many years. This he naturally resented, but Angria and Báláji Vishvanáth invaded his territory and compelled him to submit.

In 1720 the rights of the Maráthás were acknowledged by the Emperor of Delhi, and the Konkan was included in what was called the Svaráj or Home-rule, over which from this time forward the Musalmáns retained no authority whatever. The various provinces were then assigned to the different great officers of state, and the Chitnis thus got charge of a great part of the Konkan, Angria retaining the part already granted to him and being very formidable to all his neighbours.[3] Details of the history of his family and of their relations with other powers will be found in the next section.

During the war between the Sátára and Kolhápur branches of the Maráthás no important operations are recorded in the Konkan, and it appears that the rich district of Málvan was left for Rájárám A'ngria and the Sávants to fight for among themselves. In 1731 the treaty of partition between Sátára and Kolhápur was concluded and in this Kolhápur received the whole of the Konkan south of Vijaydurg, while the fort of Ratnágiri was given to Sháhu in exchange for Kopál.[4] Vijaydurg itself of course remained with the Angriás, but by this time Kánhoji was dead, and his successors by their dissensions among themselves relieved the other powers of a formidable enemy. The Maráthás therefore under Báláji Vishvanáth, having now made peace with the Kolhápur party were able to make a real attack on the Sidi, for the bombardment of Janjira was a periodical performance which scarcely deserved the name of serious warfare. The Sidi had retained the districts of Mahád, Ráygad, Dábhol, and Anjanvel. The Pratinidhi in 1733 with the connivance of a notorious pirate called Shaikhji, who was well in the Sidi's confidence, took a force into the districts of the latter which

---

[1] Bruce, III. 649.
[2] Kloguen, 49-50.
[3] Grant Duff, 186, 193, 200, 203.
[4] Grant Duff, 223 : Aitchison's Treaties, VI 87.

Section VII. The Marathas, 1680-1739.

ravaged the country but did little else, and the Sidi's troops gained the fort of Govalkot while the Pratinidhi was close by at Chiplún.[1] The Bombay Government in December of this year entered into their first formal alliance with the Sidi, but this was directed chiefly against Ángria and does not seem to have included the defence of the Sidi's territory against the Marátha state.[2] From this time however there was no interruption of the good understanding between the Bombay Government and the Sidis, and the alliance was at this time chiefly valued by the English because it enabled them to obtain supplies of beef, which they could not obtain from the Hindu governments in their more immediate neighbourhood.[3] It was stipulated that, on A'ngria being conquered, Khánderi should go to the English and all the rest of the forts to the Sidi except Kolába, which was to be entirely demolished and never rebuilt except with the consent of both governments. It is remarkable that this treaty was signed by seven of the Sidis and without any reference to their being one head of the government.[4] A writer of that time accordingly speaks of the Janjira government as a republic, and there is no doubt that up almost to the present time (1894) the *gádi* has been looked upon as to some extent elective. Immediately after this the reigning Sidi died, and the dissensions among his sons enabled the Peshwa Bájiráv to interfere. In 1735 he took Ráygad, which had been lost to the Maráthás since 1690, as well as the forts of Tala and Ghosála, and eventually those of Avchitgad and Birvádi were also ceded and a provision made for Sidi Rahman whom the Maráthás had supported.

Thus the rule both of the Sidi and of Ángria being broken, and the Moghals got rid of, the Marátha state had again become the chief power in the Konkan. The time had arrived when they might hope to make a successful attack on the Portuguese and by driving them out of their old possessions unite the whole province under Native rule. No particular pretext for attacking the Portuguese was necessary, for war was the natural state of these powers on the coast and peace the exception, and it was not likely that the "Government of the Konkani Bráhmans," as it was called since the Peshwás had become virtually the rulers of the state, should much longer endure the presence of foreigners in their native district. It appeared also in the result that, except in two or three places, the Portuguese were not in a position to offer much defence,[5] although trusting rather to their old prestige than to their present strength, they did not scruple to give the Maráthás provocation. In 1737 they again allied themselves with Sambháji A'ngria and attempted to take Kolába from Mánáji, whom the Peshwa was sent to support.[6] The intolerance as to religious matters from which the native subjects of Portugal suffered has already been described, and it is said that the Hindu inhabitants of Sálsette complained of "the intemperate zeal with which it was attempted to convert them to the

---

[1] Grant Duff, 231. [2] Aitchison's Treaties, VI. 200. [3] Grant Duff, 288.
[4] Bombay Government Records, XXVI. 10. [5] Bom. Quar. Review, IV. 78, 80.
[6] Grant Duff, 237.

Section VII.

The Marathas, 1680-1739.

Roman Catholic faith, and to subject them to the terrors of the Inquisition."[1] The Maráthás therefore invaded Sálsette in April 1737, and having taken Ghodbandar and put the garrison to the sword speedily got command of the Bassein river, and so prevented any succour being sent from Bassein. The fortifications of Thána were incomplete as has already been mentioned, and the Governor of Sálsette retired to Karanja with unnecessary haste.[2] Thána was however defended, and not taken till two assaults had been repulsed, the capitulation being assisted by the Maráthás seizing the families of the defenders and threatening to slaughter them.[3] The English sent men and ammunition to assist in the defence of Bándra, but finding it untenable they induced the Portuguese to destroy the fortifications and abandon the place.[4] The great church of St. Anne with the Jesuits' college, standing on the site of the present slaughter-houses, was then destroyed, and also the church of Our Lady of the Mount now generally known as Mount Mary, which was rebuilt in 1761, the great crosses of the two older buildings alone remaining. There being no other places of much strength in the island, Sálsette was thus practically lost to the Portuguese. The Peshwa thought it necessary to send a very large force to the Konkan, but being at the time much pressed in the north of India was soon obliged to withdraw a great part of it. Encouraged by this the Portuguese in 1738 made some gallant efforts, and at Asheri defeated the Marátha army and were preparing to attempt the recovery of Thána, but it was too late.

In January 1739 Chimnáji Appa assumed command in the Northern Konkan, and took Khatalvada, Dáhánu, Kelva, Shirgaon, and Tárápur. At all these places there were forts, that of Tárápur being the most considerable, and the defence there was very obstinate. There still seemed a chance for the Portuguese, for the Peshwa alarmed at the approach of Nadir Sháh recalled Chimnaji Appa and his force from the Konkan to help to resist the invaders in the north of India. But by this time Vesáva and Dharávi, the last forts in Sálsette, had surrendered, and the siege of Bassein had commenced and Chimnáji Appa was hero enough to disregard the order of recall.[5] The commandant of Bassein offered to pay tribute to the Maráthás and to humble himself as the Sidi had done, but this was of no avail. The city was invested on February 17, and the capitulation took place on May 16. During the interval the Portuguese showed all the heroism that was possible to a besieged force, and repulsed the attacks which were made with constantly increasing obstinacy. Had they been supported by a fleet they might have held out till the rains should necessitate the retreat of the Marátha army, but Mánáji Angria blockaded the sea approach and their provisions were exhausted. They made frequent and urgent appeals to the Bombay Government to assist them, which, unfortunately for our national fame, were disregarded,[6] and two

[1] Reg. I. of 1880.
[2] Grant Duff, 237.
[3] Bom. Quar. Review, III. 273.
[4] Bom. Quar. Review, IV. 78, 80.
[5] Grant Duff, 237, 240, 242.
[6] Bom. Quar. Review, IV. 82.

different treaties were entered into during the month of April ceding territory near Goa, but were not apparently ratified.[1] They are believed to have lost 800 men during the siege and the Maráthás acknowledge to 5000.[2]

With the surrender of the Capital of the North not only the glory of the Portuguese departed, but also every vestige of their power in the Northern Konkan, for the greater part of the European fazendars abandoned their estates and left the country.[3] Nor were they long allowed to keep their isolated position at Chaul though no operations were conducted against it in 1740. But in that year the Portuguese fleet was destroyed by Angria,[4] and in January 1741 Chaul was attacked and taken (under the direction of Chimnaji Appa [5]) by Khandoji Mánkár, who in the next year in consideration of his services received the village of Kharoli in the Thal district in inám.[6] After the rains, while on their march from Chaul to Goa, the wretched remains of the Portuguese armies were attacked by Khem Sávant and numbers of them perished.

It does not appear that this destruction of the Portuguese power in India was much regarded by the Portuguese in Europe. In 1744 the King in giving orders to a new Viceroy said scarcely anything about recovering the lost territories except that opportunities were to be watched, but gave minute and particular orders as to commerce, and suggested that the artisans of Thána should be induced to settle in Goa.[7] On two subsequent occasions however the Portuguese made some show of vigour. In 1756 the Maráthás under the influence of Sadáshivráv Bháu had resolved to take Goa. To anticipate them in this the Portuguese Viceroy attacked the Marátha districts near Goa but was defeated and killed.[8] His attack had however the effect of putting an end to the hostilities of the Maráthás. In 1774 the Portuguese Government provoked by the capture of one of their forty-gun ships by the Maráthás determined in revenge to take not only their old province of the North but also Gheria and Suvarndurg, and for this purpose large reinforcements were sent from Europe. The only result was that the Bombay Government in order to forestall them took Thána.

From what has been said in the earlier parts of this work it might reasonably have been expected that the Maráthás, who have never had much reputation for clemency, would have treated the Christians with rigour after the conquest, and that the faith of the great

---

[1] Jervis, 129.

[2] Grant Duff, 240, 242. The first man who planted the Peshwa's flag on the fort is said to have been Ranoji Bháburáv Khanvilkar, who for his services received eighteen villages in the Northern and Southern Konkan The present representative of the family was notorious as the prime minister of Malhárráv the late Gaikwár of Baroda.

[3] East India House Selections, III. 774. [4] Kloguen, 51.

[5] Grant Duff, 256. It is stated in the Bombay Quarterly Review, IV. 89, that Chaul was delivered to the English for surrender to the Maráthás, and this implies that no siege took place, but the writer has thought it safer to follow Grant Duff.

[6] Sadar Adálat Civil Reports (1825), II. 76. [7] O Chronista, II. 158.

[8] Grant Duff, 294.

majority of these Christians would not have been steady enough to stand against adversity. The facts however are equally creditable to the Maráthás and to the Christians. The Governor of Bassein indeed in the articles of capitulation got no better terms for the converts than the privilege of three churches within the city, one in the district and one in the island of Sálsette,[1] and the Maráthás are said to have destroyed some of the churches as soon as they invaded Sálsette. The Portuguese monks and other white priests abandoned the district with the fazendárs, as if knowing that they had little to expect from the affection of their flocks when the secular power would no longer help them. But their place was taken by 'Canarins' or black priests from Malabár under a Vicar General, who was also a Canarin, and twenty years after the conquest when Anquetil du Perron travelled through the district the Christian congregations were all flourishing and in no way molested in the exercise of their religion. A good many of their churches and convents were more or less in ruins, and of course Hindu temples had sprung up where none were allowed before, but at Thána the church fêtes and ceremonies were celebrated with the same pomp as at Goa, fifteen native priests being assembled at a function in which Du Perron assisted in the choir: and at Agáshi he found the roads full of people "going to church with as much liberty as in a Christian state."[2] It is clear from this that if the Maráthás were ever inclined to avenge the cruelties of the Jesuits and the Inquisition, they desisted as soon as the European leaders had been got rid of, and allowed their subjects full liberty of conscience.

The Marátha state had now possession of the whole Konkan, except that part held by the Sidi and Ángria, and these powers were, as shown above, so weakened as to be formidable only at sea. The state of Jawhár must also be excepted, for it is said to have had command of all the country between the Gháts and the Bassein boundary from the latitude of Bassein to that of Daman. Still it is evident that this large tract was left to Jawhár simply because it was always considered almost valueless, the total revenue being only 3½ lakhs,[3] and eventually the Maráthás got possession of nearly the whole without any particular opposition. The possessions of the Shirké family must also be mentioned, as they continued to hold territory yielding a revenue of Rs. 75,000 a year down to 1768, when the Peshwa put an end to the small state.[4] The *ináms* were however continued to them, and their representatives now live in a very reduced condition at Kutra, immediately below their old Ghat capital Bahirugad, and are known by the surname of Ráje Shirké. It is now necessary to return to the Ángriás as their downfall in 1756 is the next event of importance in the history of the Konkan.

[1] Bom. Quar. Review, IV. 84.
[2] Du Perron, I. 384, 426.
[3] Bom. Gov. Sel. XXVI. 15.
[4] Sadar Adálat Civil Reports (1825), II. 458.

SECTION VIII.

THE A'NGRIA'S.

Section VIII.
The Angrias, 1700-1756.

The family of Ángria is by caste Maráthа, and its splendour may be considered almost to have begun and ended with Kánhoji, although his father Tukáji had early distinguished himself in Shiváji's fleet.[1] It has been already stated that Kánhoji's power rapidly increased during the unsettled days of Sambháji and Sháhu, and in 1713 he was recognised as virtually independent, and was in fact master of all the coast with the forts on it from Bombay to Vijaydurg besides a good deal of the inland country. He made Vijaydurg his capital and in doing so showed himself a sailor of a different sort from Shiváji. It may probably also be owing to the same uncompromising spirit that he was from the first on terms of enmity, more or less pronounced, with the Bombay Government. As early as 1717 the English had already made an attempt on Vijaydurg, but were not successful.[2] In 1719 a force from Bombay attempted to take Khanderi from Ángria, but failed.[3] The then Viceroy at Goa is vaguely said to have chastised Ángria,[4] but in November 1720 the Portuguese found it advisable to unite with the English against him, and they burnt sixteen of his vessels which were lying in the Vijaydurg river, but could do nothing against the fort. In 1722 the same allies attacked Kolába with three British ships of the line and a Portuguese army but failed, and in 1724 the Dutch attacked Vijaydurg with a fleet of seven ships of the line, two bomb ketches and some land forces, but they succeeded no better than the others. Kánhoji was naturally encouraged by these failures, and in 1727 he took the *Darby*, a richly-laden English ship besides many Dutch and French ships at different times, and our East India Company are said at this time to have been put to an annual expense of £50,000 in keeping up an armed squadron to protect their trade against the pirates, of whom Kánhoji was the acknowledged chief. In 1728 however he died and his possessions were soon all in confusion. His eldest legitimate son Sakhoji retained possession of Kolába until his death soon afterwards, when his illegitimate brothers Mánáji and Yesáji were put in charge by Sambháji, the second legitimate son, who lived at Suvarndurg. Mánáji and Yesáji having quarrelled, Mánáji with the assistance of the Portuguese took Kolába and put Yesáji's eyes out. Sambháji then attacked him, but Mánáji got assistance from the Peshwa, to whom he yielded

[1] Grant Duff, 163. [2] Milburn, I. 295. [3] Bom. Quar. Review, III. 57. [4] Kloguen, 50.

Section VIII.

The Angrias, 1700-1756.

the forts of Kutla (probably Kothigad) and Rájmáchi, and repulsed Sambháji.[1] The war between these two continued for a good many years with various alternations of alliances, but the Bombay Government appear always to have opposed the whole family. In 1730 they made an offensive and defensive alliance with Phond Sávant against the Ángriás generally, and in 1733 a similar one with the Sidi,[2] but these appear to have had no particular result. The next hostilities we hear of were in December 1738 when Commodore Bagwel with four grabs was cruising in search of Sambháji's fleet, and on the 22nd came upon nine of his grabs and thirteen gallivats issuing from the Vijaydurg river. They stood up the coast, but the Commodore immediately bore down on them, and they took refuge in the Rájápur river, displaying all their flags. They ran up the river further than the English vessels could follow them, and the Commodore could only give them a few broadsides, which however did much damage and killed their Admiral.[3] After this it was Mánáji's turn to be troublesome, and he took Karanja and Elephanta, but soon afterwards Sambháji attacked him and took Chaul, Álibág, Ságargad, and Thal. Báláji Bájiráv was sent from the Dakhan to help to defend Kolába, and distinguished himself in an attack on an outpost, and with his assistance Mánáji held his own.[4] In the meanwhile the English drove Sambháji's fleet down as far as Suvarndurg, where they cannonaded his camp and refused to allow him to retire to the fort. He however managed to effect his escape. In 1740 Sambháji took possession of Bharatgad, Bhagvantgad, and the greater part of the Vádi possessions in the Sálshi province, and these were not recovered till 1748.[5] About this time Sambháji died and was succeeded by his half-brother Tuláji. He like the rest, whether rendering or refusing obedience to the Peshwás, never failed to plunder the ships of all those who were not too strong for him. The Sávants and the Kolhápur captains did the same, and these both now and later went among the English by the general name of Málvans,[6] as at an earlier period other pirates were called Sunguiceers from Sangameshvar their principal station.[7]

Matters went on in this way till 1755, when the Portuguese having entirely lost their power, and the Maráthás being on unusually good terms both with the English and the Sidi, the two powers determined to reduce Tuláji Ángria by a joint expedition. The Maráthás were to keep Vijaydurg and the English to receive Bánkot with the sovereignty of the Mahád river and a few villages on its banks.[8] Orme has given a long and interesting account[9] of the operations that followed, and his description of the equipment and manœuvres of the pirates is also too apt to the purpose of this history to allow of much curtailment. Facts related by other authorities and in particular by Ives, who was surgeon on board

---

[1] Grant Duff, 231; Macpherson, 181.
[2] Aitchison's Treaties, VI. 119, 200.
[3] Bom. Quar. Review, IV. 75.
[4] Grant Duff, 247.
[5] Hutchinson, 157.
[6] Grant Duff, 288; Field Officer, 163.
[7] DeCoutto, XII. 30.
[8] Grant Duff, 288.
[9] History, I. 407-417.

Section VIII.

The Angrias, 1700-1756.

Admiral Watson's ship at the taking of Gheria, will be interpolated in Orme's narrative:

"The piracies which Ángria exercised upon ships of all nations indifferently, who did not purchase his passes, rendered him every day more and more powerful. The land and sea breezes on this coast, as well as on that of Coromandel, blow alternately in the twenty-four hours, and divide the day, so that vessels sailing along the coast are obliged to keep in sight of land, since the land winds do not reach more than forty miles out to sea. There was not a creek, bay, harbour, or mouth of a river along the coast of his dominions in which he had not erected fortifications and marine receptacles to serve both as a station of discovery and as a place of refuge to his vessels; hence it was as difficult to avoid the encounter of them as to take them. His fleet consisted of grabs and gallivats, vessels peculiar to the Malabár coast. The grabs have rarely more than two masts, although some have three; those of three are about 300 tons burthen, but the others are not more than 150. They are built to draw very little water, being very broad in proportion to their length, narrowing however from the middle to the end, where instead of bows they have a prow, projecting like that of a Mediterranean galley, and covered with a strong deck, level with the main deck of the vessel, from which however it is separated by a bulk-head which terminates the forecastle. As this construction subjects the grab to pitch violently when sailing against a head sea, the deck of the prow is not enclosed with sides as the rest of the vessel is, but remains bare, that the water which dashes upon it may pass off without interruption. On the main deck under the forecastle are mounted two pieces of cannon of nine or twelve pounders, which point forwards through the portholes cut in the bulk-head, and fire over the prow; the cannon of the broadside are from six to nine pounders. The gallivats are large row-boats built like the grab but of smaller dimensions, the largest rarely exceeding seventy tons: they have two masts, of which the mizen is very slight; the main mast bears only one sail, which is triangular and very large, the peak of it when hoisted being much higher than the mast itself. In general the gallivats are covered with a spar deck, made for lightness of split bamboos, and these carry only petteraroes, which are fixed on swivels in the gunnel of the vessel: but those of the largest size have a fixed deck on which they mount six or eight pieces of cannon from two to four pounders. They have forty or fifty stout oars, and may be rowed four miles an hour. Eight or ten grabs, and forty or fifty gallivats, crowded with men, generally composed Ángria's principal fleet destined to attack ships of force or burthen. The vessel no sooner came in sight of the port or bay where the fleet was lying, than they slipped their cables and put out to sea. If the wind blew, their construction enabled them to sail almost as fast as the wind; and if it was calm, the gallivats rowing towed the grabs. When within cannon shot of the chase they generally assembled in her stern, and the grabs attacked her at a distance with their prow guns, firing first only at the masts, and

Section VIII.

The Angrias, 1700-1756.

taking aim when the three masts of the vessel just opened all together to their view, by which means the shot would probably strike one or other of the three. As soon as the chase was dismasted, they came nearer and battered her on all sides until she struck; and if the defence was obstinate, they sent a number of gallivats with two or three hundred men in each, who boarded sword in hand from all quarters in the same instant.

"The Maráthás who were in possession of the main land opposite to Bombay, had several times made proposals to the English Government in the island, to attack this common enemy with their united forces, but it was not before the beginning of 1755 that both parties happened to be ready at the same time to undertake such an expedition. The Presidency then made a treaty with Rámáji Pant, Báláji Peshwa's general in these parts, and agreed to assist the Maráthás with their marine force in reducing Suvarndurg, Bánkot, and some others of Ángria's forts, which lie near to Chaul, a harbour and fortified city belonging to the Maráthás. Accordingly Commodore James, the commander-in-chief of the Company's marine force in India, sailed on the 22nd of March in the *Protector* of forty-four guns, with a ketch of sixteen guns and two bomb vessels; but such was the exaggerated opinion of Ángria's strongholds, that the Presidency instructed him not to expose the Company's vessels to any risk by attacking them, but only to blockade the harbours whilst the Marátha army carried on their operations by land. Three days after the Marátha fleet, consisting of seven grabs and sixty gallivats, came out of Chaul, having on board 10,000 land forces, and the fleets united proceeded to Comara-bay, where they anchored in order to permit the Maráthás to get their meal on shore, since they are prohibited by their religion from eating or washing at sea. Departing from hence they anchored again about fifteen miles to the north of Suvarndurg when Rámáji Pant with the troops disembarked in order to proceed the rest of the way by land. Commodore James now receiving intelligence that the enemy's fleet lay at anchor in the harbour of Suvarndurg represented to the Admiral of the Marátha fleet, that by proceeding immediately thither they might come upon them in the night, and so effectually blockade them in the harbour that few or none would be able to escape. The Marátha seemed highly to approve the proposal, but had not authority enough over his officers to make any of them stir before the morning, when the enemy discovering them under sail, immediately slipped their cables and put to sea. The Commodore then flung out the signal for a general chase; but as little regard was paid to this as to his former intention; for although the vessels of the Maráthás had hitherto sailed better than the English, such was their terror of Angria's fleet, that they all kept behind, and suffered the *Protector* to proceed alone almost out of their sight. The enemy on the other hand exerted themselves with uncommon industry, flinging overboard all their lumber to lighten their vessels, not only crowding all the sails they could bend, but also hanging up their garments, and even their turbans, to catch every breath of air. The *Protector*,

Section VIII.

The Angrias, 1700-1756.

however, came within gun-shot of some of the sternmost, b the evening approaching, Commodore James gave over the chas and returned to Suvarndurg which he had passed several miles. Here he found Rámáji Pant with the army besieging, as they said, the three forts on the main land; but they were firing only from one gun, a four-pounder, at the distance of two miles, and even at this distance the troops did not think themselves safe without digging pits, in which they sheltered themselves covered up to the chin from the enemy's fire. The Commodore, judging from these operations that they would never take the forts, determined to exceed the instructions which he had received from the Presidency, rather than expose the English arms to the disgrace they would suffer, if an expedition in which they were believed by Angria to have taken so great a share, should miscarry. The next day, the 2nd of April, he began to cannonade and bombard the fort of Suvarndurg situated on the island;[1] but finding that the walls on the western side which he attacked, were mostly cut out of the solid rock, he changed his station to the north-east between the island and the main; where whilst one of his broadsides plied the north-east bastions of this fort the other fired on Fort Goa, the largest of those upon the main land. The bastions of Suvarndurg however, were so high, that the *Protector* could only point her upper tier at them, but being anchored within a hundred yards, the musketry in the round tops drove the enemy from their guns, and by noon the parapet of the north-east bastions was in ruins, when a shell from one of the bomb vessels set fire to a thatched house, which the garrison, dreading the *Protector's* musketry, were afraid to extinguish; the blaze spreading fiercely at this dry season of the year, all the buildings of the fort were soon in flames, and amongst them a magazine of powder blew up. On this disaster the inhabitants, men women and children with the greatest part of the garrison, in all near 1000 persons, ran out of the fort, and embarking in seven or eight large boats, attempted to make their escape to Fort Goa, where the enemy after suffering a severe cannonade, hung out a flag as a signal of surrender; but whilst the Maráthás were marching to take possession of it, the governor, perceiving that the Commodore had not yet taken possession of Suvarndurg, got into a boat with some of his most honest men, and crossed over to the island, hoping to be able to maintain the fort until he should receive assistance from Dábhol which is in sight of it. Upon this the *Protector* renewed her fire upon Suvarndurg, and the Commodore finding that the governor wanted to protract the defence until night, when it was not to be doubted that some boats from Dábhol would endeavour to throw succours into the place, he landed half his seamen under cover of the fire of the ships, who with great intrepidity ran up to the gate, and cutting down the sallyport with their axes, forced their way into it; on which the garrison surrendered: the other two forts on the

[1] The fort of Suvarndurg had at this time fifty guns mounted on the ramparts, and the three forts on the shore eighty between them. Milburn, I. 295.

Section VIII.

The Angrias, 1700-1756.

main land had by this time hung out flags of truce, and the Maráthás took possession of them.[1] This was all the work of one day, in which the spirited resolution of Commodore James destroyed the timorous prejudices which had for twenty years been entertained of the impracticability of reducing any of Ángria's fortified harbours. On the 8th of April the fleet and army proceeded to Bánkot which surrendered on the first summons, and the Maráthás consented that the Company should keep it. Rámáji Pant was so elated by these successes, that he offered Commodore James 2,00,000 rupees if he would immediately proceed against Dábhol and some other of the enemy's forts a little to the southward of that place; and certainly this was the time to attack them, during the consternation into which the enemy were thrown by the losses they had just sustained. But the monsoon was approaching, and the Commodore having already exceeded his orders, would not venture to comply with the Marátha's request without permission from Bombay. But the Presidency, notwithstanding the unexpected successes of their arms, was so solicitous for the fate of one of their bomb ketches, a heavy flat-bottomed boat incapable of keeping the sea in tempestuous weather, that they ordered him to bring back the fleet into harbour without delay. Accordingly on the 11th he delivered the forts of Suvarndurg to the Maráthás, striking the English flag, which for the honour of their arms he had hitherto caused to be hoisted in them, and on the 15th sailed away with his ships to Bombay: the Marátha fleet at the same time returned to Chaul.

"The Maráthás had in the meantime sent a force from Poona and taken some other forts in the Suvarndurg district and threatened Ratnágiri.[2] Bánkot was not given up till after the rains, when the name of the fort was changed from Himmatgad to Fort Victoria, and eventually the sovereignty of the river and ten villages on it were ceded. This was, excepting Bombay, the first territory the English possessed on the west side of India, and besides being valued for the bullocks that could be obtained there, it soon afterwards was found most useful as a recruiting[3] ground for our native regiments. It was probably also valued as a harbour, for the anchorage was then much better than it has since become, and the river was navigable for large vessels.[4] A treaty regulating the trade of the river was concluded in the following year.[5] After the rains the Maráthás under Rámáji Pant again commenced operations in the Konkan, and early in the year 1756 they took Anjanvel and Dábhol after a siege, and reported the prospect of the immediate capture of Govalkot.[3] They then continued their operations, and before the expedition against Vijaydurg started had reduced all the coast forts north of that without any particular loss, except at Rájápur, where 300 men were killed by an accidental explosion of gunpowder.[6]

[1] The land forts were of little value except as appendages to Suvarndurg. An examination of the fort at Harnai will prove that the present gateway on the land side is quite modern, the only original gateway having opened on to the rocks facing Suvarndurg. The walls on the land side are much stronger and higher than those towards the sea. [2] Grant Duff, 290. [3] Bánkot Manuscript Diaries.
[4] Milburn, I. 294; Forbes, I. 103. [5] Aitchison, VI. 4. [6] Grant Duff, 291.

Section VIII.

The Angrias, 1700-1756.

"After the rains it was determined to attack Gheria, but it was so long since any Englishman had seen this place, that trusting to the report of the natives, they believed it to be at least as strong as Gibraltar, and like Gibraltar situated on a mountain inaccessible from the sea. For this reason it was resolved to send vessels to reconnoitre it, which service Commodore James, in the *Protector* with two other ships, performed. He found the enemy's fleet at anchor in the harbour, notwithstanding which he approached within cannon shot of the fort, and having attentively considered it, returned at the end of December to Bombay, and described the place such as it really was, very strong indeed, but far from being inaccessible or impregnable.[1] Upon his representation it was resolved to prosecute the expedition with vigour. The Marátha army under the command of Rámáji Pant marched from Chaul, and the twenty-gun ship, and the sloop of Mr. Watson's squadron, were sent forward to blockade the harbour where they were soon after joined by Commodore James in the *Protector* and another ship which was of 20 guns belonging to the Company. On the 11th of February the Admiral with the rest of the ships arrived. The whole united fleet now consisted of four ships of the line, of 70, 64, 60, and 50 guns, one of 44, three of 20, a grab of 12, and five bomb-ketches, fourteen vessels in all. Besides the seamen, they had on board a battalion of 800 Europeans with 1000 sepoys under the command of Lieutenant-Colonel Clive. Ives says that the Marátha army consisted of 5000 or 6000 horse and as many foot. Their fleet was three or four grabs and forty or fifty gallivats, and was lying in the Rájápur creek (about four miles north of Gheria), the small fort of which they had taken before the English fleet arrived.[2] On its appearance Angria was so terrified that he left his town to be defended by his brother and went and put himself into the hands of the Maráthás who having crossed the river at some distance from the sea, were already encamped to the eastward of the *peta*. Here he endeavoured to prevail on Rámáji Pant to accept of a ransom for his fort, offering a large sum of money if he would divert the storm that was ready to break upon him. But the Marátha availing himself of his fear, kept him a prisoner, and extorted from him an order directing his brother to deliver the fortress to the Maráthás, intending if he could get possession of it in this clandestine manner to exclude his allies the English from any share of the plunder. The Admiral receiving intelligence of these proceedings, sent a summons to the fort on the morning after his arrival, and receiving no answer, ordered the ships to weigh in the afternoon as soon as the sea wind set in. They proceeded in two divisions, parallel to each other, the larger covering the bomb-ketches and smaller vessels from the fire of the fort. As soon as they had passed the point of the promontory, they stood into the river, and anchoring along the north side of the fortifications, began, at the distance of fifty yards, to

[1] Ives wrote that there was a large town south of the fort crowded and populous and the houses covered with cadjans. Ives, 80. [2] Ives, 82.

Section VIII.

The Angrias, 1700-1756.

batter them with 150 pieces of cannon; the bomb-ketches at the same time plied their mortars, and within ten minutes after the firing began, a shell fell into one of Ángria's grabs, which set her on fire; the rest being fastened together with her, soon shared the same fate, and in less than an hour this fleet, which had for fifty years been the terror of the Malabár coast, was utterly destroyed. In the meantime the cannonade and bombardment continued furiously, and silenced the enemy's fire. But the governor did not surrender when the night set in. Intelligence being received from a deserter that he intended to give up the place the next day to the Maráthás, Colonel Clive landed with the troops; and in order to prevent the Maráthás from carrying their scheme into execution, took up his ground between them and the fort.

"Ives states with regard to the occurrences of this day that the Admiral summoned the fort to surrender on the day he arrived (the 11th) but received only a defiance. Next morning he sent another message, which was not replied to. The engagement began about two o'clock by the fort firing on the *Kingfisher.* The firing went on over half an hour before the *Restoration* grab, which had belonged to the East India Company and had been taken by Ángria caught fire. From the grabs the fire was communicated to a large ship lying on the shore, and from that to the arsenal, storehouse, suburbs and city, and even to several parts of the fort, particularly a square tower, where it continued burning all night with such violence that the stone walls appeared like red-hot iron. About 6-30 the fire of the fort was entirely silenced, but the bomb vessels continued throwing in shells till daylight. Clive landed about 9 P.M.[1]

"Early in the morning the Admiral summoned the place again, declaring that he would renew the attack and give no quarter if it was not delivered up to him in an hour: in answer to which the governor desired a cessation of hostilities until the next morning, alleging that he only waited for orders from A'ngria to comply with the summons. The cannonade was therefore renewed at four in the afternoon; and in less than half an hour the garrison, unable to stand the shock any longer, called out to the advanced guard of the troops on shore that they were ready to surrender, upon which Lieutenant-Colonel Clive immediately marched up and took possession of the fort. It was found that notwithstanding the cannonade had destroyed most of the artificial works upon which they fired, the rock remained a natural and almost impregnable bulwark; so that if the enemy had been endowed with courage sufficient to have maintained the place to extremity, it could only have been taken by regular approaches on the land side. There were found in it 200 pieces of cannon, six brass mortars, and a great quantity of ammunition and military and naval stores of all kinds: the money and effects of other kinds amounted to 120,000 pounds sterling. All this booty was divided amongst the captors, without

1 Ives, 82.

any reserve either for the nation or the Company. Besides the vessels which were set on fire during the attack, there were two ships, one of them of forty guns, upon the stocks, both of which the captors destroyed.

"Ives describes the cannonade on the second day as longer than Orme says. A magazine in the fort was blown up by it about 2 P.M. and the signal of surrender shown at 4. But the governor not being willing to admit the troops that night fire was again renewed, and full submission made at 5-15. Clive had been making his approaches all this time and had greatly annoyed the enemy with his cannon. The colonel and the whole army marched into the fort on the 14th at sunrise, and found in it ten English and three Dutch prisoners. Our loss in killed and wounded amounted to about twenty.

"Whilst the fleet were employed in taking on board the plunder, the Maráthás sent detachments to summon several other forts, which surrendered without making any resistance. Thus in less than a month they got possession of all the territories wrested from them by Ángria's predecessors, and which they had for seventy years despaired of ever being able to recover. In the beginning of April the fleet returned to Bombay, where Mr. Watson repaired his squadron."

Orme in this says nothing of the charges of treachery and bad faith which have so often been made against the British leaders at Gheria.[1] It is not necessary here to go into the question, but the following seems a fair statement of the case: "The allies (Maráthás and English) seem to have been quite as desirous of outwitting each other as of overcoming the enemy. Both parties meditated an exclusive appropriation of the booty which was anticipated and both took much pains to attain their object. The English were successful. The place fell into their hands, and their Marátha friends were disappointed of the expected prize."[2] This capture of Vijaydurg is one of the few events that have taken place in the Konkan which is thought worthy of mention by all the historians of British India, and it may be mentioned that after Admiral Watson's death in the following year the East India Company erected a monument to him in Westminster Abbey, and that a pillar commemorative of the capture of Suvarndurg is still standing at Shooter's Hill near London.

Tuláji Ángria's family were taken in the fort and he himself sent as a prisoner to a fort near Ráygad and kept in confinement till his death.[3] The tombs of Tuláji and his six wives, one of whom became a *sati*, are shown outside the fort at Vijaydurg. His two sons escaped after twelve or fourteen years' captivity and were protected in Bombay.

The Bombay Government were now exceedingly anxious to keep Vijaydurg and give back Bánkot, but the Maráthás could not be induced to consent to this, as the possession of this fort had been

[1] Grant Duff, 291; Mill, III. 172 & note. [2] Thornton, I. 182. [3] Grant Duff, 292.

Section VIII.

The Angrias, 1700-1756.

the Peshwa's chief object in making the treaty and the expedition with the English.[1]

As the other branch of the Ángria family which retained the Kolába principality for nearly a hundred years longer never took any prominent part in the affairs of the coast, it is as well to mention here the little that need be said about them. Mánáji was in alliance with the Maráthás till his death in 1759, when he was succeeded by his son Rághoji, who lived and reigned till 1793. He did not forget the piratical instincts of the family, but Forbes who passed through his territories in 1771 on his way from Dásgaon to Bombay heard from some Europeans who were in his service that he was generally beloved by his people and less oppressive than most Marátha princes. He resided in the island of Kolába (as his successors continued to do), where were the palace treasury and other public buildings, but the stables gardens and larger edifices for which the fort could afford no accommodation were at Álibág.[2] Rághoji was succeeded by his son Mánáji, who was first rejected and then acknowledged by the Peshwa and finally deposed by Daulatráv Sindia in 1799 in favour of another member of the family. But the grandson of the last Mánáji eventually succeeded, and died just before the conquest of the Peshwa's territories by the English.[3] By this time the state had been reduced by gradual encroachments to a very small compass, and the whole revenue did not exceed three lákhs of rupees. The Rája was however considered independent but received investiture from the Peshwa.[4] In 1840 on the death of the last of the Ángriás of the direct and legitimate line the state lapsed to the British Government. Since that the buildings in the fort of Kolába have gone to ruin.

The fort of Ságargad, four miles from Álibág, which is said to have been built by Kánoji Ángria, must have dominated the whole of the Álibág sub-division, except so much as was protected by the Chaul forts. It is very extensive and might certainly have held a large number of troops, but the fortifications cannot be called strong, and the unsubstantial walls and gateways differ much from those of Shiváji's fortresses. The appearance of the fort however from some points is remarkably fine. The outer walls surround the top of the hill, which in many places has a good natural scarp. At the south end the hill stretches out in a narrow tongue, and at the end of this is a tapering pinnacle of rock detached from the hill by a narrow chasm to a considerable depth. It may be assumed that there was no fort here in the sixteenth century as the hill is never mentioned by Portuguese writers.

---

[1] Grant Duff, 292. [2] Oriental Memoirs, I. 225.
[3] Grant Duff, 506, 531; Aitchison's Treaties, VI. 181.
[4] Elphinstone in East India House Selections, IV. 153.

SECTION IX.

THE MARATHÁS FROM THE FALL OF THE ANGRIÁS TO THE ACCESSION OF BÁJIRÁV.

1756 TO 1796.

Section IX. The Marathas, 1756-1796.

THE chief events in the history of the Konkan between 1739 and 1760 have been related in the last section as referring mostly to the Angriás. A little more must be said to show the general condition of the country during that period, and then the regular course of its history subsequently to 1760 will be taken up.

From the time that the Maráthás by expelling the Portuguese became the paramount power in the North and a great part of the the South Konkan, a period of comparative peacefulness, and therefore of prosperity, began. The English Government at Bombay now first appear on the scene with sufficient influence to interfere with effect among the coast powers. The first treaty they entered into with the Maráthás was concluded at Bassein in 1739 immediately after the capture of that place. It was chiefly occupied with the commercial relations of the two governments, the admission of the Maráthás to the Máhim river (Bándra creek), and the granting of passes by each government to trading vessels. One stipulation shows in a strong light the insecurity of the seas outside Bombay, and the little command the Maráthás had over it, namely that their fishing boats carrying provisions or goods from Máhim to Vesáva should be protected by two fighting gallivats of the English.

The Maráthás however seem to have made as good arrangements as were practicable for the defence of their new possessions and the protection of their subjects. In 1760 the fort of Bassein was in good repair and the gate on the south-east had been closed. The fort at Dáhánu had just been repaired in order to protect the inhabitants against the pirates. The fort at Tárápur was also repaired and a new fort was being built at Kelva.[1] As to their treatment of their subjects other than Hindus mention has been already made of their tolerance towards the Christians of Sálsette and Bassein. Towards the Musalmáns of the North Konkan their conduct was equally praiseworthy. The Portuguese had allowed no *kázis* in their territory, but Báláji Bájiráv re-established the office, bestowing it apparently on Musalmáns who had done service to the Maráthás, and endowing it with *ináms*. He made the *kázi* of Trombay the head of all those in the North Konkan, the *kázis* of Kalyán Bhiwndi and other places being his *náibs*. Similarly, though probably dating from earlier times, the *kázi* of Thal was the head of those in the present Kolába district. The condition of Sálsette in 1760 is said

[1] Aitchison's Treaties, III. 10.

Section IX. The Marathas, 1756-1796.

to have been such that it was full of villages almost all Christian and returned to the cultivators of its soil more than twenty-four lákhs of rupees a year.[1] This must have been an exaggeration, but it is likely that the toleration in religion shown to the inhabitants of whatever creed made them endure without much complaining the additional taxes which the Maráthás imposed immediately after the conquest.

The state of the district between Bombay and Gheria may be gathered from the last section, and all that can be said about the district of Málvan is that it was, as ever, distracted by the strifes of the Angriás, the Sávants, and the Kolhápur Maráthás, but until the downfall of the A'ngriás their influence over it appears to have been the strongest.

In 1760 the Maráthás thought it time to recommence operations against Janjira, and Rámáji Pant Phadnavis, the Sar Subhedár of the Konkan, besieged the island assisted by a corps of Portuguese. The English took part with the Sidi and hoisted the British flag at Janjira[2] and thus the Maráthás had a good cause of quarrel with the Bombay Government. But the disastrous battle of Pánipat in 1761, the death of the Peshwa Báláji Bájiráv, and the succession of a minor, with the internal dissensions which followed, restrained for a time the aggressive spirit of the Maráthás. Raghunáthráv, during the youth of the Peshwa Mádhavráv, aspired to rule the Marátha state, and was anxious to keep on good terms with the English, who now desired to possess territory. As most convenient to Bombay their first designs were on Sálsette and Bassein,[3] but Raghunáthráv was not yet prepared to yield places so valuable and so lately conquered, and therefore the articles of agreement now concluded with him contained no territorial concession except a very doubtful one of the island of Underi or Hennery.[4] The whole tone of the agreement, however, shows that the English were now in a much stronger position than they had ever been before, and the independence of the Sidi was so far secured that the Maráthás undertook to restore his territories and not again molest them. By 1766 the Peshwa Mádhavráv had established his own power and so far retrieved the position of the state that the wish of the English to become possessed of Sálsette or even of the islands in Bombay harbour received no attention. Thus matters continued till 1771, when with the death of Mádhavráv began those misfortunes which ended in the destruction of the Marátha state in 1818.

Grant Duff looks on Mádhavráv as superior in character and abilities to any of his predecessors, and though he was only twenty-seven when he died, "he is deservedly celebrated for his firm support of the weak against the oppressive, of the poor against the rich, and, as far as the constitution of society permitted, for his equity to all. He made no innovations; he improved the system

[1] Du Perron, I. 380, 335. [2] Grant Duff, 324. [3] Grant Duff, 324.
[4] Aitchison's Treaties, III. 22.

established, endeavoured to amend defects without altering forms, and restricted a corruption which he could not eradicate."[1] So also Elphinstone says of him that "he was the first who introduced order into the internal administration, and showed a sincere desire to protect his subjects from military violence, and to establish something like a regular dispensation of justice."[2] It will be useful therefore here to consider the Marátha system of government as it existed at this time for the Konkan, for it is certain that in the troubles which henceforward more or less encompassed the state under such degenerate descendants of the first Peshwás as Raghunáthráv and his son Bájiráv, the limits of authority were but little attended to and the good of the country was entirely neglected; yet while Nána Phadnavis' power was untramelled, the revenue management of some of the districts at least was regular and systematic.[3]

There was from the first a Sar Subhedár of the Konkan, four or five other provinces being ruled by an officer of the same rank and title. His residence was at Bassein,[4] the new town of which was after its occupation by the Maráthás called Bájipur. Under the Sar Subhedár were the *mámlatdárs,* whose districts were much larger than those of the present officers of the same name, and generally yielded about five lákhs of rupees. The amount of revenue expected was fixed by the government at the beginning of the year, and the *mámlatdár* was allowed to levy a moderate extra percentage for himself. He was encouraged in Mádhavráv's time, but apparently not obliged, to live in his districts.[5] There was generally no one in authority between the *mámlatdár* and the *pátils* of the villages; and as criminal and civil justice and police were also administered by the Sar Subhedár the *mámlatdárs* and the *pátils*, it is evident that the latter class must in many cases have had great power. Under this system a few powerful officials ruled large districts in which they were not necessarily resident, holding office only from year to year and with power to pay themselves by percentages: and although this may have worked well enough under the strict and intelligent supervision of Mádhavráv, yet under such rulers as his immediate predecessors and successors it must have been oppressive in the highest degree. And judging by what we are told of the Marátha government of Sálsette it was so,[6] for it is not likely that the administration would be more severe on the people there than in the older possessions which were valued less highly. The ablest of the *mhátrás* who have already been mentioned as village headmen under the Portuguese were made *pátils* by Khandoji Mánkar the first *subhedár* of Sálsette,[6] and this officer began by raising the assessment of all lands ten per cent above what it had been under the Portuguese, and by establishing a house-tax, a tobacco-tax, and

---

1 Grant Duff, 326, 352.
2 East India House Selections, IV. 146.
3 Chaplin's Report (1824), 144.
4 Grant Duff, 324.
5 Grant Duff, 354. Thus Forbes states that in 1771 the governor of Mahád lived at Poona, while his diván cruelly oppressed the people. Oriental Memoirs, I. 194.
6 Reg. I. of 1808.

a shop-tax or *mohtarfa*. Many additional taxes were afterwards imposed,[1] and wherever there seemed room for getting in a fresh one it was levied, even although it might apply only to two or three villages. Sálsette was divided into seven districts, each under a *haváldár* and *kárkuns*, and it would appear from this also that there were no regular civil officers between the *subhedár* and the *pátils*. The island, however, notwithstanding these heavy taxations is said to have been prosperous till the death of Báláji Bájiráv in 1761. Returns of the year 1768 show that the district of Kalyán, which extended from the Pen river to the Vaitarna and from the Gháts about thirty miles towards the sea and contained 742 villages, besides the towns of Kalyán and Bhiwndi, had a revenue of 4½ lákhs from the land and 2½ from customs.[2] This was undoubtedly a very large amount for such a district considering the circumstances of the times. On the other hand Forbes' description of the districts he passed through in 1771 between Álibág and Dásgaon does not give one the idea of the country being much worse off as to cultivation and population than it is now.[3]

The first event in the Konkan after the accession of Náráyanráv in 1771 was the reduction of Ráygad, the *haváldár* of which had been for some months in rebellion. About the same time a British envoy was sent to reside at Poona, with the chief object of obtaining the cession of Sálsette Bassein and the islands of Bombay harbour,[4] which the Court of Directors had now for several years looked on as a matter of the highest importance, declaring in 1769[5] that Sálsette Bassein and their dependencies and the Maráthás' proportion of the Surat provinces were all that they sought for on the west side of India. Sálsette was wanted because its produce almost supplied Bombay, and with Karanja and Bassein quite sufficed for the wants of the English. Bassein was necessary for the provision of timber for the Company's dockyard.[6] Some of the inhabitants of the island are said to have treated with the Bombay Government for its delivery a little later than this.[7] After the death of Náráyanráv the ambition and unpopularity of Raghunáthráv made the alliance of the English very necessary to him, notwithstanding which he at the end of 1774 positively refused to surrender the coveted territory. But just at this time it was rumoured that a Portuguese armament was on the way from Europe to recover Sálsette, and the Bombay Government being determined that no European nation should again settle themselves so close to Bombay resolved to take the island by force. Thána had just been reinforced by 500 Maráthás: but on December 12 a force of 600 European and 1200 Native troops were sent up the creek from Bombay. The batteries were opened on the twentieth; on the twenty-seventh an attempt was made to fill up the ditch, but was repulsed with the loss of 100 Europeans. On the following evening, however, the fort was carried by assault with

[1] Reg. I. of 1808. [2] Kalyán Manuscript Diaries. [3] Oriental Memoirs, I. 204.
[4] Grant Duff, 359, 371. [5] Mill, III. 603. [6] Historical Account, 9.
[7] House of Commons Reports, VIII. 43.

trifling loss on our side and the greater part of the garrison was put to the sword. Commodore Watson who commanded the naval force had previously been mortally wounded.[1] More than a hundred cannon were found on the walls, but most of them had been damaged or dismounted during the siege.[2]

In the meantime a small force under Colonel Keating had been sent against Vesáva, and two attempts at escalade were repulsed. But on the fourth day when our batteries opened the fort surrendered. Colonel Keating then took another detachment against Karanja, the fort on the top of which was small, badly constructed, and mounted only fourteen guns. This was soon evacuated, and Elephanta and Hog Island were then surrendered without resistance.[3] Thus by New Year's Day of 1775 Sálsette and its dependencies, including Bassein, were in the possession of our Government, and as if to show that Sálsette was not to be given up, the fortifications of Thána were immediately improved by the construction of a glacis and esplanade.[4] Three months later Raghunáthráv, now hard-pushed by what was called the ministerial party of the Marátha state, ceded Sálsette and other possessions to the English[5] by a treaty signed at Surat, and from this arose what is known in history as the First Marátha War. Bassein was, however, restored to the Maráthás[5] and Dásgaon and Kumla, two of the villages belonging to the English on the Bánkot river which had been taken by the Maráthás in February 1775, were retained by them till 1784, it may be presumed by arrangement.[6]

No mention is made anywhere of a declaration of war against the Maráthás but in the same month (December 1774) in which Thána was taken there was a rather serious sea fight off Gheria. The *Revenge* of twenty-eight guns and the *Bombay* grab of twenty-four fell in there with the whole Marátha fleet consisting of the Admiral's ship of forty-four guns, three of twenty-four to thirty-two each, five ketches of twelve to fourteen each, and ten gallivats of six to ten each. The four largest bore down on the English ships, but after a warm engagement the Admiral's ship took fire and blew up, and the rest of the fleet fled and got under shelter of Gheria fort. The two English ships saved thirty-four men out of 420 on board the Admiral's ship and sent them into Gheria.[7]

In 1776 the internal dissensions of the Marátha state enabled an impostor to obtain some power, and circumstances made him choose the Konkan as the field of his exploits. He was known as Sadáshiv Chimnáji professing to be the son of Chimnáji Appa and to have escaped from the field of Pánipat, and he had been for

---

[1] Grant Duff, 373-74. [2] Forbes, I. 452. [3] House of Commons Reports, VIII. 166.
[4] Grant Duff, 376; Aitchison's Treaties, III. 24.
[5] Mill, III. 608, 619. As nothing is said of the taking of Bassein by any of the authorities it must be assumed that it was effected by arrangement.
[6] Bánkot Manuscript Diaries.
[7] Parsons, 217. Parsons sailed in the *Revenge* not long after this, so his account may be relied on. Grant Duff (page 386) seems to make the date a little later.

Section IX. The Marathas, 1756-1796.

some time in confinement at Ratnágiri in charge of the Subhedár Rámchandra Paránjpe. This man released him and he soon got a large force together, and by the end of the rains had taken twenty of the Konkan forts and had a following of 20,000 men. He marched through the Konkan and soon had possession of most of it, and in October went up the Borghát. There however he was attacked, and being driven down again tried to get protection at Bombay, as the Government had to some extent countenanced him, but not getting admittance he went on to Kolába. Rághoji Ángria there took him prisoner and sent him to Poona, where he was soon afterwards put to death. A force was then sent into the Konkan under Bháuráv Phanse and speedily reduced it to obedience. Raghunáthráv, now an exile, and ready to ally himself with any one, had left Surat with the ostensible purpose of joining the pretended Sadáshiv Bháu, but had been compelled to seek shelter at Tárápur, from whence he came in November to Bombay in one of the Company's vessels.[1] There was at this time owing to the treaty of Purandhar peace between the English and Maráthás, but in January 1777 it was reported from Goa that the Marátha fleet had left Gheria with the design of attacking the *Revenge* and the *Bombay* grab, so the two vessels sailed off to look for them. After searching in vain about Gheria the Marátha fleet was found on February 16 at the entrance of a port of theirs called Cole Arbour, three frigates, five ketches and ten gallivats. The two ships went within gunshot of them, but they declined action.[2]

To the year 1777 also belongs the account of a curious intrigue carried on by an adventurer named St. Lubin in the name of the French Government. It is not clear how far he was authorised by that Government, but it appears certain that his enterprise was made with their knowledge. He arrived on the coast in a French merchant ship in March or April 1777, the port of landing being called "*Collaby*, a place at the entrance into the river of Chaul." The cargo consisting of artillery, firearms, copper, and cloth, was landed at Chaul, and an escort of twenty-five Arab sepoys, an elephant, twenty camels, and some horse was sent from Poona, with a palanquin, to conduct St. Lubin thither. On his arrival he was well received by Nána Phadnavis, and he presented credentials from the King of France, which the French authorities in India, as well as the English, declared to be forgeries. Nána Phadnavis, however, favoured him, probably with no other object than to annoy the English, whose jealousy of French influence in India was notorious. In January 1778 the Bombay Government were informed that an agreement had been signed at Poona between the ministers and St. Lubin by which Revdanda or Chaul was to be made over to the French, so as to serve them as a port for the disembarkation of troops, and this information is said to have strengthened our Government in their resolution to support Rághoba. But negotiations were still going on with the ministers, and St. Lubin

[1] Grant Duff, 395, 398.

[2] Parsons, 243.

was at last dismissed from Poona in July or August 1778, having before this unsuccessfully applied to the Portuguese authorities to allow French troops to march through their possessions. By this time it had apparently become plain to the Marátha government that they would gain nothing by further negotiations with him.[1] But the question of the cession of Chaul and Revdanda to the French was again under discussion in 1786:[2] so that the French, who were at this time pressing us so hard in the south of India, would seem to have entertained the idea of opposing us near Bombay also.

By the autumn of 1778 Raghunáthráv was again in the ascendant, and on the pretext that the ministerial party had not observed the treaty of Purandhar a new engagement was entered into by our Government with him under which he was to be recognised as Peshwa, and the province of Bassein and the island of Khánderi were to be ceded to Bombay.[3] This led two years later to the only serious campaign in the Konkan in which our troops were ever engaged. The advanced party of the force intended to conduct Raghunáthráv to Poona, took possession of the Borghát, and the main body of the troops left Bombay on November 23, and after taking the fort at Belápur and leaving in it a garrison of sixty men disembarked at Panvel where they remained for several days. After a further unnecessary delay the force went up the Ghát on December 23.[4] The unfortunate events that followed, including the disgraceful convention of Vadgaon do not belong to the history of the Konkan, but while the army was above the gháts all supplies had to be sent from below, and to keep the road open between Panvel and Khopavli (Campolee) a company of Europeans, three of sepoys, and two guns were sent out under the command of Colonel Egerton. Raghunáthráv had also a force at Kalva opposite to Thána, but the enemy had about the district five thousand horse which had come down the Kására Ghát. It appears on the whole that communications between Panvel and Khopavli were not generally kept open, and that the two parties in the Konkan were pretty equally matched.[5]

Negotiations occupied the whole of 1779, and in October of that year the ministerial party at Poona were so assured of their position that Nána Phadnavis[6] told General Goddard that the surrender of Sálsette and of Raghunáthráv were essential preliminaries to

---

1 Grant Duff, 399, 404; Historical Account, 115-170.
2 Grant Duff, 468.
3 Aitchison's Treaties, III. 40.
4 Grant Duff, 412.
5 Hist. Account, 176, 179.
6 Báláji Janárdhan Bhánu, commonly called Nána Phadnavis, was a native of Velás, a village adjoining Bánkot and within three or four miles of Shrivardhan, the birthplace of Báláji Vishvanáth the first Peshwa of the family that afterwards ruled at Poona. He built a temple at Velás in a romantic situation and supplied it with water brought from the cliff above. He also built at a cost of twelve lákhs the large tank at Cámpoli, and a rest-house for Brahman travellers close by. Nána's brother Gangadhar was Subedhár of Vijaydurg and there built the temple of Rámeshvar, which is remarkable by its gloomy position, and by the road down to it being cut through the solid rock at a very steep incline.

Section IX.

The Marathas. 1756-1796.

the making of any treaty. Active operations being then begun various posts between Sálsette and the Gháts were occupied by our troops early in 1780,[1] chiefly to prevent the Maráthás from cutting off supplies from Bombay; for Sálsette which had formerly been so flourishing and prosperous was now pining in decay, so that a few years afterwards it is described as "not cultivating a sufficient quantity of grain to maintain the town and garrison of Thána."[2] This may no doubt be attributed to our Government having held to the Marátha system introduced after the death of Báláji Bájiráo of farming the lands to the highest bidder. The main part of the army was employed in Gujarát, and it was not till May that Colonel Hartley was sent into the Konkan.[2] A small detachment had possession of Kalyán, and was besieged by a large Marátha army, which was to make the attack on May 25, but Colonel Hartley fortunately arrived on the twenty-fourth, and beating up the Marátha camp in the night drove them out of that part of the Konkan. Two battalions were left at Kalyán for the rains, and on August 3 an attempt was made to surprise the fortress of Malangad (Bhau Malan) which was not successful.[3] Our force, however, occupied the lower works of the fort, and was there surrounded by 3000 Maráthás until relieved by Colonel Hartley on October 1. The next day the Maráthás again took up a threatening position, but Hartley attacked them with such spirit that they shortly afterwards retreated up the Gháts. The rigours of this war are shown by the fact of three emissaries of the Poona government having been blown from guns at Thána in October.[4]

The whole army was now ordered down from Gujarát to the Konkan, the Europeans coming by sea; but General Goddard with the rest of the troops marched from Surat to Bassein. He took twenty-eight days doing this, from the roads being still so deep and the rivers full, and arrived before Bassein on November 13. The fortress at this time is described as a regular polygon without outworks of any description,[5] but it was strong enough to require the siege to be carried on by regular approaches. The first battery of six guns and six mortars was 900 yards distant from the fort and was opened on November 28. On December 9, a battery of nine heavy guns at a distance of 500 yards was opened, and at the same time another battery of twenty mortars. On the tenth, when a breach was nearly effected, a conditional offer of surrender was made but refused, and next morning the garrison surrendered at discretion. The loss on the British side was but small.[6] In the meantime the Marátha chiefs had made great efforts to send down troops, and Hartley had been constantly engaged in the neighbourhood of Kalyán and the Borghát and had a large number of sick and wounded. He however on December 8 moved to Titvála in the direction of Bassein to prevent the Marátha force cutting him off

---

[1] Grant Duff, 428, 433-34.
[2] Reg. I. of 1808; Hové, 12-14.
[3] Grant Duff, 437.
[4] Bánkot Manuscript Diaries.
[5] Field Officer, 137.
[6] Mill, IV. 299; Thornton, II. 191.

from Goddard;[1] and having taken up a strong position in the hills east of Bassein, afterwards known as Hartley's Trap,[2] was for the next three or four days exposed to the constant attacks of the Maráthás, whom he always repulsed with heavy loss though suffering but little himself. In one of these attacks Rámchandra Ganesh was killed, and Haripant Phádke succeeded to the command of the Marátha army. Immediately on the surrender of Bassein Goddard hastened to join Hartley, and on the thirteenth the army was united.

The next operation was the reduction of the small island-fort of Arnála, ten miles north of Bassein, and it was not until preparations were made for bombarding it from Agáshi on the mainland that the commandant on January 18, 1781, surrendered.[3] It was now determined to threaten Poona rather than secure the Konkan, and the army marched across to the Gháts, and having met with little opposition forced the Borghát on February 8 and occupied Khandála, General Goddard with the head-quarters remaining at Khopavli. Some negotiations followed, after which 12,000 men under Parashrám Bháu Patvardhan were sent into the Konkan, and getting between Goddard's force and Bombay, they, on the night of March 15, attacked a detachment of two regiments with a convoy of stores which had reached Chauk on their way from Panvel. The English force suffered severely, but with the assistance of a reinforcement from Khopavli the whole convoy was brought into the head-quarters camp on the seventeenth. Soon after this Holkar arrived to reinforce Parashrám Bháu, and the Marátha force now amounting to 25,000 cavalry attacked a large detachment which had been sent to Panvel with unloaded bullocks to bring up stores. The convoy got back from Panvel after a three days' march in which the constant attacks of the Maráthás caused a loss of 106 killed and wounded. The army was now ready to return for the rains to Kalyán and Bombay, but the Maráthás had in the meantime assembled all along that part of the Gháts in great force, and immediately on Goddard leaving the Borghát open, Haripant Phádke followed, and took a considerable quantity of baggage and ammunition, and though the Maráthás dared not molest the army when in camp, yet on the 20th 21st and 23rd of April during the march they so harassed our troops that Goddard's loss before reaching Panvel was 466 killed and wounded, including eighteen European officers. A great part of the army was from here sent down the coast, and the rest after remaining some weeks encamped at Panvel, were sent to Kalyán for the rains.[4]

During the progress of these events Residents had been appointed at Belápur, Kalyán, and Karanja, and from their reports some idea of the state of the country may be gained. The chief object of the Residents was of course to collect the revenues, and in February

---

1 Grant Duff, 439. 2 Field Officer, 137.
3 Grant Duff, 440, 442; Field Officer, 321. 4 Mill, IV. 301; Grant Duff, 444.

Section IX. The Marathas, 1756-1796.

1781 (before the operations of that year about Kalyán and the Ghát had begun) it is reported that "Badlápur and Dámod, which were considerable towns, and every village hut and stack on the high road between Khopavli and Kalyán had been burnt, and the inhabitants for the most part fled." The non-return of seventy-five carts and forty-four oxen which had been taken from Ágáshi by the army, would, it was said, cause great distress to the district of Bassein.[1]

No further operations took place in the Konkan after the rains, and in March 1782 the treaty of Salbye was concluded[2] by which all the recent conquests including Bassein were restored to the Maráthás, though the restoration was not absolutely made for upwards of a year,[3] and the cession of Sálsette, Elephanta, Karanja, and Hog Island to the English finally confirmed. No further change of any importance was made in the governing powers of the Konkan for the next thirty-five years, but it may here be mentioned that in 1782 the Maráthás, who had gradually taken from the Jawhár Rája the greater part of his territories, confirmed him in the possession of the small remainder, which he holds to this day.[4] In 1783-84, a dispute which the Marátha state had with the Pant Pratinidhi of Vishálgad about the districts near Ratnágiri held by them jointly was settled by a treaty. These districts included a considerable part of the Sangameshvar Ratnágiri and Rájápur sub-divisions, the Peshwa's *subhedár* at Ratnágiri being the chief authority of that government. The river and port of Sangameshvar are mentioned in this treaty as if they were of importance, and among other stipulations is one that the *khots* and the *pátils* who used to be kept two months in Vishálgad fort for the settlement of their accounts, must not in future be detained more than four days.[5]

It is now time to return to the affairs of the coast, where piracy still flourished not less than before the fall of Ángria. In 1765 the piracies on the coast south of Vijaydurg induced the Bombay Government to send a force which took Málvan from the Kolhápur authorities and Ráiri from the Sávants.[6] The name of the island-fort at Málvan was changed from Sindhudurg to Fort Augustus, but in the beginning of the following year the place was restored on payment of Rs. 3,60,000.[7] A promise to pay a further sum was made, and permission given for the establishment of a factory at Málvan, which does not appear to have been made use of. Ráiri was not returned till October 1766, because our Government and the Sávants could not agree as to the price of it.[8] Eventually Rs. 80,000 were paid, and the village and the district of Vengurla was made over and mortgaged for thirteen years.[9] The mortgagee however was not permitted to realize the revenues, and the agreement to abstain

---

[1] Belápur Kalyán and Karanja Manuscript Diaries.
[2] Aitchison's Treaties, III. 49 ; Mill, IV. 411.
[3] Grant Duff, 457.
[4] Government Selections, XXVI. 15.
[5] Thomas' Treaties, 558.
[6] Grant Duff, 508-510.
[7] Aitchison's Treaties, VI. 91.
[8] Ráiri Manuscript Diaries.
[9] Aitchison's Treaties, VI. 125.

Section IX. The Marathas, 1756-1796.

from piracy was not observed either by the Kolhápur state or the Sávants.[1] The Bombay Government therefore at the end of the thirteen years refused to restore Vengurla, on which the Sávants in 1780 took it, plundering both public and private property. The Peshwa had in the meantime established a fleet at Vijaydurg under a Marátha named Anandráo Dhulap, whose family remained in power until 1812, and whose descendants still have a small property in the neighbourhood, and though entirely impoverished are considered fit to marry with the families of the Gáikwár and other princes. The Peshwa also had another fleet under the Sar Subhedár of Bassein[2] and after 1775 his officers paid no respect even to English ships, which they took if they could, and only restored if the capture was quickly and clearly proved against them. On account of these various piratical fleets the coasting vessels could not at this time ply without being convoyed by the Company's vessels. Sixty or eighty of them generally sailed from Bombay to Surat under a convoy of one or two ships. In 1774 five or six Portuguese merchantmen sailed from Goa to Surat convoyed by a sixty-four gun ship, but were attacked by the Maráthás, the frigate put to flight, and the rest taken into Gheria.[1] In 1780 a ship carrying despatches from the Court of Directors was taken off the coast and carried to Vijaydurg, and the officer sent as a prisoner to Rasálgad, one of the Konkan forts visible from Mahábaleshvar. A more serious affair took place in 1783 after peace had been concluded between the Bombay Government and the Maráthás. The *Ranger*, a ship of the Bombay Marine, siled from Bombay on April 5 with several military officers on board: on the eighth when near Gheria she was attacked by Dhulap, and after a fight of five hours was captured and taken into Gheria, where Dhulap denied all knowledge of the peace. Two officers were killed and three besides the commander of the vessel wounded, and no communication was received at Bombay from the survivors till May 23, when a letter of May 5 arrived. The prisoners were released on the twenty-seventh, and arrived in Bombay in the *Ranger* on the twenty-ninth, she being too much disabled to proceed on her voyage. The bad faith of the Poona government was shown by Dhulap having displayed in the presence of some of the officers the ornaments sent to him from Poona in honour of the achievement.[3]

The Ángriás who still held Kolába were dependent on the Peshwa, and the Sidis retained their old independence, but were allies of the English. In 1784, however, the latter were parties to an agreement by which the rightful heir to the throne who had been dispossessed by another of his family gave up all his rights in the Janjira territories to the Peshwa in exchange for an estate in Gujarát, and he thus became Nawáb of Sachin, and the alliance between Bombay and Janjira was dissolved. But the usurper was

[1] Government Selections, X. 4. [2] Grant Duff, 504, 506, 509.
[3] Annual Register for 1783, 289 ; Grant Duff, 457.

Section IX.

The Marathas, 1756-1796.

in point of fact never dispossessed, and his descendants still rule Janjira, which the Maráthás never succeeded in taking.[1]

In 1777 the Málvan district was overrun by the Kolhápur troops after an insurrection by the chief of Vishálgad and others, and in 1782 there was another expedition in which the chiefs of Vádi were for a time subdued. In 1786 however disturbances again took place, and the Rája of Kolhápur himself took a large army into the Konkan. He stormed Bharatgad, the fort which commands the beautiful and very fertile valley of Masura, Nivti a well-known fort on the coast between Málvan and Vengurla, and Vishálgad which commands the most level part of the Southern Konkan.[2] On account, however, of the Sávants getting assistance from Goa he evacuated Nivti and Vengurla, but appointed *mámlatdárs* and other officials to the rest of the newly-conquered territory. Khem Sávant, instead of going on fighting as was usual to him, negotiated with Sindia, and eventually the district was restored to Vádi in 1793. Málvan was however retained by Kolhápur[3] and for a few years this part of the Konkan enjoyed peace. In 1792 while these events were in progress the Bombay Government had prepared an armament against Kolhápur, but this was not despatched, as a treaty was made by which the English were allowed to have a factory at the island of Málvan (Sindhudurg) and to hoist their flag there till all claims were paid.[4]

A few facts worth recording come into this period and are here mentioned without particular arrangement. In May 1790 a force left Bombay to co-operate with the army which had just invaded Tippoo Sultán's territory. It was disembarked at Sangameshvar, and after halting there five days marched up the A'mba Ghát, the steepness of which is proved by the march up taking only an hour and a half.

Although there was artillery with it, a second detachment went by the same route in the following November. The entrance to the river at Jaygad was at this time defended by forts on each side. A wall of communication ran up the side of the hill on the south shore from a battery of eleven embrasures on a level with the water, which like the other fortifications was in very bad repair.[5] The factory at Fort Victoria was found useful during this war as the Resident purchased and received from Poona between eleven and twelve thousand bullocks,[6] and sent them down the coast for the use of the army.[7] At this time Thána is described as a straggling town with several Portuguese churches and a number of Christian inhabitants. It was garrisoned by a battalion of sepoys and a company of European artillery. The fort is

---

[1] Aitchison's Treaties, VI. 208; Grant Duff, 507. [2] Account of Kolhápur, 499.
[3] Hutchinson, 159. [4] Aitchison's Treaties, VI. 94; Grant Duff, 509.
[5] Field Officer, 183; Moor, 2, 9, 47.
[6] The average price paid was Rs. 32 per bullock, which seems high for the time.
[7] Bankot Manuscript Diaries.

described as small, well built and, although not a complete, yet a strong fortification and always kept in the highest order.[1]

In 1790 the Konkan, in common with other parts of Western India, was visited by a great scarcity amounting almost to famine,[2] but in this respect this district with its generally very heavy rainfall and its easy water communication suffers much less than the dry plains of the Dakhan. Between 1771 and 1790 a survey and assessment in cash of a great part of the Kalyán district was made by Sadáshiv Keshav, Sar Subhedár of the Konkan, and an assessment in grain of part of the Kolába district by a *subhedár* of Rájpuri in 1784-85.[3] But the general survey and assessment of the Konkan proposed by Nána Phadnavis never went further.

There is nothing more to record of the Konkan either of a warlike or peaceable character until the accession of Bájiráv, whose eventful reign, including the fall of the Marátha state, requires a section to itself.

---

1 Moor, 369. 2 Report on Famines, 117.
3 Jervis, 125; Government Selections, XCXVI. 78, 346.

SECTION X.

THE REIGN OF BA'JIRA'V AND THE BRITISH CONQUEST.

1796 TO 1818.

Section X.

Bajirav, 1796-1818.

In 1796 Nána Phadnavis, unable to secure his own power or to prevent the accession of Bájiráv, fled to the Konkan, and put garrisons in Pratápgad and Ráygad. He himself stayed at Mahád till October, by which time he had collected an army of 10,000 men.[1] These efforts were so far successful that, under the treaty of Mahád concluded in the same month when Bájiráv was enthroned as Peshwa, Nána Phadnavis returned to Poona as minister.[2] But from this time the chiefs and *jághirdárs* were utterly uncontrolled and assumed independence, while the Dakhan was overrun with banditti. This state of affairs culminated in October 1802 with the victory of Yashvantráv Holkar over Sindia and the flight of Bájiráv from Poona.[3] He first went to Sinhgad, but after staying there only three days he hastily retreated to Ráygad, and having released Mahádevráv Ráste, who had been confined there since April of the previous year, he went down to Mahád.[4] He had with him 6000 or 8000 men, and at his request an English vessel was sent down to Bánkot to take him up to Bombay. He wished to send his family and the families of his attendants to Suvarndurg, but the commandant refused to receive them. Grain for the subsistence of his force had to be sent from Bassein and Bombay, this being the year of the great famine. The Sar Subhedár of the Konkan, Khanderáv Ráste, joined him at Mahád from Bassein. About November 22 Holkar with his army came down the Pár Ghát, on which the Peshwa fled to Suvarndurg, while some of his followers took refuge in the English factory at Fort Victoria. Suvarndurg, however, was found to be in a defenceless condition, and the Peshwa therefore embarked in one of his own vessels escorted by two belonging to the Bombay Government. He put into Chaul and stayed there some days, and on again embarking was so harassed by contrary winds that on December 15 he put into Manori in Sálsette, from whence he went on to Bassein, arriving there with about thirty followers on the seventeenth. In the meantime Holkar with 5000 troops had taken with very little resistance Ráygad and Savarndurg and in the latter the Peshwa's family.[5] Colonel Close who had been awaiting the Peshwa's arrival in Bombay with Mountstuart Elphinstone[6] then his

---

[1] Grant Duff, 525; Asiatic Annual Register (1803), 58.
[2] Grant Duff, 285.
[3] Elphinstone in E. I. House Selections, IV. 147.
[4] Grant Duff, 558.
[5] Blue Book relating to Marátha War of 1803, 350-463; Asiatic Annual Register (1803), 23.
[6] Bom. R. A. S. Journal, VI. 97.

Section X.

Bajirav, 1796-1818.

assistant, went to him at Bassein immediately on his arrival, and there on December 31 was concluded the treaty of Bassein.[1] A field detachment which had been sent to Ghodbandar in the expectation that the Peshwa might find it convenient to take refuge in British territory, was then sent to Bassein, where the Peshwa remained till April 27, 1803.[2] Entrance into the Bassein island being then as now obtainable only by the bridges at Sopára and Gokhivade "a considerable stockade of palmyra trees" was erected to defend the Sopára bridge.[3] Affairs at Poona being at last settled, Bájiráv left Bassein escorted by a British force of 2200 men, including the 78th Regiment, part of the 84th, and some artillery. He stayed at Kalyán for a week and from there marched up the Borghát.[4]

Neither the treaty of Bassein nor either of those concluded in the following year made any difference in the position of the Konkan powers, but the Peshwa had now become to a considerable extent dependent on the British Government, and being supported by them he was able from this time to take vengeance on the chiefs, whose armies were much reduced.[5] A Marátha force was sent against Suvarndurg on account of the Killedár Hari Ballál Kelkar having thrown off his allegiance, and after an unsuccessful investment a small British force returning from the Malabár coast was ordered to take the island and the ports on the mainland.[6] The Peshwa's force was encamped at Kelshi, eight miles north of Suvarndurg, and the garrison of the island was said to be 800 men, Arabs and Maráthás, but it was eventually surrendered without resistance, and 200 Native Infantry put in until the orders of the Peshwa should be received. It would appear from all these last events that the fort had not been kept in a proper state of repair, and although both Nána Phadnavis and the Peshwa had followed the old Marátha custom of retiring into the Konkan when too hard pressed above the Ghâts, yet neither their habits nor their mode of government led them either to maintain the forts when in prosperity or to turn them to good account in adversity. These strongholds were often made useful as prisons, of which instances have already been given, but neither now nor at the final fall of the Peshwa's power were they found of much use from a military point of view.

The famine of 1802-3, which was so devastating in some parts, appears to have been very partial in the Konkan, as one of the chief causes was absent, the ravages of Holkar. The influx of starving people from the Dakhan is mentioned as causing much of the scarcity in the Northern Konkan and Kolába. In the latter district many deaths are said to have occurred, and the same is stated of the Khed petha, the most rugged of the whole Konkan and the most easily affected by famine. The Málvan district is

[1] Aitchison's Treaties, III. 63. [2] Blue Book as above.
[3] Dickenson's Manuscript Report. [4] Mill, VI. 419.
[5] Elphinstone in E. I. House Selections, IV. 147. [6] Manuscript Records.

Section X.

Bajirav, 1796-1818.

said also to have suffered severely, and here the ravages of war no doubt assisted the famine. But on the whole it is doubtful if any villages were deserted or depopulated.[1]

On the death of Khem Sávant in 1803 the district of Málvan again fell into its usual distracted condition, and in 1806 the Rája of Kolhápur before the end of the monsoon descended into the Konkan and took Bharatgad and Nivti, but as he soon returned above the Gháts the Vádi troops quickly retorted by overrunning the district and burning the suburbs of Málvan. The cruelties committed on this occasion were something uncommon even in that district, and the Kolhápur Rája then returned and carried on the war in the Vádi districts, while an advanced party raised the siege of Bharatgad just begun by the Vádi troops. Nivti and Ráiri however had fallen to the Sávants. In 1808 the Kolhápur troops had to retreat, and in the next year Phond Sávant had to fly before Mánsinghráv Pátankar who followed him as far as Rájápur and levied a heavy contribution on that town though generally quite beyond the range of Vádi politics. In 1810 the Dakhan troops had again to leave the Konkan, and Ráiri and Nivti were retaken by the Vádi chiefs.[2] The piracies of both these powers had continued unchecked,[3] and their serious import to this Presidency may be judged of by the fact that the Duke of Wellington only two days after the battle of Assaye wrote (with his own hand as was usual to him) a short despatch on the subject to the Bombay Government.[4] The pirates appear to have been equally bold on the seas north of Bombay, for in 1803 an officer going to Cambay had a guard of sepoys with him who kept their muskets loaded and were constantly on the look-out for pirates.[5] The remedy adopted was the blockade of the ports belonging to Kolhápur and Vádi, but this of course could not continue for ever, and in 1812, when the settlement between the Peshwa and Kolhápur was made, the harbour and forts of Málvan were ceded to the English by Kolhápur, and the fort of Vengurla with some land adjoining by the Sávants.[6] Nivti was left to the latter but a guard of British troops was stationed there to see that no piratical vessels made use of the port. From this time till the cession of the whole Konkan, the Bombay Government kept a civil and military establishment both at Málvan and Vengurla. The cession brought to an end the troubles of this district from the Kolhápur state, but the Sávants by their internal quarrels kept the country in confusion for several years longer.[7] The claims of the different governments on the district were complicated and extraordinary, the revenue being divided among the Peshwa, the Rája of Kolhápur, the Sávants, and the Pant of Bávda, with separate payments for the forts at Málvan. In January 1813 the

---

[1] Report on Past Famines, 116. [2] Hutchinson, 161-165.

[3] Two brothers named Bápuji and Hiráji, who are remembered by persons still (1883) living, as having spent their last days at Málvan in great poverty, were, when young, noted for the cruelty and daring of their piracies.

[4] Manuscript Records. [5] Field Officer, 458.

[6] Aitchison's Treaties, VI. 97, 129. [7] Asiatic Journal, VIII. 78.

Section X.

Bajirav. 1796-1818.

Sávants again took Bharatgad from the Kolhápur authorities, and it was not restored till a British detachment was sent from Kolhápur in March. This force afterwards went on to Ráiri, but returned above the Gháts before the monsoon.[1] In 1815 the districts belonging to Vádi in two *tarafs* north of Málvan were occupied by a force from Málvan,[2] but this was only to prevent aggression on the part of the Sávants.

Before coming to the events which led immediately to the overthrow of the Peshwa it is necessary to say something about the management of his districts in the last years of the Marátha government. Long previously to this all the districts had been let out on farm, but Bájiráv allowed every aggravation of this evil, for leases of districts were often summarily annulled on a higher offer being made, and thus the element of uncertainty was added to the other inducements the farmer had to extortion. And if a farmer failed in his payments, not only his own property but that of his securities was confiscated, and very frequently he himself sent to a hill-fort. To the farmers was committed the superintendence of both civil and criminal justice in their districts, which enabled them to increase their exactions by fines. And, as the complaints of the people were never listened to by those in authority at Poona, the farmers would seem to have had no inducement towards leniency, and it may be thought strange that they ever failed to make their contracts pay.[3]

Bráhmans and other influential people got their lands at lower rates than the common cultivators, and were also exempt from many of the cesses, and this gave rise to what was called the Pándharpesha tenure.[4] As an instance of summary repression of crime it may be mentioned that the *pátil* of Chauk in 1810 caught two Bhils (more probably Khátkaris) and hung them up by the heels in the sun naked till they died. This is said to have had a good effect on the Bhils.[5]

Among the minor results of the loose system of government that prevailed, may be mentioned the frequent changes in the stations of *mámlatdárs*, of which the following is an instance. Nasrápur was originally the head-quarters of the district about Karjat, but on a Devrukhi Bráhman getting the farm of the district he removed his office to Dahivali close to Karjat, where there was a large settlement of Devrukhis. But about 1811 a Chitpávan became farmer or *mámlatdár*, and a Devrukhi village not been agreeable to him he removed his head-quarters to Kadva. Places may often be found in tolerable proximity, which have at one time or other been the head-quarters of a district, and this may probably often be accounted for by reasons similar to the above.

But notwithstanding the badness of the government the districts below the Gháts were so much better off than those of the Dakhan that they derived considerable advantage from the contrast. There

---

[1] Hutchinson, 161-165. [2] Hutchinson, 6; Grant Duff, 621.
[3] Grant Duff, 624. [4] Manuscript Records. [5] Seely, 36.

Section X.

Bajirav, 1796-1818.

was so little cultivation in the Dakhan owing to the constant movements of Pendháris and armies, and the population of Poona was so large that the Konkan *tálukás* below the Gháts where the peace was but little disturbed became the chief granaries of the Marátha government. The Nasrápur division in particular benefited by this state of things, and the average price of rice received by the cultivator in the later days of Marátha rule is said to have been as much as two rupees a *man.*[1]

Chatursing, brother of the Rája of Sátára, had for several years carried on predatory operations against the Peshwa's government, but he was taken prisoner in 1812 by Trimbakji Dengla, who seduced him to a conference, and was confined until his death in 1818 in the fort of Kángori, where two European officers were also imprisoned in 1817. After Chatursing's imprisonment an impostor carried on the rebellion in his name, and the Rámoshis under him were very active in taking forts and plundering the country. Troops were constantly out after them, but they were never suppressed as long as the Peshwa's government lasted, and the districts of Suvarndurg and Anjanvel are said to have suffered particularly from their raids.[2] In the beginning of 1817 three or four distinct bodies of Pendáris descended into the Konkan intending to sweep the whole coast as far as Surat. One band completely sacked some large villages near Suvarndurg ; another body plundered Mahád in February, but did not venture to attack Dásgaon which was defended by a body of invalids.[3] At the same time a body of six or seven hundred was at Panwel, and either this or another force of them advanced as far as Bhiwndi, but were prevented by the rivers from entering the rich coast districts of Bassein and Máhím. They however marched by Asheri to Tárápur and from there up to the Portuguese frontier, the inhabitants of course fleeing before them, and at Bordi, a rich coast village, only a few of the latter had come back in the following year.[4]

Bájiráv three or four years before his deposition had built a palace at Guhágar,[5] six miles south of Dábhol, both as a hot-weather retreat and to enable him to perform his religious rites on the sea-shore. Every one who has been to this delightful place will acknowledge Bájiráv's good taste in fixing on the "Bay of the Bráhmans" as it was called by the Portuguese and early navigators.[6] He visited it for some years in succession,[7] his route being down the Kumbhárli Ghát and through Chiplún, where the building now used as the *kacheri* was erected for his accommodation. The greater part of the palace at Guhágar was pulled down shortly after our Government took the Konkan, and the materials used for Government buildings at Ratnágiri.[5]

---

1 J. M. Davies' Manuscript Reports of 1836.
2 Grant Duff, 632, 654, 678 ; E. I. House Selections, III. 783 & IV. 140, 148.
3 Asiatic Journal, III. 626 & IV. 315.
4 Dickenson's Manuscript Report.
5 Waddington's Manuscript Report.
6 De la Valle, III. 143.
7 Grant Duff does not mention these expeditions, but Thornton says that Bájiráv went there every year between his restoration and final deposition. History. IV. 431.

Section X.

Bajirav, 1796-1818.

Trimbakji Dengla, when given up by the Peshwa to our Government, was for his many enormities confined in the fort at Thána. The story of his escape thence in September 1816 is told by Bishop Heber with a tinge of romance which certainly makes it more agreeable reading than the official report of the circumstance would be: "Trimbakji was kept in confinement at Thána near Bombay; and while there a common-looking Marátha groom with a good character in his hand came to offer his services to the commanding officer. He was accepted, and had to keep his horse under the window of Trimbakji's prison. Nothing remarkable was observed in his conduct except a more than usual attention to his horse, and a habit while currying and cleaning him of singing verses of Maráthi songs all apparently relating to his trade. At length Trimbakji disappeared, and the groom followed him; on which it was recollected that his singing had been made up of verses like the following:

> 'Behind the bush the bowmen hide
> The horse beneath the tree,
> Where shall I find a knight-will ride
> The jungle paths with me?
> There are five and fifty coursers there,
> And four and fifty men;
> When the fifty-fifth shall mount his steed
> The Deccan thrives again.'"[1]

The treaty of Poona in June 1817 which was concluded after several months of resistance to the British demands, gave our Government possession of the whole of the North Konkan, described as "the districts of Bailapoor, Autgong, and Culleaun, and all the territories to the north of those districts as far as Gujarát lying between the Ghâts and the sea."[2] It was intended also to procure the cession of the Southern Konkan to complete our command of the coast and because it was believed to be "a fertile country full of strong military positions," but being the native country of the Peshwa and of almost all the principal Bráhman families[3] connected with the Poona government so much opposition was made that the cession could not be insisted upon.[4] The delivery of Ráygad as well as Sinhgad and Purandhar had in the previous month been demanded as an earnest of the Peshwa's intention to act fairly by us,[5] and Mr. Elphinstone in a despatch of May 9 wrote that in the event of war there was little doubt that Bájiráv would fly to Ráygad where he might establish himself during the rains without the possibility of military operations being

[1] Heber's Journal, II. 8. The story is told at greater length but in a less romantic form in the novel Pandurang Hari. [2] Aitchison's Treaties, III. 87.

[3] Besides the Bráhmans and Maráthás already mentioned as Konkanis, Haripant Phadke was a native of Guhagar, as was Gangadhar Shástri murdered at Pandharpur. The Patvardhan chiefs of Miraj originally came from the village of Ganpati-pula near Ratnágiri; the Ghorpáde chiefs of Ichalkaranji from Mhápan near Vengurla. The chiefs of Ramdurg and Nargund of the Bháve family were also Konkani Bráhmans, and Bájiráv's second wife was of the Ok family of Guhágar, if not herself a native of that place.

[4] Blue Book Pendhari and Marátha Wars, 112. [5] Grant Duff, 634.

Section X.

Bajirav, 1796-1818.

undertaken against him.[1] As however on this occasion the Peshwa yielded at the last moment he lost his last chance of saving himself by the old Marátha safeguard of retreating to the Konkan forts. It is possible that his experiences of Ráygad and Suvarndurg in 1802-3 rendered him less ready to shut himself up in the Konkan than Mr. Elphinstone anticipated. It was said that he had entrusted the principal forts to some of his chief officers, Revdanda being made over to Angria's diwán, and it was believed that the forts were in a better state of defence than proved to be the case.[2]

Ráygad was restored to the Peshwa in August,[3] but after the rains the Bhils and Rámoshis were enlisted by him, and employed in shutting up the passes through the Gháts.[2] They also invaded the Kalyán district, and numbers of the inhabitants took refuge in the forts of Bassein and Máhuli.[4] Early in November these marauders held the Borghát. The Bombay troops kept open communications between Khopali and Panwel, but a despatch from General Smith near Poona to the Commander-in-Chief in Bombay had to be sent round by Bánkot.[5] When the Peshwa moved northwards in December, preparations were made to prevent him from going down into the North Konkan,[6] and in point of fact he was on one occasion close to the Nánaghát.[4] The fort of Kotligad in the North Konkan was at this time taken for the Peshwa by a Sardár named Bápuráv Lámbia, but on December 30 was retaken by Captain Brooks without loss.[7] No other operations were necessary north of Bombay, but small forces were prepared for the reduction of the forts in the Southern Konkan. Hostilities were begun by the capture, at the end of November, of Suvarndurg, which made little resistance. In January 1818 a force under Colonel Prother, consisting of 380 Europeans 800 Native Infantry and a battering train, took Karnála, and within a month afterwards the forts of Avchitgad, Songad, Páli which was bombarded for two hours, and Bharap, the last a strong place the fall of which hastened the surrender of the Pant Sachiv to the British authority.[8] It was cannonaded for twenty-four hours before surrendering, and an immense store of provisions found in it.[9] About the same time Mandangad, where there were two forts with a triple stockade in the space between,[10] was taken by escalade by a small force from Suvarndurg under Colonel Kennedy,[11] and here a seaman was killed and nine or ten sepoys wounded.[9] These operations were in many cases very difficult from the necessity of dragging guns up to the top of the hills on which the forts stood. The acquisition of these was considered especially necessary, because the families of our sepoys belonging to this district had been so persecuted by the Peshwa's officers that in January 1818 proclamation was made offering pardon to all sepoys who might on that account have

---

1 Blue Book as above, 94 - 98.
2 Blue Book relating to War in India (1819), 80.
3 Grant Duff, 646.
4 Dickenson's Manuscript Report.
5 Blue Book, 119, 120.
6 Grant Duff, 656 ; Blue Book, 140.
7 Asiatic Journal, VI. 96.
8 Blacker, 246 ; Blue Book, 128, 177, 245.
9 Manuscript Records.
10 As. Journal VI 320.
11 Blue Book, 206.

deserted from our army.[1] It was also rightly anticipated that outside of the forts we should meet with no opposition.

The Peshwa had now fled so far to the north that fears were no longer entertained of his descending into the Konkan, and Colonel Prother's force was therefore called up into the Dakhan.[2] There he reduced many forts, including Rájmáchi and Kuári which commanded the two most direct routes from Bombay to Poona.[3] In the meantime a detachment under Major Kennett took the fort of Nawapura by escalade. Captain Barrow defeated at the Kasur Ghát (which had for many years been much used by troops passing between the Dakhan and Gujarát) a body of Arab Musalmáns and Kolis commanded by Bápuráv Lámbia, which had plundered and burnt villages in that part of the Konkan. Colonel Kennedy's force reduced Rámgad and Pálgad in the Khed district and paid the *killedár* Rs. 5000 for the possession of Rasalgad, a place of strength in the same neighbourhood, after which the force occupied Khed.[4] In April Colonel Prother's force returned to the Konkan with the chief object of taking Ráygad where the Peshwa's wife was. He was reinforced by six companies of the 67th Regiment, and a detachment of the 89th which up to this time had been at Málvan.[5] The force first destroyed a stockaded post near Indápur, and there slaughtered a number of the enemy, and after taking the forts of Tala and Ghosála reached Mahád on April 24. On the morning of that day a detachment of the force carried a stockade at the foot of Ráygad and occupied the *petha* and thus cut off the escape of the Peshwa's family for which two elephants and a number of camels and horses were found prepared. A passport was sent to the Peshwa's wife, which however did not reach her, as the Arabs fired on the flag of truce. On the twenty-sixth the whole force besieged the fort, and after ten days the garrison began to treat for the surrender, being chiefly impelled to this by a shell from our batteries having set the palace on fire and done a great deal of damage. The negotiations were carried on till May 10, when the fort was surrendered and five lákhs of rupees taken in it. The garrison consisted of 100 Arabs and about 800 other troops. Nearly all the buildings had been destroyed, but there were "marks of grandeur where streets of length with apparently once beautiful and regular buildings had been." The temples and tomb of Shiváji could with difficulty be made out, but most of the destruction had been caused before this siege. The work of Colonel Prother's force, which from first to last had suffered very few casualties, was concluded by the capture of the forts of Lingána, Kángori, Chandangad, and Mahipatgad.[6] The European troops then returned to Bombay, the Native Infantry were cantoned for the rains at Páli, and a new battalion, composed of those who had deserted from our regiments and had been allowed to return, was formed at Kuári.[5]

---

[1] Blue Book, 212; As. Journal, VI. 219. [2] Blue Book, 235; Wilson, II. 324.
[3] Hamilton, II. 152. [4] Asiatic Journal, VI. 320. [5] Blacker, 246, 310.
[6] Blue Book, 264-341; Wilson, II. 324; Grant Duff, 679.

Section X.

Bájiráv, 1796-1818.

In the meantime a force from Málvan under Colonel Imlach had taken the forts belonging to the Peshwa in the Salshi district. Siddhagad was at first unsuccessfully attacked, but with the help of a detachment of the 89th Regiment, which put into Málvan on account of adverse winds, a second attack was successful.[1] Bhagvantgad made some resistance, and its capture was followed by the occupation of Achra. Devgad was taken and an attempt made on Vijaydurg, but so heavy a fire was opened on our vessels that they were forced to cut their cables and return to Devgad. There a number of the enemy held some stockades on the opposite side of the river and commanded the harbour, but a party attacked and defeated them with considerable loss.

The force under Colonel Kennedy having got possession of all the forts in the Suvarndurg district took Anjanvel on May 17, and from there went on to Govalkot, where it was found that a large body of Rámoshis had been plundering through the district and had taken possession of Chiplún. They however professed peaceable intentions and evacuated the town. The force then took the forts of Bairamgarh and Bháwangarh, and an order was obtained from the Deshmukh of Ratnágiri at Sátára for the surrender of the forts in that táluka, namely Ratnágiri, Purangad, Jaygad, and Sátavli. These were not in our possession till the beginning of June,[2] and in that month the conquest of the Southern Konkan was completed by the unconditional surrender of the district and fort of Vijaydurg,[3] which were held by two brothers of the Dhulap family, one of whom was *subhedár* of the district and the other *killedár* of the fort and Admiral of the Peshwa's fleet. The Dhulaps are said not to have been in the fort at the time of our force appearing before it, but two Musalmán brothers fired a few shots from the walls till they were both killed on the spot by the bursting of one of the guns, after which no further resistance was made.[4] The Admiral's vessel of 430 tons burden, 156 feet long and 33 feet beam, was taken in the river, and the dock, 355 feet long and 257 feet in the broadest part, remains to this day. There was also a small building-yard and a mast-house.[5]

While the South Konkan forts had thus been falling into our hands one by one, Captain T. Dickenson, of the Engineers, had been examining those in the North Konkan ceded to us in the previous year. The chief of these was of course Bassein, but that fortress formerly so much coveted was now found to be "an acquisition of no military importance." Its circumference was upwards of a mile and a half, but it had "fundamental weaknesses in the too great distance between the main defences and the absence of any ditch or parapet of greater pretensions than a breastwork, while the ramparts were in many places overgrown

---

[1] Asiatic Journal, VI. 320.
[2] Asiatic Journal, VI. 418; Blue Book, 210, 218-264, 286.
[3] Asiatic Journal, VII. 57. [4] Local information.
[5] Asiatic Journal, IX. 123; Waddington's Manuscript Report.

Section X.

Bajirav, 1796-1818.

with jungle, and there was scarcely a public building habitable." Arnála was the next in importance of the coast forts, and Tárápur the next, both from its better state of repair and its central position, being about 500 feet in length and breadth, with walls about ten feet thick and, including the parapet, thirty feet high. There were eight other forts on the coast between the Vaitarna and the Daman frontier, and these were generally in rather better condition than those inland, but of little use from their small size, being chiefly kept up as a security against pirates and to command creeks. Of inland forts there were sixteen, mostly insulated and in the middle of the jungle, and there were four which might be called Ghát forts. The gateways of all were said to be the best part, but "it is hardly possible to conceive a more neglected state than the forts generally are in. It would seem that for the last twenty years not the labour of a single person or the expenditure of a rupee has been sanctioned by the Peshwa's government either upon the works themselves or the interior buildings. Even the water in many places has been allowed to become unfit for use." Asheri Malangad and Máhuli Captain Dickenson considered impregnable, but owing to their isolated position useless under our Government, and of the whole he said that "the most insignificant is adequate against a siege by a native enemy, but the best in their present state untenable perhaps for any length of time against Europeans."[1] In the end it was decided that the coast forts should not then be destroyed, as the inhabitants might have a feeling of insecurity without them, and they mostly remain untouched except by natural decay to the present time. Of the inland forts the interior parts were destroyed as far as possible, but the outer works being left, the hills have scarcely lost in picturesqueness. Bassein-Arnála and Tárápur, and the Ghát fortresses of Gorakgad Kotligad and Siddhagad held small detachments of soldiers for a short time,[2] but all have now for many years past been abandoned to solitude.

Thus the operations in the Konkan were brought to an end, and the whole of the districts which had been the Peshwa's came under the British Government. There were still parties of marauders wandering about, and in September 1818 a body of 500 Arabs Maráthás and Patháns were attacked at Poládpur by Lieutenant Crosby, who had been left at Mahád with seventy-five sepoys and 140 horse, and were defeated with considerable loss.[3]

Two prisoners of importance were kept in the Konkan during the rains of 1818, Chimnáji Appa the Peshwa's brother, who was allowed to remain at Bassein till the season should admit of his proceeding to Benáres,[4] and Trimbakji Dengla who more than any one else might be called the cause of the Peshwa's destruction. He was again confined in Thána fort, from which he had escaped in 1816, and after the rains was sent to a prison more distant from the scene of his exploits.[5]

---

[1] Dickenson's Manuscript Report. [2] Manuscript Records.
[3] Asiatic Journal, VII. 134. [4] Blue Book Pindhari and Marátha War, 347.
[5] Wilson, II. 365.

SECTION XI.

THE ENGLISH ESTABLISHMENTS IN THE KONKAN PREVIOUS TO 1818.

Section XI.

The English, 1611-1818.

WE have now reached the period when the successive Native governments had given place to the English throughout the whole Konkan. Before proceeding with the history of the Konkan under British rule it is necessary to go back and describe the early settlements made for purposes of trade, and the measures taken for the management of the small possessions of our Government in this part of the Presidency previous to 1818.

As early as 1611 the English East India Company had directed their attention to Dábhol with a view to the establishment of a factory, but they were opposed by the Portuguese.[1] Sir Henry Middleton with three ships went there in February 1612, and stayed some little time, receiving great civility from the Sidi governor, and procuring some trade.[2] But the Company's settlement at Surat was for some years sufficient for their requirements. In 1618 further attempts were made to trade at Dábhol,[3] and in 1624 and for two or three years afterwards difficulties both with the Dutch and the Moghals caused a proposal that the factory and establishment should be removed there from Surat, as the inhabitants had made most friendly offers of accommodation and protection.[4] This was not carried out, but ten years later a phirman for a factory at Dábhol was asked for and refused, and no further attempt seems to have been made.[5] In 1638-9 the first Freetraders or Interlopers, the association of Sir William Courten, established a factory at Rájápur in the Southern Konkan; and when, owing to the great power of the Dutch, in the following year the English East India Company desired a place which would be secure from them and capable of fortification, Rájápur was recommended as the best after Bombay. In 1649-50 the Musalmán governor offered the trade of this town to the President at Surat because of the bad character of the Interlopers, who had incurred heavy debts there. The offer was accepted as at Rájápur pepper and cardamoms could be obtained without exposure to the opposition of the Dutch,[6] and it is also said that the finest *batelás* and muslins were at that time produced about there.[7] But just about this time Courten's association was incorporated with the East India Company, so that the factory at Rájápur was continued on the same footing as before. In 1660 several factories were

---

[1] Bruce, I. 165. [2] Orme's Fragments, 323.
[3] Milburn, Introduction, xviii. [4] Bruce, I. 261, 274.
[5] Bruce, I. 334. Hamilton states that the English had a factory at Dábhol, but the writer found no confirmation of the statement, except that Grose in 1750 mentions it as one of the places at which the English have forts factories or settlements: Knox, II. 438; Pinkerton, VIII. 350.
[6] Bruce, I. 357, 568, 444; Macpherson, 115. [7] Hamilton in Pinkerton, VIII. 352.

abandoned but Rájápur was retained.[1] It appears however to have been given up after its plunder by Shiváji in 1664[2] and not re-established till 1674, though for some years previously there had been proposals for replacing it; for Shiváji, and Sambháji after him, though they oppressed the factors and hampered their trade, always professed to be very anxious to have a factory there.[3] But it did not succeed, and in 1676-77 its withdrawal was resolved on owing to the continual extortions of the Maráthás. Shiváji would not however let the factors go and the establishment was not withdrawn till 1681. The list of factories in 1702-3 includes none in the Konkan,[4] but according to Milburn[5] that at Rájápur was again established between 1698 and 1708. It could however have been continued but a short time. A French factory had also been established there in 1670.[6]

Rájápur, which has not often been mentioned in the earlier parts of this history, is by far the best preserved and oldest-looking town in the Konkan. It is built, like so many of the other towns, at the highest navigable point of a considerable river, and as the hills rise almost immediately from the water the whole town is built on a slope, except that part close to the river. The streets are steep and narrow, and the bazárs are covered over as well as paved. The old English factory, a massive stone building with an enclosure leading down to the water, is now used as the *kacheri* and the walls of another building of European construction, and equally large, are probably the remains of the French factory. Rájápur is the only Konkan port to which Arab buggalows still come direct, and to it only two or three in the year. The rest of the great trade which used to pass to the Konkan ports from Arabia, the Persian gulf, and the Red Sea is now all swallowed up in Bombay.[7]

It does not seem that our East India Company had ever any other factory in the Konkan previous to their acquisition of Bánkot or Fort Victoria in 1756 (see Section VIII). But in 1668 when the Sidi made overtures to the English at Bombay to assist him, the Factors there suggested to the Supreme Council at Surat the many advantages which Janjira possessed over Bombay.[8] No notice was taken of the suggestion, but as the history of Janjira does not come within the scope of this memoir it may here be mentioned that, after Bombay and Goa, there is no bay or inlet on the coast of the Konkan of such striking natural beauty as Janjira, while the two rocky islets in the bay are in their present condition much

[1] Bruce, I. 437, 556.

[2] Grant Duff, 80. Orme says it was plundered in 1670. Fragments, 26.

[3] Bruce, I. 366 and II. 285, 304, 442, 487.

[4] Bruce, II. 399, 472 and III. 90.

[5] Introduction, xli.

[6] Bruce, II. 285.

[7] Rájápur is also made interesting by two well-known objects of Hindu pilgrimage, a temple over an intermittent spring, popularly called Ganga, which rises at the end of the cold weather and lasts for two or three weeks, and the temple of Dhopeshvar (properly Dhutápápeshvar 'the cleanser from sin') situated in a romantic ravine, to which a very pleasant paved road has been made within the last few years. The rise of Ganga is looked for with anxiety by the inhabitants, as its non-appearance is considered a bad omen.

[8] Grant Duff, 99.

Section XI.

The English, 1611-1818.

more picturesque than any European power would have been likely to leave them.

Of the French as connected with the Konkan besides their factory at Rájápur and the intrigue of St. Lubin, given in Section IX., the only thing that can be mentioned is that in June 1696 there was an indecisive engagement off the Vengurla rocks between seven Dutch and five French ships. The Dutch retired to Goa and the French to Surat.

The successes of the Dutch against the Portuguese have already been described. After the decline of the Portuguese the Dutch still had their fortified factory at Vengurla, but do not appear ever to have come into collision with the English in the Konkan. There was always however great jealousy between the two nations, and in the treaty concluded with the Marátha state in October 1756 the first article provided that the Dutch should be excluded from the Marátha dominions, and another article forbad their admission to Dánda-Rájápur.[1] In 1767 they are said to have wished to have a factory at Bassein, and still later the jealousy between them and the English at Surat and elsewhere was very strong.[2]

As has been already stated the acquisition of Bánkot and its dependent villages in 1756 gave our Government its first territorial possessions on this coast, and from that time different arrangements, though of course at first on a very small scale, became necessary. The fort and factory however were what were chiefly considered. No provision for the administration of criminal justice was made except as regarded the most trifling offences, but the Residents were in the habit of sending offenders for examination and trial before the Courts in Bombay,[3] and in 1797 the then Resident was superseded for having gone beyond his powers in punishing a *deshmukh* for 'contumacy.'[4] The pay of the civil officers and the number of the sepoys were increased or reduced rather with reference to the finances of the Presidency than on any other consideration, and in 1772 there were but 120 sepoys with a proper proportion of officers. In 1780 the armament of the fort was two twelve-pounders, five nine-pounders, twelve six-pounders, and four four-pounders. In 1781 the financial embarrassments of the Presidency caused the whole expenses of Bánkot, including the troops, to be reduced to Rs. 2000 a month.[4] The Chiefs constantly complained of their small profits, but Dr. Hové in 1789 wrote[5] that the Chiefs of this factory commonly retired after a few years with immense sums, and that the post was calculated as good as the councilship at Bombay. In 1802 however the pay of the Chief was raised to Rs. 600, and private trade forbidden to him.

Sálsette, our next acquisition, which had been so prosperous under the Portuguese and so fertile as to have supplied not only the

---

1 Aitchison's Treaties, III. 17.
2 Stavorinus, III. 107; House of Commons Reports (1806), 42.
3 Reg. I. of 1811. 4 Bánkot Manuscript Diaries. 5 Tours, 12, 14

neighbouring islands but Goa also,[1] appears to have been in 1818, after forty years of our government, little, if any, better than those districts just taken from the Maráthás. In 1787 Dr. Hové for the space of twelve miles saw no village nor marks of present culture: remains of large buildings testified to its former prosperity, but all was now "pining in decay. Here and there are remains of wells and marks of former culture, but no person now thinks culture an honourable employment." An intelligent writer in 1794 mentioned with approval a proposal that had been made a few years before to establish a colony of Chinese in the island.[2] In 1804 Lord Valentia found that little had been done to increase the produce of the island, the greater part being useless jungle, and even wood being only procurable at a very high price, owing chiefly to want of arrangement.[3] In 1811 the Secretary to the Bombay Government wrote of "the present half-populated and half-cultivated state of Sálsette."[4] And in 1824 Bishop Heber speaks of Sálsette as "strangely unimproved neglected and uncivilised, having no towns except Thána and Ghodbandar, very little cultivation except the *tara* palm and cocoanut, which grow almost spontaneously amid the jungle, and displaying in the cottages of its peasantry a degree of poverty and rudeness which I have seen nowhere in India except among the Bhils."[5] A striking description of the wildness of the inhabitants is also given in Hamilton's Gazetteer.

It must be remembered however that Lord Valentia's visit was immediately after the famine of 1802-3, and that 1824 also succeeded two years of drought. But the records of Government show that not much had been done up to 1808 to restore the island from the condition into which it had fallen during the occupation of the Maráthás. For fourteen years after we took it no change was made in the system of revenue and collections. Lands were still farmed out to the highest bidder, and the English Chief of Sálsette was paid by the cesses called *sar deshmukhi* and *sarpáteli* imposed by the Maráthás. The grain assessment had yielded under the Portuguese 10,077 mudás of rice, under the Maráthás it fell to 7465, and under our Government in 1794-95 to 6075. In 1798 the *jamábandi* was fixed at two-thirds of the Portuguese assessment, and most of the cesses imposed by the Maráthás were abolished. But the tax on grazing lands and on wood-cutting, the *mohtarpha* or tax on trades, and that on fisheries were retained, and the result was that the village of Bándra paid altogether over Rs. 12,000 in revenue, and was said to be "most lightly assessed."[6] The fact is that our Governors, who in those days were always more or less in financial difficulties, had not foresight enough to see the virtue of really light assessments, and thought they were doing wonders when they relieved the people of a few of the extraordinary number of taxes imposed by the Maráthás. But the relief was insufficient, and the effect very small.

---

[1] Fryer, 73. [2] Moor, 442. [3] Travels, II. 198. [4] Manuscript Records.
[5] Journal, II. 128-9. But the cocoanut tree does not grow wild in the Konkan.
[6] Reg. I. of 1808.

Section XI.
The English, 1811-1818.

In 1801 a permanent settlement was offered to the then holders of land in Sálsette, with a decennial settlement of commutation rates, but it was accepted by only four individuals,[1] although *sanads* had been prepared and printed at an expense of several thousand rupees.[2] In 1807 the grain assessment had risen to 8320 mudás, but apparently with less land under cultivation. At the end of the previous century large estates had been granted to a few British subjects in Sálsette with a view to the improvement of the country, and several of the present (so-called) khots of Sálsette derive their rights from these original grantees. Between 1798 and 1803 the Sion causeway was built,[3] which was undoubtedly the greatest possible benefit to Sálsette, and in the last-mentioned year the customs duties which had been hitherto levied on all goods passing between the two islands were abolished.[2] Thus it will be seen that the Bombay Government of those times were not so much indifferent to the welfare of the territory they had gained as ignorant of the greatness of the abuses which the Maráthás had allowed, and slow in removing them.

But where their financial position was not affected, they showed more consideration, for provision for the administration of criminal justice was made very soon after the acquisition of territory. In Sálsette and Karanja the Residents had from the first been empowered to investigate all offences and misdemeanors not capital with the assistance of two native assessors, while capital cases were sent to Bombay for trial by the Mayor's Court. In 1799 a Judge and Magistrate was appointed for the islands vested with civil criminal and police jurisdiction.[4] In civil suits an appeal was reserved to the Governor in Council sitting as the Sadar Adálat, while the more serious criminal cases were committed to the Court of Session, which consisted of the Junior Member of Council and two civilians nominated for the occasion. Quarterly sessions were held at the stations of the Magistrates, and capital sentences required the confirmation of the Governor in Council. Provision was even made for the trial of suits against Government, and the jurisdiction of the Judge and Magistrate of Sálsette was in 1803 extended to Bánkot and its dependencies, and the Court required to sit in that district for 20 days in each year.[5] In 1807 the junior member of Council became sole Session Judge of Sálsette.[6] The arrangement however only lasted till 1810, and after that the Provincial Court of Circuit and Appeal at Surat received jurisdiction over Sálsette.[7] By the same Act separate Magistrates were appointed for Káranja, as inconvenience was felt from the island being dependent on the periodical visits of the Sálsette Magistrates, and from there being no communication with the other stations for three months in each year. These arrangements continued till the cession and conquest of the rest of the Konkan in 1817-18, and the history of the district since that era may now be continued.

---

1 Reg. I. of 1808. 2 Manuscript Records.
3 It was at first constructed with a drawbridge in the centre. Hamilton, II. 169.
4 Reg. V. of 1799. 5 Reg. III. of 1803. 6 Reg. I. of 1807. 7 Reg. II. of 1811.

SECTION XII.

BRITISH RULE.

Section XII.

British Rule, 1818-1884.

In 1818 the whole Konkan, with very little more exception than at the present time, was under the British Government. The state of Sálsette has been described in Section XI, and it is also of importance to show the condition of the rest of the Konkan at the time of its acquisition. No one who knows the Konkan now will suppose that it can have been very flourishing under the Maráthás, and it is in fact easy to prove that bad as was the condition of Sálsette that of the rest of the district was far worse.

The system of farming out offices to the highest bidder was in the later years of the Peshwa's government rendered still more odious by the insecurity of the possession of these farms: for so-called leases were often summarily annulled on a higher offer being made. At the same time the taxation was exceedingly oppressive: in the Northern Konkan a list of thirty-six different taxes is given, cesses being levied even on cattle, vegetables, and poultry. The poverty of the people in general and the number of deserted villages were sufficient evidence of the evils of this system. "The Kolis, Bhils, Kátkaris, Thákurs, and other almost savage tribes who inhabit the jungles" were in the habit of plundering the villages at every opportunity, and were said to be in the most degraded state of human nature.[1] In the neighbourhood of the forts (which it must be remembered were scattered all over the districts) "the country was for miles round with scarcely an inhabitant, almost without an implement of any kind, or an artificer of the humblest description."[2] Only one exception is mentioned to the generally wretched state of the country, the island and sub-division of Bassein, where sugar-cane and plantains were as now produced in abundance. "From Bassein to Dántivra every inch of the ground is highly cultivated, and the comparative and well-known wealth of the inhabitants is ascribable to the fertility and highly cultivated state of the island."[3] There was also an excellent road from Dantivra to the Damanganga, but here the coast villages seem to have been freely plundered by the Pendháris.[2]

The Southern Konkan, which had of late years suffered less from the miseries of war, appears to have been in a better condition,

---

[1] East India House Selections (1826), III. 767, 770.
[2] Dickenson's Manuscript Report. [3] East India House Selections, III. 770.

Section XII.

British Rule, 1818-1884.

though even there very few of the villages consisted of "more than a rude cluster of thatched mud huts," and it was stated as their misfortune that there were no village walls for defence, so that the Thags and Rámoshis were frequent visitors.[1] "A man wearing a decent turban or ever so coarse a dress attracts one's attention as being above the lower orders."[2] The sub-divisions of Suvarndurg and Anjanvel were said to be the most prosperous of all in the Southern Konkan, and the revenue there soon after the establishment of our Government was "easily and punctually collected."[1] It seems probable that the *khots*, while themselves forming a body of men less poverty-stricken than the ordinary ryots, protected the latter to some extent from the rapacity of the Peshwa's officers.[3] The produce of the whole district was reported as very small: still the natural remark was made that "on viewing the face of the country, which to a cursory observer presents little less than bare hills, rocks, ravines, jungle, and mountains, the surprise is rather that there is so much, than that there is no more." The population was put down at 640,000, and as this included some part of the present Kolába district, while the present population of Ratnágiri alone is put down as over a million, the difference will be seen to be very great.

This being the general state of the country it must be stated that at least three causes concurred to depress rather than to improve the condition of the people during the first years of British rule. In the first place the Konkan suffered in a very excessive degree from the return of the military men now thrown out of employ, as, besides numbers who had served in the cavalry and infantry, most of the forts in the Dakhan as well as along the Ghâts and in the Konkan had been in a great measure garrisoned by Konkanis.[2] Secondly the great demand for grain, especially rice, in the Dakhan and particularly at Poona which resulted from the absence of cultivation above the Ghâts and the presence of a great Court and army at Poona, suddenly ceased, for the Court and army disappeared together, and the immediate increase of cultivation in the Dakhan made it independent of the supply of Konkan grain, so that it soon became an exporting instead of an importing country.[4] Thirdly the ruin of the Chitpávan dynasty which had always kept the great offices of the State to a great extent in the hands of members of that caste and had favoured other natives of the Ratnágiri district, could not have been otherwise than a most serious loss to so poor a country as the Southern Konkan. The measures taken for the improvement of the district were to a great extent counterbalanced by these inevitable causes of distress.

Before entering on the general settlement of the country it was necessary to define the rights of those Marátha states which under

---

[1] Pelly's Manuscript Report. [2] E. I. House Selections, III. 765-769, 784, 790.
[3] Wingate's Manuscript Report. [4] J. M. Davies' Manuscript Reports.

the supremacy of the Peshwa had held a great part of the coast of the Southern Konkan. Málvan, the sea-port of the Kolhápur territories, had been ceded since 1812, so that the arrangements now made with that state did not affect the Konkan. But to gain the forts of Nivti and Ráiri in consequence of the injuries committed on the inhabitants of our villages by the Sávantvádi state, a force under Sir William Grant Keir, consisting of a wing of the 89th Regiment, 2½ battalions of Native infantry, and three troops of Native cavalry and artillery, entered the Konkan in January 1819. The heavy stores and ordnance were sent by sea. Nivti which had a garrison of 300 men, was invested and surrendered on February 4 without resistance, and the force proceeded by sea to Ráiri, the defences of which were found to be formidable. On the thirteenth at day-break fire was opened on the fort by four battery guns and four eight-inch mortars, which in an hour dismantled the whole of the guns in the outworks, and then directed their fire against the general defences till 3 P.M., when the storming party of 330 men of the 89th Regiment in two columns assaulted the fort, and gained the outworks with a loss of eight killed and twenty-seven wounded, the latter including two officers. The enemy retained possession of the inner works that night, but most of them escaped before morning, and the remainder then surrendered.[1] A treaty was concluded by which the whole of the coast villages from Málvan to the Portuguese frontier were ceded and about twenty inland villages composing the districts of Pát and Ajgaum. These last however were restored in the following year and the coast villages alone retained.[2]

It was not found necessary to deprive the Kolába state of any part of its territories, which by gradual encroachments of the Poona government had been much curtailed, but a treaty defining the conditions of its dependence on the British Government was concluded in 1822. Finally, the Pant Sachiv of Bhor, who had rights over many villages in the Konkan, was settled with on the principle of exchange of villages and revenue.[3]

For several years after this and up to 1830 the Kolis and other forest and hill tribes in the North Konkan gave constant trouble by their depredations both above and below the Gháts, and made it necessary to send out small detachments for the protection of the country.[4] Notwithstanding this the generally peaceable character of the Konkan may be gathered from the fact that as early as 1820 there were not more than three battalions scattered over its whole extent, the Northern Konkan and down to Bánkot being included in the Poona Division of the Army and the Southern Konkan remaining a separate command, only because of its distance from Poona and Bombay.[5] Thána had of course been maintained as a military

---

1 Wilson, II. 446; Asiatic Journal, VIII. 291; Blacker, 484.
2 Aitchison's Treaties, VI. 132.
3 Aitchison's Treaties, VI. 182, 45; East India House Selections, IV. 153.
4 Bom. Geo. Soc. Trans., 327. 5 Bombay Selections, CIV. 4. 7.

Section XII.

British Rule, 1818-1884.

station ever since our Government got possession of Sálsette, and at the beginning of this century there was also a military establishment at Vesáva,[1] fifteen miles north of Bombay.[2] Vesáva had been spoken of by Gemelli[3] as one of the three forts of Sálsette and the harbour is mentioned by Hamilton as deep enough to receive ships of the greatest burden.[4] A small force was kept at Bhiwndi for some time and also at Panwel. There have now for many years been no troops in the district, except a wing of a Native Infantry Regiment at Thána.

In the Southern Konkan small detachments were kept for some years at Bánkot Málvan and Vengurla, which had all been for some time in our occupation, and also at Harnai. It was thought necessary, however, to make one regular military station, and Dápoli was fixed upon. About 1840 the regular troops were removed, and the veteran battalion alone kept there, and after 1857 this also was abolished, and the Southern Konkan left without any military force whatever.

Thána had from the first been the civil station of Sálsette, and became naturally the capital of the North Konkan. On July 11, 1825, Bishop Heber consecrated the church which had just been finished, and which he describes as "extremely elegant and convenient, and the effect very pleasing."[5] It was necessary also after we took the country in 1818 to fix on a place for civil head-quarters in the Southern Konkan. Bánkot Málvan and Vengurla were out of the question as being at the extremities of the district. Officers sent to report on the matter considered that Jaygad Vijaydurg and Ratnágiri were the three most suitable spots,[6] and eventually the choice fell on the last-named, which has since been the head-quarters of the district. About 1830, however, the North and South Konkan were joined into one collectorate, but this arrangement did not last long.

The first Collector of the North Konkan, Mr. Marriott, lost no time in recommending the abolition of a great number of the taxes, and within a year or two a rough survey was made of the whole collectorate.[7] But even in 1833 Sir John Malcolm wrote of "the hitherto unproductive island of Sálsette," and only looked forward to its improvement by "respectable and opulent natives of Bombay" settling in it.[8] Yet for several years after he had left India our Government levied duties at the rate of twenty-five per cent on all goods imported from the east into Sálsette and the other parts of the district which had belonged to the Portuguese. This was a Marátha impost, and our rulers apparently thought it so harmless as

---

[1] The proper name of the village in which the fort is situated is Madh, which a military author romantically translated "Isle de Mer." The Native Regiment stationed there in 1810 "had every amusement and comfort that men could require, an excellent mess, good houses &c." Seely, 2.

[2] Lord Valentia, II. 182. [3] Churchill, IV. 198. [4] Pinkerton, VIII. 343.

[5] Heber's Journal, II. 144. [6] Manuscript Records.

[7] E. I. House Selections, III. 769. [8] Government of India, 81 and Appx. 63.

Section XII.

British Rule, 1818-1884.

to retain it when many other taxes were abolished.[1] The ruggedness of both Konkans and the intersection of the country by large tidal rivers prevented the improvement of the greater part of it by road-making, so that it is only within the remembrance of the present generation that anything has been done to open out the inland parts of the district. But before the end of 1830 a great military road had been constructed from Panwel to Poona, and the Borghát opened for wheeled vehicles, which the Poona Government had on political grounds refused to let our Government repair as long as it was in their power.[2] This new road was said by Sir John Malcolm "to break down the wall between the Konkan and the Deccan." About the same time the road from Thána to Násik (afterwards part of the Ágra road) was made, and the opening of the Talghát, though it was not available for wheeled vehicles, had the greatest effect on trade, for up to that time Berár cotton used to reach Bombay by the circuitous route of Surat. The Kumbhárli Ghát was also made at this time, although not then passable for carts, and the road across Mahábaleshvar from Sátára to Mahád was completed at the joint expense of the Rája of Sátára and our Government.[3]

Thus something was done to improve the inland parts of the province, and the coast villages have from the beginning of our rule flourished and increased. The Konkani Bráhmans had not lost their old aptitude for government, nor the Konkani Maráthás their inclination towards military employ: so that, though a great part of the district had not, up to a few years ago, made much progress, and a small portion was and still is inhabited by some very uncivilised tribes, yet as a whole the Konkan probably felt the blessings of peace and strong government as much as most other parts.

In 1836-38 a new assessment was made all over the Thána district, chiefly by Mr. J. M. Davies. It was found that owing to the fall in the price of grain in the Konkan Sadáshiv Keshav's assessments of 1788 which had then represented one-third of the produce were now equivalent to one-half, and a reduction of rates had to be made accordingly. Up to this time and for several years after the cultivation of the hill lands, which is now so largely carried on, was of very trifling extent, and scarcely any restrictions were placed on the destruction of trees which from their abundance were thought of little value.[1] In the Southern Konkan owing to the peculiarity of the tenures the survey was delayed almost up to the present time.

The two political events of chief consequence in the Konkan between 1820 and 1850 were the lapse of the state of Kolába in 1840 on the death of the last of the A'ngriás of the direct and legitimate line,[4] and the insurrection and military operations in the Vádi district in 1844-45. The sub-divisions of the Kolába state with those of Pen, Rájpuri, Mahád, and Thal, which had hitherto been

---

[1] J. M. Davies' Manuscript Reports.
[2] Seely, 59.
[3] Malcolm, 107, Appendix 86, 69.
[4] Aitchison's Treaties, VI. 182.

Section XII.

British Rule, 1818-1884.

the charge of the First Assistant Collector of Thána, were formed into a sub-collectorate and recently into an independent collectorate. The Sávantvádi disturbances scarcely extended to the Málvan sub-division although its villages are much mixed up with those of the Vádi state, but one of the insurgent leaders attempted to raise the people of Málvan against our Government.[1] The Konkan was only affected by the mutinies of 1857 by a wing of the Native Infantry Regiment which mutinied at Kolhápur being at Ratnágiri and the fears entertained that the mutineers would march down. A steamer was sent to take away the ladies and children from Ratnágiri, but no disturbance took place. The ruffian, afterwards known as Nána Sáheb, was the son of a poor Bráhman of Vengaon a village of Karjat, and was adopted at the age of four by the Peshwa Bájiráv. Nána with his parents and brothers then went to live with his adoptive father in Bengal, and the Konkan had no more to do with him. The gifted French naturalist Victor Jacquemont in October 1832 contracted the illness of which he died two months later by his botanical exploration in "the pestilential jungles of Sálsette."

Since 1850 the condition of the Northern Konkan has been entirely changed by the railways that pass through it, and the roads which now render most parts accessible. Sálsette in particular now (1883) presents a very different appearance from that described forty years ago. The hills are still covered with jungle, but are therefore more valuable than if scanty crops were grown on them, and much even of the better land is every year left uncultivated, but only because the grass gives a valuable return without the trouble and expense of tillage. The great numbers of carts which during the whole fine season pass along the roads and the flourishing appearance of the villages prove that Sálsette has now to a great extent at least recovered the prosperity it had 200 years ago. The rest of the Northern Konkan is in various stages of progress, part having improved nearly as rapidly as Sálsette and two or three sub-divisions being still, owing to want of population, not much better than the whole was described as being in 1818. Of the Southern Konkan the two northern sub-divisions, that is those nearest Bombay, are but little behind Sálsette, but the greater part of it is, and by the nature of its position must remain much isolated, while its greater poverty prevents the rapid extension of its communications, so that up to about 1860 it was probably but little different from what it was in 1818. But a cart-road now runs through the whole length of it, and steam navigation has of course been in its favour. The district still manages to attract to itself money earned in other parts of India, while those of the natives who take service elsewhere generally return to end their days in the place where they were born. During the years of the great public works in Bombay thousands of labourers used to go up there for the working season

---

1 Bombay Selections, X. 19.

and return home for the rains, and though this practice declined with the decline of speculation in Bombay, greater numbers than ever find their subsistence in the factories of Bombay.

Looking at the future prospects of the Konkan it must be said that the Northern Konkan at present suffers in its inland parts from a want of population and capital, but the whole of it may in time be as flourishing as the coast villages are now. The Southern Konkan is overpopulated, and nothing can make any but a small part of it fertile, nor does it seem likely that it will be ever distinguished by manufactures, or that mineral wealth will be developed. But it holds a race of men who in the last century conquered nearly the whole of India, and who show no signs of degeneration, and no one can for a moment suppose that the progress of education and science will leave the country of the most intelligent and industrious of Indian races unknown and unimproved.